GERMANY

NETH.

POLAND

CZECH
REPUBLIC

SLOVAKIA

UKRAINE

FRANCE

SWITZER-
LAND

AUSTRIA

HUNGARY

SLOVENIA

CROATIA

MOLDOVA

ROMANIA

ITALY

BOSNIA-
HERZEGOVINA

YUGOSLAVIA

BULGARIA

Black
Sea

Adriatic Sea

ALBANIA

MACE-
DONIA

TURK.

CORSICA

SARDINIA

GREECE

Aegean
Sea

TURKEY

Mediterranean Sea

Kozarac
× Trnopolje
Prijedor
× Omarska
Bihac
Banja Luka
Manjaca ×

Doboj

Brcko

Tuzla

Travnik

Zenica

• City
× Camp

Sarajevo

Visegrad

Gorazde

Foca

The following camps are
the most notorious of the 184
camps noted by the U.N.
Commission of Experts on War Crimes:

OMARSKA
  Death camp from
  late May to early
  August, 1992

TRNOPOLJE
  Detention camp from late
  May to early October, 1992

MANJACA
  Prison camp since the Croatian war (July,
  1991), currently a military prison

Mostar

Capljina

0   40
        miles

Mass Rape

The War against Women in Bosnia-Herzegovina

Edited by Alexandra Stiglmayer

Translations by Marion Faber

Foreword by Roy Gutman

Massenvergewaltigung – Krieg gegen die Frauen

University of Nebraska Press, Lincoln and London

"Making Female Bodies the Battlefield," by Susan Brownmiller, was first published in *Newsweek*, Jan. 4, 1993, p.37. © 1992 by Susan Brownmiller. "Turning Rape into Pornography: Postmodern Genocide," by Catharine A. MacKinnon, was first published in *Ms.* 5 (July/August 1993): 24–30. © 1993 by Catharine A. MacKinnon. © 1993 Kore Verlag GmbH. © 1994 by the University of Nebraska Press. All rights reserved. Manufactured in the United States of America. The paper in this book meets the minimum requirements of American National Standard for Information Sciences – Permanence of Paper for Printed Library Materials, ANSI Z39.48-1984.

Library of Congress Cataloging-in-Publication Data
Massenvergewaltigung. English. Mass Rape : the war against women in Bosnia-Herzegovina / edited by Alexandra Stiglmayer : translated by Marion Faber. p. cm.
Includes bibliographical references.
ISBN 0-8032-4239-5
1. Rape – Bosnia and Herzegovina. 2. Yugoslav War, 1991– – Atrocities. 3. Victims of rape – Bosnia and Herzegovina. I. Stiglmayer, Alexandra, 1964– . II. Title.
HV6569.B54M3713 1994
949.702′4 – dc20
93-45997 CIP

This book is dedicated to
all the women who lived
through the tragedy of
Bosnia and Herzegovina,
and especially to those who
found the strength to tell
about the personal anguish
they suffered.

I am saddened that their
willingness to come forward
was to no avail, for it is un-
likely that they will ever
experience justice, as the
world has chosen to close
its eyes to what has
happened in Bosnia
and Herzegovina.

Contents

Foreword

Roy Gutman

As a skeptical world looked on, in May 1993 the United Nations Security Council set up the first international war crimes tribunal since Nuremberg. Its mission was to investigate, to indict, and where possible to try those suspected of crimes against humanity in the Serb conquest of Bosnia and the other wars that marked the breakup of Yugoslavia. Its statute was narrowly focused, authorizing the court to prosecute grave breaches of the Geneva Conventions of 1949 and the 1948 Convention on Genocide.

There is little reason to expect that perpetrators will ever be brought to justice, and many will argue this is only one more example of the world community's indecisive response to the Serb conquest of Bosnia. Yet if it does nothing else, the tribunal should establish a historical record of what occurred in the war, naming the principal perpetrators and posting their names on a wanted list for decades to come.

The data accumulated by the news media, by the United States government, and by the UN Commission of Experts preparing the tribunal left little doubt that Serb actions in Bosnia constitute genocide. The legal definition of genocide is the attempt to destroy in whole or in part a national, ethnic, racial, or religious group. The systematic rape of Bosnian women of Muslim or Croat origin by Serb forces that Alexandra Stiglmayer has documented is a central element in the genocide; it is also one of the most chilling because of the cold-blooded way it is carried out. The Serb conquest in the spring of 1992 was a well-executed blitzkrieg. Its pattern suggests that the extermination and expulsion of Bosnian Muslims and Croats from their ancestral lands was not a by-product but the aim of the campaign.

Bosnia was totally unprepared to defend itself when it declared independence at the recommendation of the European Community and was recognized by European states and the United States. The Serb-led Yugoslav army had a near monopoly on weapons – certainly heavy arms – and attacked undefended cities, towns, and villages with long-range artillery. After days of bombardment, the army sent in irregular forces led by underworld figures and extreme nationalists. They searched out the intellectuals and political leaders of the non-Serbs, executed them on the spot, or sent them to camps. They seized the men of fighting age and sent them to detention camps, where thousands died of beatings, executions, or starvation.

Rape occurs in nearly every war, but in this one it has played a unique role. The degradation and molestation of women was central to the conquest. Often, irregular forces kept women under house arrest in their villages or towns; sometimes they transported them to other places and held them for days, weeks, or months. A great many of the women were raped while held captive, unprotected and vulnerable, their husbands and fathers having been taken away.

Women of childbearing age were the primary targets. In the conservative society in which the Muslims of rural Bosnia grew up, women traditionally remain chaste until marriage. Rape is a trauma with far-reaching consequences for these victims, who have well-founded fears of rejection and ostracism and of lives without marriage or children. In this regard the pattern of the rapes of unmarried women of childbearing age fulfills another definition of genocide – the attempt to block procreation of the group. Yet so many cases have come to light of women of sixty and girls under twelve being raped, gang-raped, often in front of their relatives, that genocide seems too dry a description of unreined savagery. Sexual humiliation was not restricted to females; in repeated instances, men held in detention camps report being forced to commit sexual acts on each other and to witness public castrations that prisoners had to carry out against each other.

The variants in the systematic rape presumably reflected the predilections of local commanders or their political bosses. At a rape camp in Vogosca, near Sarajevo, women were killed after being raped, according to numerous witnesses. In Foca, Serb authorities held women for months on end in an indoor sports arena at the center of town, next door to the police station. Nightly, men in uniform slunk into the hall, picked out their victims with flashlights, and led them off at gunpoint to another location where they raped them.

In the town of Brezovo Polje in northeastern Bosnia, Serb paramilitary forces first arrested the men and took them to the notorious Brcko Luka death camp, then, with no one left to fight, turned their terrorism on the women. They took forty young women with their mothers to Caparde, another small town, then sent the mothers across the front lines to the nearby city of Tuzla. As guards menaced the young women with guns, soldiers took them one by one to private houses nearby and raped them once or more. They then gathered the women together, loaded them into buses, and drove them to the front lines, where they had to walk across a mined road before reaching safety.

At Omarska, in northwestern Bosnia, one of the most dreaded of the Serb concentration camps, thirty-three professional women, including doctors, political leaders, and other intellectuals, were held in quarters where Serb "investigators" used to question and beat civilian prisoners. By day the women washed dishes for the 2,200 or more men being held. At night they were prey for the guards, who raped them as if according to a schedule, once every four days. These are cases I have reported and corroborated by interviewing multiple witnesses. Alexandra Stiglmayer has other tales of women raped while in captivity from Trnopolje in northern Bosnia to Miljevina in eastern Bosnia. Her research and that of other journalists alerted the world to these events, and though it has now been replicated in material collected by the United States government and submitted to the UN Commission of Experts preparing the war crimes tribunal, almost nothing has been published except for the media accounts and material gathered by human rights watchdogs such as Helsinki Watch.

The rapes are not exclusive to the Serb forces in Bosnia, and there have been examples on a smaller scale by the other national groups. The distinction made by international relief workers and human rights analysts is that the Serbs set the pattern in 1992 – organizing the conquest to achieve a Greater Serbia, setting up concentration camps, and practicing systematic rape. Bosnian Croats in western Herzegovina adopted the pattern starting in spring 1993, as they went on the offensive to create an ethnically pure Croatian sector. Forces of the predominantly Muslim government of Bosnia also have been charged with atrocities, but not as a tool of government policy.

In a sense this should be self-evident, for Serbs have an ideology of ethnic dominance that they themselves called "ethnic cleansing." Croats began aping the Serbs to carry out the partition plan drafted by United Nations mediators Cyrus Vance and David Owen, who proposed to settle the dispute by breaking Bosnia up into ethnically dominated ministates. The Bosnian government, by contrast, insists that its goal is to retain a multiethnic society. The abuses by its forces have tended to be unauthorized and unplanned.

How is one to explain the sudden reappearance of genocide on European soil less than half a century after the Nazi Holocaust and after three generations of Europeans and Americans have come of age accepting the motto "never again"? There are undoubtedly historical roots and diplomatic explanations, but many insights into mass movements are likely to come from psychologists and sociologists.

One of the characteristics of the crimes against humanity in the former Yugoslavia, other than the number of victims – as many as 10 percent of the Muslim population of 2.2 million in less than a year – was the number of perpetrators. Until the United States government and the UN War Crimes Commission publish their data, it will be impossible to obtain a real overview, and one must rely on anecdotal evidence. But the stories of massacres where as many armed men took part as there were victims and of mass rapes where individual soldiers used the alibi that they were acting under orders suggest a regime of terror, regimentation, and a pattern of criminality that easily recalls the Third Reich. The Serb government's near monopoly on television and other news media played a role; no doubt the politicians responsible for the madness also feel there is safety in numbers. But extreme nationalist movements do not spring into being overnight, and the suggestibility that leads large numbers of individuals to join in an orgy of crime must also be sought in songs and poetry, rituals and folklore, and mores stretching back generations.

As shocking as the genocide itself is the lack of reaction by Western governments, which have ratified the Conventions that oblige them to prevent acts of genocide from occurring. In fact, even though the leading governments agreed to set up the war crimes tribunal, no government has been willing even to characterize the events that led to that decision.

It is but another of the half measures taken by the UN Security Council, many of whose members have shown a willingness to come to terms with the Serbs at any price.

One difference between this genocide and the Nazi Holocaust is that the news media have reported the destruction of Bosnia in real time and with photographs and gripping detail that the public can grasp. The similarity is that governments now as then have preferred to divert public attention by revising facts, by painting deliberately inaccurate pictures of events, by refusing to reveal the information they have. In their search for alibis for inaction, the United States and other leading nations have mischaracterized the fighting as a civil war or religious war, terms appropriated from the Serb conquerors.

So it was left to the tribunal to determine the truth and to chart a path that will allow history to render a verdict on the victors. It was a bizarre assignment. Even more grotesque, as the tribunal was being organized to investigate them, the crimes against humanity were continuing, and the world community, paralyzed by indecision, continued to look on. The world's reaction, in short, was not a harbinger for stability and order in the post–Cold War era. It seemed rather to be a formula for encouraging future state-sponsored crimes against humanity, sowing the seeds of disorder, war, and more suffering.

Acknowledgments

I would like to thank everyone who has contributed to this book: Roy Gutman, who was the first journalist to report on mass rape in Bosnia and has been foremost in drawing public attention to the atrocities perpetrated there; the German filmmaker Helke Sander for her fictional letter to Lysistrata, which illustrates how many controversial questions the rapes in Bosnia-Herzegovina raise; Paul Parin, who examines the war in the former Yugoslavia and its hatreds from an ethnopsychological perspective; Ruth Seifert for her analysis of rape in war; Catharine A. MacKinnon for her all-encomposing explanation of the phenomenon of Bosnian mass rape; the Muslim journalist Azra Zalihic-Kaurin, whose work concerns the conflicting status of Bosnian Muslim women; the Croatian psychiatrist Vera Folnegovic-Smalc, who reports about her experiences working with the victims of rape; Susan Brownmiller, who reminds us that women have been raped in all wars; Rhonda Copelon, who goes into the legal possibilities of prosecuting rape as a war crime and holding the perpetrators accountable; Cynthia Enloe for her afterword, which deals with the public response to the Bosnian mass rape and its meaning and implication in political, feminist, and human rights terms; the journalists Heidi Hecht and Seska Stanojlovic, who carried out investigations on the Serbian side; and Dr. Mladen Loncar from the Croatian Ministry of Health and the American journalist George Rodrigue, who placed their interviews at my disposal.

Thanks to the efforts of all these good people, this book is a solid first approach to the topic of mass rape in Bosnia-Herzegovina.

In addition I would like to thank my friends, especially Wade and George, as well as my parents, who always stood by my side when I came to despair over the suffering of the people in Bosnia-Herzegovina and the world's inaction.

Prologue

Helke Sander

An excerpt from a letter to Lysistrata. According to Aristophanes, it was she who brought the Peloponnesian War to an end: when Athenian and Spartan soldiers returned home from the front on leave, she persuaded their wives to withhold sexual intercourse from them until they ended the war. She was successful on both counts.

Dear Lysistrata,

I would like to know whether your strategy would make any sense today in the war zone of the former Yugoslavia.

And so I am enclosing a book with a set of essays that illuminate the problem from different sides and give you some idea of the extent and variety of the conflicts. I would particularly like you to consider the following points:

1. The Peloponnesian War took place between men on the battlefield and not in the middle of the civilian population, as is now the case in the former Yugoslavia. When you women denied your belligerent husbands' desires, your strategy was quite clearly based on your own desire for them. You wanted them back in your beds again. You did not have the hint of a suspicion that your men might be rapists. And so you were able to concentrate together on trying to end the war.

2. You women of Athens and Sparta, kin to the hostile groups of men, spoke with one another. Your unquestionable lack of power in the public sphere bound you together; you were all aware of it, and you used it as an

opportunity to join forces. In the war I'd like to discuss with you, women have nothing to say. In virtually no political leadership council are they represented. (Filed away in drawers are plans to ban them from public life altogether and restrict them to the role of mother.) Although they are not the ideologues of nationalism, and although they have no privileged position to defend, unlike you they scarcely speak to one another anymore, and instead play the role of their husbands' cheerleaders. It was not always like that.

In the beginning the only strong and serious resistance to the Serbian-Croatian conflict came from the women in both countries. But the propaganda machinery in both lands has now succeeded in tying women to the camps of their nationalistic leaders. Earlier, women had the right political instinct, but they were inexperienced and easy to manipulate. Today they are above all badly informed, because the only reading materials they receive are the chauvinistic newspapers of their respective countries. Those radically democratic women who do not automatically believe the official statements, who conduct their own research, like my Croatian friend the journalist Vesna Kesic, for example, are blacklisted and publicly defamed as traitors to the fatherland.

3. With the support of the Serbian Serbs (the rump Yugoslavia), Bosnian Serbs are conducting a war of aggression, expulsion, and annihilation against the Bosnian Muslims and also in part against the Bosnian Croats. Meanwhile the Serbian Serbs have not officially declared their military support for the Bosnian Serbs. Even the Serbian peace movement does not consider itself at war, because no Serbian Serbs are officially fighting in Bosnia. In addition, Bosnian Serbs apparently continue to ally themselves with Bosnian Croats. There are sufficient examples to show that nonnationalistic Serbian men and women are being killed (by Serbian soldiers) if they help or speak with Muslims. The issue that must be clarified is whether the Muslim and Croatian women who are being raped in great numbers are raped because they are Muslims and Croats or because they are women. The legal argument would probably be different depending on the answer. Meanwhile, it seems that those who argue that the women are raped because of their ethnic membership are also the ones who want to intervene militarily to end the rapes; but they are deluding themselves about the consequences of military intervention and are tailoring the facts accordingly.

Despite propaganda and serious disinformation, Serbian women are capable of knowing, they do know, that their country (Serbia) – however serious the Croatian provocations might once have been – has instigated a war of aggression against Croatia. Even a nationalistic and uninformed Bosnian Serb woman can know that if her husband belongs to the Chetniks, to Arkan's or Seselj's people, or to the volunteers from Serbia, he is with almost 100 percent certainty a multiple rapist. It is no comfort to know that a Croatian woman's husband, if he is a Paraga man, is also quite certainly committing rape. If the Serbian woman's husband is with the Bosnian Serb territorial army or with the rump Yugoslavian army (which is officially not even at war) then she might reckon with the probability that her husband is not an active rapist, since these armies usually punish rapes as undermining military discipline.

When we talk about systematic rape, we still have to prove that this systematic aspect can be attributed in some form or other to the Bosnian Serb leadership; we have no substantive quarrel with this assumption. But the question is whether it can be proved that the rape camps are under official military orders or whether they are controlled by the different fighting groups – at least on the outside. In their interviews the raped Bosnian women speak more frequently about Chetniks than about regular soldiers. But perhaps these Serbian women feel the way the rest of the world does: no one knows anymore whether there is any difference between criminal bands acting independently and the regular army. Perhaps the raped Bosnian women could answer these questions; they could say whether the responsibility for the brothels and the rape camps is to be placed with the Chetniks, the partisan soldiers, or the troops. If we are to undertake effective action, these differences are important; for the raped women, however, they are perhaps unimportant.

4. I have spoken about active rapists. For me those are the men who use women voluntarily and get an erection in the presence of captured, intimidated, possibly injured little girls and women. Those men who say they were "forced" to rape also belong to this group. They too apparently have an erection. Passive rapists would then be those who watch, who let it happen, without moving heaven and earth to put an end to the rapes.

5. We know that large numbers of rapes also occur in so-called peacetime. I do not intend to lay out the evidence for you now, Lysistrata. According to the women who work in women's shelters, "normal" domes-

tic violence in Serbia and in Croatia is said to have risen 100 percent since the beginning of the war. Nearly every man is armed and, if he is at home, sleeps with a weapon "under his pillow." Women, meanwhile, are not only beaten but also killed with these weapons.

At this point I would like to make a little, not unimportant, digression, so that we understand the kind of times we live in. I think we are all brainwashed to the extent that we do not see clearly how deep misogyny goes, even in countries that are not at war. If a husband kills his wife, we will read something or other about it in the newspaper under "miscellaneous." We read the daily reports of rapes in the local news and not, for example, on the first page, under "political news." True, the authors of lead stories and commentaries argue about the causes of xenophobia, but not about the obvious connections between misogyny and xenophobia; no magazine monitoring the zeitgeist would think of calling for vigils against misogyny or even of designing buttons to protest it. (To tell you the truth, I personally find such buttons tasteless, but it is interesting that within this spectrum of tastelessness they are not to be found.) Similarly, there are no tables in the daily newspapers to record the year's crimes against women from January to December, tables that regularly appear about right-wing extremism or the vandalism of Jewish cemeteries.

6. There is something else that should be mentioned: today we are speaking about the war in the former Yugoslavia. Somewhat farther away from us, and not noted as much in the press, other wars are being waged: in Tajikistan, Armenia, Azerbaijan, invariably too in Afghanistan or in those Caucasian regions with unpronounceable names. In these countries too there is murder, rape, mutilation, with hatchets and pickaxes and modern military equipment. When we begin making sustained efforts against violence, then, even violence against women, we must realistically expect that our cause will occupy us for a long time to come. Nor is it at all the case that systematic mass rapes are anything new. We need only think of Bangladesh or Uganda or Iran, where in the early 1980s young girls were raped before they were executed because it is said that the Koran forbids the execution of virgins. Unfortunately it has taken a very long time for women themselves to grasp what it means when something like this occurs. For the first time, it is women who are now forcing this topic into public awareness. Until now, all the mass rapes mentioned above were simply too far from Europe to frighten us. Television and the

press do not linger in every crisis area, and whatever they do not report seems not to exist. And so the problem will not be solved within a few excited weeks through a few exceptional efforts.

7. From the essay by Paul Parin you will learn, Lysistrata, why all the warring parties in the former Yugoslavia are afraid of one another and why – unfortunately – you can believe virtually all the horror stories, no matter who tells them to you, and no matter what the nationality of the teller. That notwithstanding, and no matter what the (perhaps justified) fear motivating them, the Bosnian Serb army did the attacking. Those who interpret this war as a war of annihilation – and in my opinion they are correct – base their wish for military intervention on a comparison to Nazi Germany, whose terrible politics of aggression and annihilation could likewise be stopped only by the Allies.

But even if one agrees with the first assessment, the second need not be correct. In the war in Bosnia we are not dealing with clearly defined battling armies. Iraq had armies. But as we know, the military objectives were not attained in the Gulf War, not even with the most modern military technology, with a regulation army as an opponent, and on surveyable terrain. Thousands of people are dead, the environment is destroyed, and the dictator is enjoying even greater respect than before. In Bosnia and in all of the former Yugoslavia there seems to be no dearth of weapons. According to reports that I cannot check, but which I hope others can, the Croats and Serbs now waging war against each other, together with the Slovenes, are still bound to other countries by common contracts for the production and delivery of weapons. Certain weapons factories in the former Yugoslavia are spared from bombing by either of the warring parties, because these factories are allegedly still supplying all the warring parties. This war cannot be resolved by a few airport bombings.

On the other hand, it seems to be asking too much to expect the Muslim and Croatian women who are being threatened, displaced, and raped in a war of aggression to simply sit down together at one table with the wives of their enemies. Just imagine if anyone had demanded the like of German and Polish women after World War II.

We have to analyze the problem. The attempt at a commonality is supported on the one hand by the common wish to end the war and on the other by women's common political impotence. We must also consider the fact that disinformation is a real force, completely underestimated in this discussion.

So in summary, Lysistrata, here are a few points that we are discussing with an eye toward nonmilitary measures for bringing the war to a close:

• Many people wonder whether the Bosnian Serb leaders who travel to Western democracies that have incorporated into their own legislation those acts condemned by international law as war crimes should be arrested as war criminals rather than having a red carpet laid down for them internationally, thereby giving the false impression that these leaders are simply nationalistic Serbs.

• If it can be proved that the Serbian Serbs are also participating in these war crimes, then the same thing would apply to them and their traveling politicians. (These are the thoughts of laymen.)

• We are discussing the immediate publication in all newspapers of running lists to record the names of known torturers and rapists (war criminals) according to the criteria that, for example, Amnesty International applies in similar publications. Again and again, the raped women or tortured men from the camps say that they knew some of their tormentors. The rapists and torturers must understand clearly that they cannot get away with their actions under any circumstances – that they will be brought to international justice.

• We are discussing how to substitute truthful reporting quickly, effectively, and powerfully for the official as well as the private disinformation and propaganda on all belligerent sides (through the press, faxes, letters, mail to those who are able to read reports in other languages).

• We are discussing how we can bring our own defense ministry to engage with commitment in a systematic, institutional, long-range exploration of exemplary nonmilitary conflict resolutions, while ensuring that women are equal participants in these efforts.

• We are also discussing how we can persuade politicians in our own countries to institute a quota rule for the participation of women in international as well as bilateral negotiations with the belligerent parties. In that connection the international community might take a fresh look at a suggestion by a Saudi Arabian (!) politician: during a disarmament debate at a general session of the United Nations in 1978 he called on every country to establish an emergency council of "mothers over forty" in order to avoid warlike conflicts, and in addition to extend compulsory military service to the age of thirty-five at least, the age of the men who normally make decisions about war and peace. This suggestion was naturally made to appear ludicrous; the press reported it with a smirk, and the politician is said to have died a short time later.

• We are naturally discussing all measures likely to offer long-term help to women.

I look forward, Lysistrata, to what I hope will be your detailed reply.

Warm wishes,

Helke Sander

Mass
Rape

The War in the Former Yugoslavia

Alexandra Stiglmayer

The war in the former Yugoslavia is presented to us by the media as a "war of psychopaths," of madmen who delight in slaughtering one another, and as the "Balkan powder keg" that has exploded once again, turning the rest of the world into helpless, perplexed spectators. And yet there are rational explanations for this war, as well as for its escalation.

A nation of many peoples, with its colorful mix of nationalities Yugoslavia seemed to represent a stable bridge between the Orient and the Occident; its particular path to socialism and its independence from both East and West were regarded with respect throughout the world. To understand why it is now being destroyed in a bloodbath, we need to review its history. Only by going back more than a thousand years will we find the reasons for the antagonism among the South Slavic (Yugoslavian) peoples,[1] the roots of their historical claims and longings, and the causes of their mutual hatred, mobilized now by their adept nationalistic leaders.

Historical Review

The history of the South Slavic peoples begins in the sixth and seventh centuries during the great migrations,[2] when the Slavs came out of what is today Ukrainian-Byelorussian territory into the Balkan region, ruled at the time by eastern Rome (Constantinople, Byzantium).[3]

I

There is no longer any way to know whether Serbs, Croats, and Slovenes already existed back then, or whether the new settlers on the territory of what was later Yugoslavia were simply Slavs. We do know that they drove out the provincial Roman population and, at least very soon after settling the Balkan peninsula, formed Serbian, Croatian, and Slovenian tribes.[4] (At that time the other Yugoslavian peoples, the Montenegrins, Macedonians, and Bosnian Muslims, did not yet exist.) The Slovenes and the Croats lived in the north of the Balkan peninsula, the Serbs in the south, and they soon came under the influence of two different cultures that were to shape them: the eastern Roman and the western Roman.

THE MEDIEVAL KINGDOMS

In the ninth century the Serbs were converted by the eastern Roman church and became orthodox Christians like the Russians, Greeks, and Bulgarians. They adopted the Slavonic liturgy of the eastern Roman Slavic apostles Cyril and Methodius, who had developed the Glagolitic script for transcribing church texts. The Cyrillic script, which is today used by the Serbs, developed from Glagolitic.

The Slovenes and the Croats, on the other hand, came under the influence of the Franks, whose King Charlemagne (768–814) advanced south to Split about the year 800. His missionaries brought western Roman Christianity,[5] and the Slovenes and Croats became Catholics and today still use the Latin alphabet.[6] Although from this point on until 1918 the Slovenes remained under German influence (the Frankish rulers were later replaced by the Habsburgs), the Croats were able to found an independent kingdom in 925. This Croatian kingdom also covered the present territory of Bosnia-Herzegovina. Croatian claims to Bosnia-Herzegovina go back to this time, as does Croatia's desire for independent statehood, which has now been realized.

In 1102 Croatia fell to Catholic Hungary, and from 1526, when a Habsburg became king of Hungary, until 1918 it belonged to the Austro-Hungarian empire; yet it was always able to preserve a certain autonomy.[7]

In the twelfth century, the Serbs, ruled by the eastern Romans, also fought successfully for national independence The center of the Serbian kingdom was Raska, the present-day Kosovo; this is why Serbs think of it as the "cradle of Serbian nationhood." Soon the Serbian kingdom also achieved ecclesiastical independence from Byzantium. In 1209 Saint

Sava was ordained as archbishop by the Greek patriarch, thus founding the autocephalous Serbian Orthodox Church.

Medieval Serbia attained its greatest power and expansion under Stefan Dusan (r. 1331–55), who extended his kingdom to the Dubrovnik/Belgrade line in the north, the present-day border of Bulgaria in the east, and central Greece in the south. In 1346 he had himself crowned emperor of the Serbs and Greeks in Skopje (today the capital of Macedonia).

The great Serbian empire lasted only a few decades, however. On June 28, 1389, the Serbs were defeated by the Ottomans in the famous battle on Kosovo Polje (the Field of the Blackbirds, near Pristina, the present-day capital of Kosovo). The nearly five hundred years of Turkish rule over the Serbs would begin with this battle. Today June 28, *Vidovdan,* is still the most important national holiday in Serbia. Over the course of centuries the memory of the battle of Kosovo, kept alive primarily by the Serbian Orthodox Church, has become a legend. All patriotic songs and poetry refer to the battle, and it has become a national objective to erase the "curse of Kosovo" and restore Serbia's former greatness.

TURKS AND HABSBURGS: CENTURIES OF FOREIGN RULE

In the Ottoman Empire the Serbs, who made up the *raya,* the Christian population, were deprived of their rights. They were kept out of all high offices and were not permitted to develop an administrative or educated class, but remained at the developmental level of smallholders. As Christians they had to pay a head tax and turn over some of their newborn boys to the Turkish rulers – the feared "levy of boys." At the sultan's court the boys were trained to be janissaries, elite fighters in the Turkish army, and were raised in the Islamic faith.[8]

Only to the Serbian Orthodox Church did the Ottoman rulers grant a certain autonomy, even entrusting it with administrative tasks such as collecting head taxes. The Serbian Church became the bearer and preserver of the national Serbian heritage, offering moral support to the people and keeping alive the memory of the past: almost all Serbian kings are revered as saints.[9]

Under Austrian and Hungarian rule, the Croats and the Slovenes had more freedom. They had their own feudal class; in Croatia the *ban,*[10] who was of Croatian nationality, represented the Hungarian king, and the administration and army were in the hands of the Croatian nobility. Croatia and Slovenia took part in the cultural, intellectual, and economic development of the rest of Europe.[11] This centuries-long separate development had a decisive influence on the economic and cultural north-south split in the former Yugoslavia.

Many Serbs fled to Croatia to escape Turkish oppression. They settled at the Austrian military frontier (*vojna krajina*), the "bulwark of Christianity." The military frontier denotes the well-secured border area of Croatia. Because its inhabitants had the task of repulsing the recurrent Turkish advances, they were given land and such privileges as personal freedom, freedom from taxes, religious freedom, education, and self-government.[12] The military frontier, which was up to eighty kilometers wide in some places, coincides almost exactly with the present-day Serbian settlement areas in Croatia (currently occupied for the most part by Serbs), for the Serbs who live in Croatia are usually direct descendants of the frontier settlers. The name Krajina for this region has remained, too.

Some Serbs also fled from the Ottomans into Vojvodina, which at the time belonged to South Hungary (today Serbia). In 1690, for example, 80,000 Serbs fled to Vojvodina from Kosovo because a Serbian rebellion against the Turks there had failed and the Serbs were afraid of retaliation. Islamicized Albanians moved into the depopulated Kosovo territory.[13] Today they make up 90 percent of the population there, but as Edgar Hösch writes, "the abandonment of a province that in the Middle Ages was the nucleus of the Serbian state and whose famous Field of the Blackbirds (*Kosovo Polje*) near Pristina is one of the most symbolically important sites of Serbian history can be entertained by the Serbs only with great difficulty."[14] The problems of nationality in later Yugoslavia were not caused solely by these population displacements under Turkish rule. During the same period, new peoples were emerging in the territory that would become Yugoslavia: the Montenegrins and the Bosnian Muslims. The Montenegrins are Serbs who lived in the impassable mountain world of Montenegro, where the Ottoman Empire was never able to establish its power completely. In the seventeenth century the hostile tribes of the Montenegrins began to unite and, with the help of Russia, formed a national state. In 1799 the Turks recognized the autonomy of Montenegro. Many Montenegrins, however, continue to think of themselves as ethnic Serbs: Radovan Karadzic, for example, the leader of the Bosnian Serbs, is a Montenegrin.[15]

The Bosnian Muslims are descended from the Slavs who settled the Balkan peninsula in the sixth and seventh centuries. Presumably the tribes of the Serbs and Croats intersected on the territory of Bosnia-Herzegovina. Afterward the territory belonged alternately to the Croatian-Catholic-western Roman and the Serbian-Orthodox-eastern Roman spheres of influence.

The Bosnians too intermittently attained independence for short periods. Their first well-known ruler was Ban Kulin (ca. 1180–1204), under whom the Bogumils' heretical teachings, condemned by the Catholic Church, were widely disseminated – probably because the various cultural influences on the Bosnians had caused religious instability.

In 1463 the Ottomans conquered the territory of Bosnia-Herzegovina. Unlike the conquest of Serbia, this conquest led to countless conversions to Islam. In 1624, according to the report of a papal delegate, two-thirds of the population were Muslims.[16] Historians explain the Islamification of Bosnia by the absence of a strong sense of identity in its inhabitants, owing to alternating Catholic and Byzantine influence, and by the weakness of the Bogumilian teaching, which had only a few, persecuted disciples in Europe.[17] Bosnians were also attracted by privileges such as the elimination of the Christian head tax and by converts' better chances for advancement. By converting, members of the Bosnian nobility were able to preserve their rights as property owners, and the Bosnian Muslims became high officials and officers (*beys*) in the Turkish empire, ruling over the *raya*.

Even today the Serbs bear a grudge against the Bosnian Muslims for taking part in their oppression under Ottoman rule. Against the background of almost five hundred years of Turkish rule over the Serbs, it is also understandable that the Serbs have a deep-seated fear of Islam.

NATIONAL AWAKENING

In the nineteenth century, when national movements were forming throughout Europe, the national consciousness of the South Slavic people was also awakened. They became aware of their linguistic and ethnic relatedness,[18] but a far more important impulse turned out to be the wish for political self-determination. In the foreground of all national ideologies stood "the exclusive interests of each respective nation. . . . Conceptions of nationality that propagated South Slavic national unity, that is, the different variants of Yugoslavism,[19] had a significantly weaker profile."[20] That Yugoslavia (South Slavia) later came into being was due more to a conjunction of various factors than to the South Slavs' purposeful work toward unification.

In 1804 and 1815 the Serbs' wish for self-determination led to uprisings against the Turks. The second uprising had Russian support and was successful. The Belgrade *pashalic,* a Turkish administrative zone of approximately 24,000 square kilometers, was liberated and recognized as autonomous by the Ottoman Porte in 1830. Yet the new Serbia was significantly smaller than the great empire that had existed before the invasion of the Turks, and it included only a fraction of all the Serbs. Most Serbs were still living under Turkish rule in Bosnia, Macedonia, and Kosovo or had moved away, like the Serbs who were now living under Austro-Hungarian rule in Croatia and Vojvodina, or else they had become autonomous like the Montenegrins.

In 1844 the Serbian minister of the interior Ilija Garasanin (1812–74) developed a plan (*nacertanije*) whose goal was to unify all the Serbs within one empire. This empire was to be achieved through clever diplomacy and the mobilization of all Serbs. Garasanin's plan was not realized, but from that time on the Serbs dreamed of a "state for all Serbs," and the idea of Greater Serbia repeatedly cropped up as a political concept: "The basic fact that the borders of the Serbian state in the 19th century did not coincide with the borders of Serbian settlements gave the idea of Serbian nationality an explosive quality. Politically and ideologically the purpose of every Serbian political program was to alter the international status quo."[21] Although Serbia continued to expand until World War I, it was only Yugoslavia that would become the "house for all Serbs." With its collapse, the Serbs who make up minorities in Croatia, Bosnia-Herzegovina, and Macedonia are once again threatened with dispersal into different states; this is one of the reasons for their resistance to the independence of Croatia and Bosnia. When the war in Croatia began, one of the insurgent Serbs declared: "If Yugoslavia collapses and the present-day borders of the republics remain intact, then we Serbs would have to live in four different republics. What people in the world wishes to be treated like the Kurds?"[22]

The Croats, too, developed national ambitions in the nineteenth century. Their attempt to free themselves from Hungarian encirclement (Croatia formally belonged to the Hungarian part of Austro-Hungary) failed in 1848. Awareness of this political weakness led to movements in Croatia that strove either for federalization of the Danube Monarchy (with Austria, Hungary, and Croatia-Slovenia as equally enfranchised parts of the empire) or for unification in a federalist state with Croatia's "Serbian brothers" who had successfully shaken off Turkish rule. In addition there was also a nationalistic movement around the Frankist Party, which had as its goal an independent Croatian state that would also encompass Bosnia-Herzegovina.[23] The present-day right extremist Croatian Party of the Right, which has its own irregular troops, the HOS (Croatian Armed Forces), refers back to this Frankist Party.

The Croatians' demands for federalization of the Habsburg Empire gained new weight when Bosnia-Herzegovina came under Austrian administration at the Congress of Berlin in 1878, thereby adding an additional South Slavic territory to Austria. This step had been preceded in 1875 by an uprising of the Bosnian Serbs against their Turkish rulers in Bosnia-Herzegovina. Russia and Montenegro had rushed to the aid of their religious brethren, and together they had driven the Turks out of Bosnia-Herzegovina and out of southern Serbia and Macedonia. Russia's influence on the Balkan peninsula had thus become very great, and Austria-Hungary and England protested vehemently. In 1878 at the Congress of Berlin, which was intended to avert this international crisis, it was decided that Austria would be permitted to govern Bosnia-Herzegovina and that Macedonia would be returned to Turkey.

Austria annexed Bosnia-Herzegovina in 1908, nearly starting a war. Russia was deterred from a declaration of war only because the German empire affirmed its loyalty to its alliance with Austria. Thereafter the two great powers of Russia (with its allied partners France and England as well as Serbia and Montenegro) and Austria-Hungary (with its allied partner Germany and the imperial components Croatia and Slovenia) opposed each other with undisguised hostility. The murder of the Austrian crown prince Franz Ferdinand by the nineteen-year-old Serbian nationalist Gavrilo Princip in Sarajevo on June 28, 1914, the 525th anniversary of the battle of Kosovo, was ultimately no more than the spark that lit the powder keg.[24]

THE "FIRST" YUGOSLAVIA

Yugoslavia came into being because of World War I, in which both the Habsburg empire and the Turkish empire disintegrated. When the war

Yugoslavia's History

1918	Kingdom of Serbs, Croats, and Slovenes
1929	Renamed "Yugoslavia"
1941	German-Italian occupation
1945	Socialist Yugoslavia, composed of six republics
1991	Independence of Slovenia and Croatia
1992	Independence of Bosnia-Herzegovina and

Map 2. History of the Yugoslav State

began, Serbia hoped to exploit the conflict to further its own expansion, but when its powerful protector Russia withdrew because of the February Revolution in 1917, it came to view more positively the alternative, a union with the South Slavic areas of the declining Danube Monarchy. This idea had been put forward by Croatian and Slovenian politicians who had formed the "Yugoslavian Commission" in London in 1915; on December 1, 1918, the Serbian prince regent Aleksander Karadjordjevic announced the founding of the "Kingdom of Serbs, Croats, and Slovenes." Montenegro joined the new state, which also included Kosovo and northern Macedonia,[25] areas that Serbia had conquered in the Balkan wars of 1912–13.[26]

Yugoslavia was born, but the people united within it had differing ideas of the new state. The Croats and the Slovenes supported a federation in which they were to be enfranchised equally with the Serbs, but the Serbs insisted they should have the leading role. After all, they had been on the winning side in the war, they could point to almost one hundred years of recent statehood, and they possessed a functioning national government, an army, a royal house, and the largest portion of the population.

The Serbs prevailed. On June 28, 1921, once again the anniversary of the battle of Kosovo, so historically meaningful for the Serbs, the constitution of the new state was passed, providing for a constitutional monarchy and a centralist state structure. Croatian and Slovenian representatives boycotted the vote. "From the outset, the principles of national authority and state centralism [laid down in the constitution] labeled the champions of recognition and equal rights for the 'littler' nations as enemies of the constitution. Even if the Serbs did not represent an absolute majority of the entire population,[27] the centralist constitution did give them an advantage as the relatively strongest group."[28] The result was a series of unending disputes between Croats and Serbs, boycotts of parliament, and collapsed governments. By the end of 1928 twenty-four cabinets had ruled, at times for no more than a week.[29]

The chaos that prevailed through the whole country exacerbated the political situation. Economically there was a strong rift between the relatively rich north and the poor south, and the measures intended to alleviate it – higher taxes in Croatia and Slovenia, investments in Serbia – "created a climate of national indignation which was at times consciously stirred up by Croatian politicians."[30] In Macedonia, faced with the politics of Serbianization,[31] the Macedonian underground organization IMRO (Internal Macedonian Revolutionary Organization) was engaged in terrorism; in Kosovo the Albanians, who the Serbs considered "national aliens," were subject to grave reprisals; and in Bosnia-Herzegovina there were violent disputes between disfranchised Muslim landowners and their Christian former peasants.[32]

The Croatian-Serbian opposition that was coming to a head culminated in the assassination of the popular leader of the Croats, Stjepan

Radic (1871–1928), whose Croatian Peasant Party had gained as much as 80 percent of the votes in elections in Croatia. A Serbian deputy shot him and four other Croatian representatives in parliament on June 20, 1928. Seven weeks later, Radic died from his wounds. The Croats took his murder personally, and a civil war was imminent. Radic's successor, Vladimir Macek, categorically demanded a new federalist reorganization of the nation.

On January 6, 1929, the Yugoslavian king Aleksander Karadjordjevic dissolved parliament, suspended the constitution, and began dictatorial rule. Freedom of the press and freedom of speech were revoked, and all national, regional, and confessional parties were forbidden.[33] As a sign of the new times the Kingdom of Serbs, Croats, and Slovenes was renamed the Kingdom of Yugoslavia. National tensions were expected to disappear.

The dictatorial monarchy brought no improvement to the tense domestic political situation. On October 9, 1934, the Yugoslavian king was finally killed in Marseilles in a joint action of the Croatian terrorist organization Ustasha and the Macedonian IMRO.[34] In the years following the royal assassination, Yugoslavia slowly returned to democracy. On August 26, 1939, in fact, a Serbian-Croatian treaty was achieved: *Sporazum* (Agreement), which provided for the creation of a Croatian *banovina* with far-reaching self-government.[35] However, because World War II began only a week after it was signed, the treaty was never put into effect.

Hitler soon pressed Yugoslavia, with its close economic connections to Germany, to join the Tripartite Pact (Germany, Italy, Japan), of which Hungary, Romania, and Slovakia were already members. After long hesitation the Yugoslavian government signed the pact on March 25, 1941. Two days later there was a military coup in Belgrade, and Hitler ordered that Yugoslavia be "destroyed militarily and as a state."[36] On April 6 the bombing of Belgrade began.

WORLD WAR II

Under the assault of German, Italian, and Hungarian troops the Yugoslavian army dissolved, since most of the non-Serbian soldiers saw no reason to fight for their unpopular state. After only eleven days, on April 17, 1941, the Yugoslavian Supreme Command signed an unconditional surrender, and the country was divided up among the victors.

In Croatia, to which Bosnia-Herzegovina was annexed, Hitler and

Mussolini set up a puppet state. Because the Peasant Party, the strongest political force in Croatia, refused to cooperate with the fascists, they put the Ustasha leader Ante Pavelic (1889–1959) in power. He turned Croatia into a state after the model of fascist Germany. In this state, all Serbs were to be rooted out. They were forced to convert to Catholicism, displaced, murdered, and interned in concentration camps. How many Serbs were sacrificed to the fury of the Ustasha is not known; estimates range up to 700,000.[37]

Acts of revenge were not long in coming. In Serbia, which was placed under German military administration, the first resistance movement against the occupation forces was formed: the Chetniks, royalists favoring a greater Serbia,[38] under the Serb officer Draza Mihajlovic (1893–1946). The allies recognized Mihajlovic as the leader of the Yugoslavian resistance. But soon the Chetniks neglected the struggle against the occupation forces, instead taking revenge on the Croatian and Muslim civilian population for the Ustasha massacres. Thus on August 19, 1941, according to army reports, they killed 1,300 innocent people in the eastern Bosnian city of Foca.[39] In the summer of 1943, when the Chetniks actually began to collaborate with the Italians, the Allies dropped Mihajlovic.[40]

Josip Broz Tito (1892–1980), who stood at the forefront of the Yugoslavian Partisan movement, was named the new leader of the Yugoslavian resistance. Tito, half Croat, half Slovene, orthodox Communist and general secretary of the Communist Party of Yugoslavia (CPY) since 1939, had been able to rally great portions of the Yugoslavian population behind him with the motto "Brotherhood and Unity" and with the promise to establish a "just" federalist Yugoslavia after the war. At the end of 1942 his troops comprised 130,000 to 150,000 men, primarily Serbs from Bosnia-Herzegovina and Montenegrins; in 1943 they were joined primarily by Croatians from Dalmatia, Slovenes, Muslims, and Croats from Croatia.[41]

With the support of the Allies, Tito led the Partisans to victory, although the road was no less bloody than before. Wherever the Partisans invaded as liberators, they liquidated their enemies and those they took to be their enemies. In spring 1945, approximately 30,000 Croatian and Slovenian soldiers in flight to Austria were delivered by the British to the Partisans near Bleiburg, who liquidated them then and there; hundreds of thousands of civilian refugees were driven back to their homeland in a death march. Somewhat later, Chetnik troops were encircled on the Serbian-Bosnian border: here too approximately 30,000 men were killed on the spot.[42]

The constitution of the Federal People's Republic of Yugoslavia was passed on January 30, 1946, dividing Yugoslavia into six component republics (Slovenia, Croatia, Bosnia-Herzegovina, Montenegro, Serbia, and Macedonia) and two autonomous provinces (Vojvodina and Kosovo) annexed to Serbia. The monolithic CPY ruled as the central power.

Although Tito had oriented himself along historical boundaries when drawing the borders of Slovenia, Croatia, Bosnia-Herzegovina, and Montenegro, Serbia had to accept sensitive losses: to guard against greater Serbian demands, Kosovo (in which Albanians composed 68 percent of the population with half a million people) and Vojvodina (in which 840,000 Serbs [50 percent], 430,000 Hungarians [26 percent], 135,000 Croats [8 percent] as well as other minorities lived) were granted autonomous status. Tito created a special component republic out of Macedonia; and Bosnia-Herzegovina, where 1.1 million Serbs (44 percent of the population), 800,000 Muslims (31 percent), and 600,000 Croats (24 percent) lived, was also raised to the level of a component republic.[43]

By federalizing Yugoslavia (if at first only formally) and by the socialist reorganization of the country, the CPY thought it had eradicated the national question.[44] After their break with Stalin in 1948, the Yugoslavian Communists remained true to this concept when they began to develop new, undogmatic forms of socialism – I mention here only the catchwords "workers' self-management," "decentralization," and "nonalignment" – and Yugoslavia became the "symbol of courageous experimentation" in the world press.[45]

All nationalistic or even patriotic movements were forbidden, and the bloody massacres of World War II, which had left deep wounds in the psyche of the people, never worked through to the surface. But behind the facade of "brotherhood and unity" the old national passions continued to smolder. "In post-war Yugoslavia," Ramet writes, "Serbia easily slipped back into the role of 'big brother.'"[46] An important player in that regard was the Serbian Aleksander Rankovic (1909–83): minister of the interior, Tito's deputy responsible for personnel policies, and the feared chief of the Yugoslavian secret police UDBA,[47] which was staffed by Serbs and Montenegrins. Under the UDBA the Croats were made to suffer, "for they are held accountable for the collapse of 'old' Yugoslavia, for Ustasha fascism, and – most weighty of all – for the cruel persecution of Serbs on the territory of the Pavelic state established in 1941. From the Serbian perspective there is something like Croatian collective guilt."[48] Rankovic had Serbs put into all mid-level and higher-level posts within the Croatian police, justice department, and administration, and he pursued a similar policy in Bosnia-Herzegovina.[49] Kosovo stood "under Serbian rule from the beginning. . . . The UDBA, governed entirely by Serbs and Montenegrins, declared Kosmet[50] 'Yugoslavia's most potentially dangerous region,' where one had to reckon at all times with attempts at armed revolution."[51] Mistreatment and murder of Albanians were the order of the day, and in the mid-1950s 100,000 Turks, or Albanians who were declared to be Turks, were deported to Turkey.[52]

In the 1960s the first consequences of socialist mismanagement in Yugoslavia became noticeable, and the party organizations of the "prosperous" component republics Slovenia and Croatia as well as Macedonia urged further decentralization and liberalization.[53] The strongest opponents of any kind of reform were Rankovic and his followers. They were aware that an economic liberalization would be accompanied by a political one and by the republics' greater independence; and that would reduce the political power of the Serbs, who were especially dominant in the federal institutions.[54]

In 1966 Tito toppled Rankovic. After his fall, demands for national self-determination were heard in all the republics: Bosnian Muslims demanded recognition as a people and received it; a short time later, Kosovo Albanians demanded more autonomy and received it; the Macedonian Orthodox Church declared itself separate from the Serbian Orthodox Church; Slovenes protested the lack of investment in their republic; and in Croatia a national movement emerged that even included the Croatian party leaders. They decried above all the "economic exploitation" of Croatia, which was traced back to the hegemony of Belgrade. Even as early as this point Croatians expressed their wish for autonomy, while the representatives of the Serbian minority in a countermove demanded the establishment of autonomous territories.[55]

In 1971 Tito intervened, crushing the "Croatian Spring." Although the voicing of any national or nationalistic sentiment was punished severely thereafter, he could no longer deny the existence of national tensions. He sought to resolve them by a wide-ranging strengthening of the economic and political rights of the republics and the autonomous provinces of Kosovo and Vojvodina, as well as by instituting parity in nominations to all leadership councils, as recorded in the constitution of 1974.[56]

The end result of this constitution was to cripple all the organs of state (every republic had the right to veto important decisions and made generous use of that right) and to splinter the Yugoslavian market into eight protectionist economic zones.[57] But Yugoslavia did remain peaceful until Tito's death on May 4, 1980. In the year of his death the inflation rate was 27 percent, the payment deficit was $4 billion, the foreign debt, calculated for the first time, totaled $19 billion,[58] and there was a troublesome lack of provisions. The catastrophic economic situation propelled Yugoslavia toward disintegration. All measures undertaken to stabilize the economy failed, since the Communist leaders of the Yugoslavian republics attacked one another and were unable to agree on any idea to overcome the crisis. This created the ideal soil for the growth of nationalism.

War!

The first national passions in Serbia were awakened by the uprising of the Kosovo Albanians in 1981. The Albanians represented 75 percent of the population in Kosovo at the time (today 90 percent) and demanded more autonomy. The uprising was put down, but in Serbia people heard that the Albanians were planning "genocide" against the Serbian people. The Serbian Orthodox Church called for the "protection" of the Serbian population and their holy places in Kosovo, and they too accused Albanian nationalists of "ethnic murder."[59] The Serbian media began to report atrocities in Kosovo: Albanians were said to be raping Serbian women,[60] slaughtering the cattle of Serbian peasants, sawing down their fruit trees, smearing walls with graffiti such as "Serbs go home to Serbia" and "Kosovo – a republic!" and driving the Serbs out by these means.[61] Not much of this propaganda was true, but it reached people's ears, catapulting to power Slobodan Milosevic, the most zealous advocate of the thesis of the "genocidal Kosovo Albanians." In 1986 he became Serbia's party leader, and one year later its president.

But Milosevic did not want just Kosovo – he wanted all of Yugoslavia. In fervent speeches he discussed the Serbs' "injuries and disfranchisement" in socialist Yugoslavia, their "historical greatness," and the "hostility toward Serbs" of the other Yugoslavian peoples. His words were not without influence on the Serbs, who were suffering from an economic crisis, and Milosevic became ever more popular. The press and national television in Serbia were taken over by Milosevic. In 1988 the political administration in the provinces of Kosovo and Vojvodina as well as in the republic of Montenegro was shuffled, and Milosevic's followers were installed.[62] Little by little Kosovo was occupied by a gigantic military machine; all educated Albanians lost their jobs, and Albanian-language schools and universities were closed.

At the same time, Milosevic had to tend to the other Yugoslavian republics.[63] The Slovenian and Croatian Communists protested most vehemently against his policies, which were shaking the foundation of Tito's legacy. They were declared "enemies of Serbia." Milosevic accused them of being "separatists, nationalists, and destroyers of Yugoslavia" who considered "Serbian greatness a thorn in the side." Circulating at Serbian demonstrations was the motto: "The weapons of Albanian terrorists are fired by Slovenes and Croats."[64]

When the Slovenian and Croatian Communists ultimately resigned and announced free elections in 1990, Milosevic unleashed a hate campaign against the Croats. In this case it was easy to conjure up the "danger of genocide," for in the Croatian fascists' Ustasha state the Serbs had been persecuted and slaughtered. Milosevic's main weapon, the Serbian press under his control, labeled Franjo Tudjman, who had been elected president of Croatia in May 1990, a Ustasha agent and repeatedly warned the Serbs in Croatia (12 percent of the population) against the "new fascism."

Tudjman and his right-wing nationalistic HDZ (Croatian Democratic Union) Party did nothing to allay the fears of the Croatian Serbs. On the contrary, they resurrected old national symbols that had once been used by the Ustasha (the red-and-white checkerboard pattern, for example, which adorns the Croatian flag today); they refused to incorporate the four Serbian *S*'s into the coat of arms;[65] and in the new constitution that was passed in December they demoted the Serbs from a constituent people to a national minority. Croatia did want to negotiate with representatives of the Serbian minority, but they refused. Instead these Serbs instigated armed uprisings and seized power in villages with Serbian populations.

At the Yugoslavian level, the Croats and Slovenes tried to put through the idea of a confederation, but Milosevic would hear nothing of this. He asserted meanwhile that Serbia existed wherever there were Serbian graves: in Croatia, Bosnia-Herzegovina, Montenegro, Kosovo, Vojvodina, and Macedonia – wherever Serbs had settled during their eventful history.[66] The Serbian minority in Croatia was armed by Belgrade, and the Yugoslavian Federal Army, in which Serbs made up 70 percent of the generals, was instructed that Yugoslavia had to be preserved at any cost.[67] Croatia and Slovenia, feeling ever more uncomfortable in Yugoslavia, held referenda and received popular support for their declarations of independence. On June 25, 1991, both parliaments reached the moment of declaring their republics autonomous states.

That was the signal for an attack by the Yugoslavian Federal Army and Serbian paramilitary troops, which had already brought many Serbian-inhabited localities in Croatia under their control. The war in Slovenia lasted only ten days, after which the Federal Army retreated.[68] But one-third of Croatia was conquered, and despite the presence of United Nations peacekeeping troops in March 1992, the fighting still goes on with varying intensity.

At the same time, Milosevic had to prepare for war against Bosnia-Herzegovina. For what good would it do to conquer Croatia if Bosnia-Herzegovina was still lying between Serbia and Croatia? Serbia's state television station once again took over the war propaganda. Once again the message was that Serbs were being threatened by "genocide." This time the danger was coming from Muslims, who according to Television Belgrade were "Islam fundamentalists, *mudjahedins,* and extremists." In Bosnia-Herzegovina, Muslims represent 44 percent of the population, Serbs 31 percent, and Croats 17 percent.

As early as November 1991, shortly before the elections in Bosnia-Herzegovina and half a year before the start of the war, the Bosnian Serbs declared their "autonomy."[69] Not long after that, Radovan Karadzic, the leader of the Bosnian Serbs, made known in which area the new Serbian state was to be established: in 62 percent of the territory of Bosnia-Herzegovina.[70] The Serbs made up only 31 percent of the Bosnian population, it was true, but even those communities in which Serbs represented a minority were to belong to the new state (as would the non-Serbian majority in these communities).

The Muslims could not agree to this, for it would have meant that more than half of the 2 million Muslims living scattered throughout Bosnia-Herzegovina would have come under Serbian rule. The president of Bosnia, Alija Izetbegovic, a Muslim who had been elected in December 1991, insisted on a multinational, territorially unified Bosnia-Herzegovina. Because of this, the negotiations over cantonizing Bosnia-Herzegovina that had been going on under the auspices of the European Community (EC) ran aground in early 1992.

On March 3, after a people's referendum in which 62.7 percent of the voters (virtually all of them Muslims and Croats) voted for independence, Bosnia-Herzegovina declared its independence. On April 6 and 7, Bosnia-Herzegovina was recognized by the EC and by the United States. Thereupon the Serbian troops attacked.

These troops consisted of 80,000 to 100,000 soldiers of the Yugoslavian Federal Army who had been moved to Bosnia-Herzegovina from Slovenia and the unoccupied two-thirds of Croatia, volunteers from the ranks of the Bosnian Serbs, and the army of the paramilitary groups directed from Belgrade – for example, the Chetniks of Vojislav Seselj, head of the ultranationalistic Serbian Radical Party and a deputy in the Serbian parliament, or the Tiger group of the former Belgrade mafia boss Zeljko Raznjatovic, called Arkan.

There were sufficient military forces to break the resistance of the Bosnian Muslims and Croats quickly. The totally unprepared and unarmed Muslims have been forced back to 15–20 percent of Bosnian territory. Because of their experiences in the Croatian motherland, the Croats were somewhat better prepared. They retain approximately 20–25 percent of Bosnian territory, western Herzegovina and its foothills, which make up an area to which the Serbian leaders for the most part have raised no claims.

Until now the Serbs' march of conquest through the former Yugoslavia has been successful. They possess a third of the land in Croatia, two-thirds in Bosnia-Herzegovina. In the process 150,000 to 200,000 people have lost their lives, among whom the Bosnian Muslims have by far the most victims. According to statistics of the UN Commission on Refugees, an additional 3.5 million people have been expelled or have fled from the war. Among these people too the Bosnian Muslims form the largest group.

"ETHNIC CLEANSING"
The Serbian military leaders are concerned not only with winning territory, but also with driving out – and permanently – all "non-Serbs" in

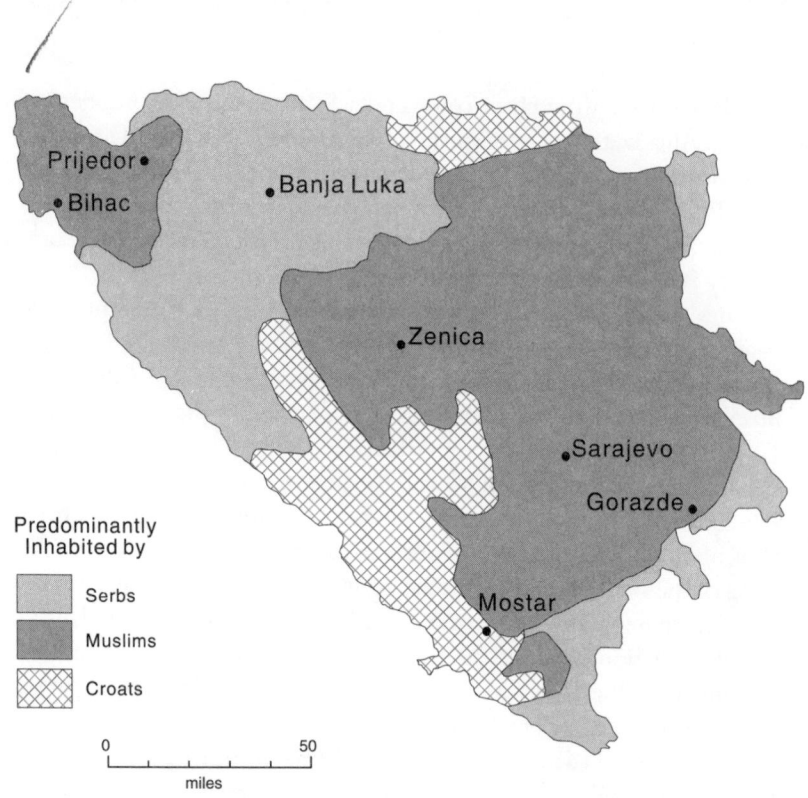

City	Population	Muslims(%)	Serbs(%)	Croats(%)	Others(%)
Banja Luka	195,139	15	55	15	16
Bihac	70,896	67	18	8	8
Gorazde	37,505	70	26	–	3
Mostar	126,067	35	19	34	12
Prijedor	112,470	44	42	6	8
Sarajevo	525,980	49	28	7	16
Zenica	145,577	55	16	16	13
Bosnia-H.	4,354,911	44	31	17	8

Map 3. Ethnic Distribution before the War. The table shows the ethnic composition of cities and of Bosnia-Herzegovina according to the national census of 1991.

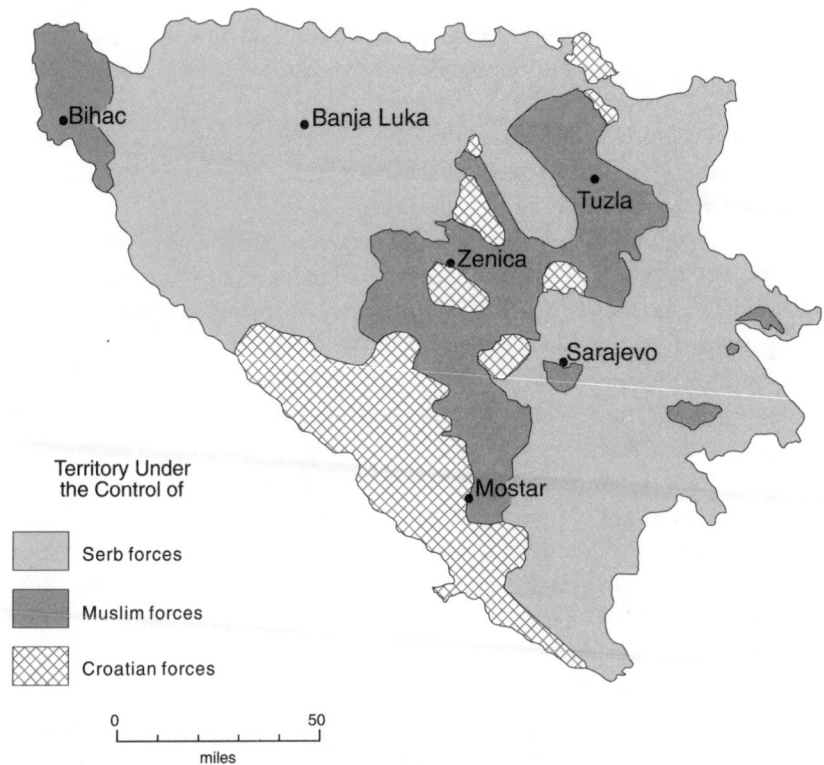

Map 4. The Combat Situation in August 1993

this territory. Muslims and Croats are murdered, imprisoned in camps, and deported; to prevent their return they are purposefully terrorized, tortured and raped; their houses and cultural sites are blown up so they will have nothing left should they want to return.

All this is based on political calculation: anticipating the possibility that the international community might not accept their conquests, the Serbian leaders are planning a people's referendum. If there are only Serbs in the areas concerned, then 100 percent of the "voters" will vote for the Serbian objective, whether it is a "Serbian republic" in Bosnia-Herzegovina or annexation to the mother republic of Serbia. At the moment it may perhaps seem absurd that any such people's referendum would be internationally recognized, but how will it be in ten or twenty years, when peace prevails again and the expelled Muslims and Croats still have not returned?

The Serbian leaders had to plan their "ethnic cleansing" carefully; they saw clearly that the native Serbs, friends and neighbors of the Muslims and Croats, would not simply go along.

Television Belgrade played and continues to play an important role, for it is the only Serbian information medium in all the war zones and far-flung sections of Serbia and Montenegro. It spreads the idea of "dangerous Muslim fundamentalists" and "fascistic, genocidal Croats." Nor does it back away from lies. Thus for two months Belgrade television did not report that Serbian troops were firing on Sarajevo – rather, it reported that "Muslim extremists" were shooting at their own people.[71]

In the past seven years since Belgrade television has been controlled by Slobodan Milosevic, it has built up a distorted image of reality, a highly complex web of lies in which everything has its own logic. Many Serbs are convinced by it that they are defending themselves against the Muslim and Croatian "danger" and must for that reason put aside sentiment and friendly feelings.

Nevertheless, the Serb public is usually kept uninformed of the brutal cleansing actions carried out by special units of the Serbian army[72] and by paramilitary groups directed from Belgrade. The latter recruits are made up of ultranationalists, criminals, the unemployed, and sociopaths, who are permitted to keep as the booty of war whatever they can take away from the Muslims and Croats they are supposed to drive off. They usually find like-minded people within the ranks of the "local Serbs." These groups doing the "dirty work" also terrorize the Serbian civilian population. Every man must join the war, and any contact with Muslims or Croats is frowned upon. Serbs who actually try to help them are stamped as traitors to the fatherland and usually suffer a similar fate: prison camp or death.

An article that appeared on July 28, 1992, in the Serbian magazine *Epoha* is an accurate example of Serbian propaganda. The Belgrade journalist Dragoljub Radanov describes his trip into those zones occupied by Serbs in northwestern Bosnia and Croatia, the so-called Krajina, and conveys the desired images of the Serbian enemies:

> The Serbs of Krajina, grown used to the constant Muslim-Croatian threat, seem to have decided this time around to reverse that history in

which some Serbs always died "in great numbers" while others then had to "escape." This time they have made a quick and clear decision that there is only one people on Krajina territory. It is unimportant whose idea it is – although everybody knows it is not a Serbian idea. It is important that it be carried out thoroughly. The Serbs have drawn their borders and struck hard; they have conquered and have kept winning. The territory is free. . . . There is no such thing as "coexistence," there are no Muslims and Croats, it is entirely a matter of indifference whether they move away voluntarily or under force, or whether they are killed in the cleansing actions. There is no pathos, none of this false cosmopolitanism that we in Belgrade are used to; there is no mercy, and no one expects any mercy either. . . .

The system of waging war is simple and efficient. The army breaks down resistance with its heavy artillery. Then the *martijevci* [special squads], who are responsible throughout Krajina for the cleansing actions, come in. The cleansing sometimes takes awhile. They say they are being slaughtered. Correct, in a certain sense. During the cleansing actions they use a knife whenever possible, to save ammunition. You have to understand that – this is not television here; this is war, rationalization.

Strangely enough, there is no real hatred in [Croatian] Krajina, in Knin. They don't hate the Croats, they have simply decided that there will be no Croats on their territory. One way or another. In the Bosnian region, hatred does exist, for the evidence seems to suggest that the Muslims took greater pleasure in torturing Serbs. When we arrived, we heard that the day before they had caught a group who roasted four boys on a grill, somewhere near Kotor Vares. They grilled them and even put a megaphone up to them, so that their screams would be heard far and wide. They chain prisoners to minarets and poke their eyes out in front of microphones. Now there are no more minarets, no mosques, either; they have been destroyed, some of them have disappeared without a trace. In every attack the minaret is the first thing to be destroyed, for the Muslims spread out in lines around the minarets. As soon as someone with a weapon falls, others take up the weapon and go on, go on and on. They use their wives and children as protective shields. They are in a holy war. In the prison camp in Prijedor approximately 290 Muslims are standing quietly in the courtyard. The Serbs say, "They are dangerous, they regret nothing, and they do not suffer. Their Allah has told them that if they die in war, they will go directly to heaven."

International Response to the War

The escalation of the war in the former Yugoslavia is the result of an unchecked act of aggression that has meanwhile grown into a campaign of annihilation. A significant share of responsibility for it must be attributed to the international community.

When the war in Slovenia and Croatia began in the summer of 1991, European Community nations took up the problem almost overzealously. Their efforts were marked by an incorrect assessment of the situation, adherence to historical friendships and alliances (e.g., France and Great Britain with Serbia, Germany and Austria with Croatia), and quarrels within their own ranks (reservations about the new Germany after reunification). The disunited members of the EC could not agree on any concrete measures, and all their attempts at a solution served only to save face. When the United Nations started discussing military intervention in April 1993, it became clear that Europe is not prepared to act: no European country wants to participate in military action.

The discussion in the United Nations Security Council, which was called upon to help, took a similar shape. Its members are confronted by the additional problem that Russia, where weapons abound and where strong Communist forces are still active, takes Serbia's side for historical, religious, and ideological reasons.

In order to mask its inability to act, the international community paints false pictures of this war, pictures of an impenetrable civil war in which no intercession is possible. The Bush administration, for example, issued a directive to maintain this false impression. This became known when George Kenney, the State Department assistant responsible for this region, resigned for reasons of conscience on August 25, 1992. "The Bush administration pronouncements on the Yugoslav crisis between February and August exhibited the worst sort of hypocrisy," Kenney wrote to explain his resignation:

I know; I wrote them. . . . My job was to make it appear as though the U.S. was active and concerned about the situation and, at the same time, give no one the impression that the U.S. was actually going to do something significant about it.

The goal from the beginning was not good public policy, but good public relations, and from that perspective, the administration's approach was a smashing success. It managed to downplay the gravity of the crisis and obscure the real issues. Of course, it did so at the expense of civilian casualties in numbers that are not yet known. . . . The trick in this instance was to ignore any facts – whether they pertained to atrocities, rumors of concentration camps, or starvation – that would complicate the policy goal of not getting involved.[73]

The UN Security Council also tries to appear shocked and busy. They pass one resolution after the other, impose embargoes, create commissions, threaten and negotiate; but all these measures are half-hearted and change little in the course of the war.

When the war began in 1991, the UN Security Council at first declared an arms embargo against Yugoslavia. It could not have done the Serbian side a bigger favor, for the Serbs are backed by the Yugoslavian Federal Army with its gigantic arms and munitions arsenals, whereas in the beginning the Croats and Muslims had no weapons at all. This is the reason the Serbian army was able to conquer large portions of Croatia and Bosnia-Herzegovina.

In March 1992 the UN Security Council sent UN soldiers into the former Yugoslavia. Their mandate, however, defines them as a "peacekeeping force" and not as a "peacemaking force"; this means that they may not use force in any of their activities. And their mere presence has not impressed anyone.

The 14,000 UN soldiers who were sent to the Serbian-occupied territories of Croatia have the task of demilitarizing the crisis zones and facilitating the return of Croatian refugees. Because they have no means of bringing pressure to bear, they are as far from their goal today as they were at the outset. The 8,000 UN soldiers who have been accompanying and protecting aid convoys in Bosnia-Herzegovina since October 1992 may use force only if a convoy is actually attacked. Every barricade at which they are "peaceably" stopped presents an insurmountable barrier. Because they may not intervene in any battles, they have to look on without acting as the civilian population is massacred. At first the flight ban over Bosnia-Herzegovina, passed by the UN Security Council in October

1992, did not dictate punishment for nonobservance. Not until six months later, after the Serbian air force had done its work, did NATO provide planes authorized to shoot down hostile military aircraft.

Because it lacks a commitment to use military force if necessary, the first Bosnia-Herzegovina peace plan, developed by the two negotiators Lord David Owen and Cyrus Vance, has failed. It provided for the division of Bosnia-Herzegovina into ten relatively autonomous provinces (three Muslim, three Serbian, and three Croatian, with the capital of Sarajevo as a neutral zone). But under the terms of the plan, Serbian leaders would have to relinquish a third of the territory they now control – and why would they want to sign on to a plan like that?

It is above all the 2 million Bosnian Muslims who are suffering because of these policies. Their politicians had thought the world would support them if it came to an act of Serbian aggression in Bosnia-Herzegovina. Again and again, Bosnian president Alija Izetbegovic had insisted that a war would not solve any problems and rejected any arming of his people. Today the Muslims are crowded together on 15–20 percent of the area of Bosnia-Herzegovina and bewail the loss of 150,000 to 200,000 of their people. For the most part these people did not die from grenades or bombs but were deliberately murdered in intentional acts of mass destruction by the Serbian military forces. To disguise the fact that genocide is occurring, the international community uses the term "ethnic cleansing."

Meanwhile the Muslims must defend themselves not only against the Serbs, but also against the Bosnian Croats, who were their allies when the war began. From the beginning the Croats pursued a two-track policy: they would either ally themselves with the Muslims or else divide Bosnia-Herzegovina with the Serbs and sacrifice the Muslims. They have decided on the second option, for they see it is not justice, but military strength and brutality that will triumph in this war.

The notion of a war of "madmen who are slaughtering one another," of a war that escalates without anyone's being able to do anything about it, is becoming ever more true. It is now only a question of time until the community of nations withdraws completely from the war, saying, "We knew it all along."

RAPES AND OTHER WAR CRIMES

The community of nations has been investigating war crimes in the former Yugoslavia only superficially. Aides on the Mazowiecki Commission the commission of experts formed by the United Nations to investigate the human rights situation in the former Yugoslavia complain about insufficient personnel and receive no support from UN member nations, although all governments, aid organizations, and human rights organizations have officially been called on to participate.

The two large organizations on the spot, the International Red Cross and the UN Commission on Refugees, are committed to neutrality and are overburdened. They are hardly able to tend to the masses of refugees and the needy, let alone ask them questions about war crimes. "Neither the International Red Cross nor any other humanitarian organization can solve this problem," said Red Cross security coordinator Didier Pradervand at the end of November 1992. "The international community itself must find the answer; it cannot rely on the humanitarian activities of the various organizations."[74]

A conscious refusal to disclose any crimes is one way to avoid having to act. Another way to avoid action is to conceal the context of the crimes. The United Nations insists steadfastly that all parties to the war are equal and tries in its reports about the human rights situation to make all sides equally responsible for the war crimes. As a rule it takes a few of the less drastic cases from the abundance of crimes committed on the Serbian side and names them in one breath with the crimes committed on the Muslim and Croatian side.

An excellent example is the treatment of mass rape. The first refugees who fled from Bosnia-Herzegovina to Croatia in June 1992 had already reported rapes. Two months later, in August, the American journalist Roy Gutman wrote the first complete report about the rapes of Muslim women by Serbian soldiers.[75] At that time co-workers of the United Nations Commission on Refugees were already familiar with these reports. Thus Anders Levinson, responsible for central Bosnia, told me on August 24, 1992, that among the 4,000 Muslim refugees who had arrived that weekend in the central Bosnian city of Travnik there were forty-nine raped women. Forty-nine women who spoke about it – how great must the real number of rape victims among the 4,000 deported Muslims have been?

No one reacted, no one began follow-up investigations. In November more and more reports about rape appeared in the press. But even at the beginning of December, both the UN Commission on Refugees and the International Red Cross repeated uniformly that only isolated cases of rape were known, and indeed on all sides. Normally such a story would end here. The journalists would write down the explanations of the international organizations and pack up. But they kept on writing.

How astonished I was in mid-December 1992 when the press spokesperson for the International Red Cross, Sylvana Foa, suddenly explained to me that the UN Commission on Refugees was receiving "*continual reports of rapes from Bosnian refugees*," that rapes "were widespread," and that it was "really a shocking thing"! It was the pressure of the publicity caused by press reports that had led to this mysterious turnaround. Thus one of the war crimes has been exposed, at least, triggering worldwide outrage.

Notes

1. *Yugo* in Serbo-Croatian means south, so Yugoslavia means South Slavia.

2. The invasion of the Huns into the greater Gothic empire in A.D. 375 was probably the occasion for the Slavic migration. The greater Gothic empire subsequently declined, and its Slavic inhabitants fled. See Georg Stadtmüller, *Geschichte Südosteuropas* (Munich, 1950), p.90.

3. In A.D. 395 the ancient Roman Empire had split into an eastern Roman empire and a western Roman empire (the end of imperial unity). In the Roman Empire the province of Illyria was the territory that eventually became Yugoslavia.

4. The eastern Roman emperor Constantine VII Porphyrogenitus (913–59) reports in his work *De administrando imperio* that the eastern Roman emperor Heraclius (610–14) had allied himself with the Slavic tribes of the Croats and Serbs. The Slovenes are mentioned in connection with the first South Slavic state, Caranthania, which they founded in 650 and which existed for one hundred years. See Peter Bartl, *Grundzüge der jugoslawischen Geschichte* (Darmstadt, 1985), pp. 1 ff. and 47 ff.

5. After the division of the Roman imperium in the year 395, the western Roman half lasted for eighty years, then to be conquered by various "barbarian tribes" – the eastern Goths and later the western Goths and Franks. The "barbarians" adopted the culture of western Rome. The Franks, who rose to be a great European power, are considered the heirs of the western Roman empire.

6. On this subject the historian Klaus-Detlev Grothusen writes: "After the storms of the great migrations of peoples, the Frankish empire (as the heir of the western Roman empire) and Byzantium (the old eastern Rome) came into direct contact for the first time on the territory of present-day Yugoslavia and therewith

began that tradition . . . that has become the basic fact of Yugoslavian history: the cultural border between the Latin western church and the Greek Orthodox eastern church." Klaus-Detlev Grothusen, "Historische Voraussetzung des heutigen Jugoslawiens," in *Jugoslawien zwischen West und Ost: Probleme seiner Geschichte, Wirtschaft und Politik,* ed. Herbert Ludat (Giessen, 1963), p.18.

7. Dalmatia, the present-day Croatian coastal area, did not belong to Austria until 1797. From the twelfth to the fifteenth century Dalmatia was alternately under Venetian, Hungarian, and Byzantine rule, and after 1421 it belonged permanently to Venice. Although their culture and language became Venetian for some time, the Dalmatians of today think of themselves as pure Croats.

8. For the positions of the Serbs in the Ottoman Empire, see Edgar Hösch, *Geschichte der Balkanländer: Von der Frühzeit bis zur Gegenwart* (Munich, 1988), p.94, and Bartl, *Grundzüge,* p.94.

9. For Serbian church history, see Ivo Banac, *The National Question in Yugoslavia: Origins, History, Politics* (Ithaca, N.Y., 1988), pp.66 ff., Grothusen, "Historische Voraussetzung," p.27, and Hösch, *Geschichte,* p.97.

10. Title of nobility.

11. For the development of Croatia and Slovenia, see Grothusen, "Historische Voraussetzung," p.20, and Peter Sugar and Ivo Lederer, eds., *Nationalism in Eastern Europe* (Seattle, 1969), pp.401 ff.

12. For the military frontier, see Bartl, *Grundzüge,* pp.44 ff., and H. ⁀ ' ᷅arby, "Croatia," in *A Short History of Yugoslavia: From Early Times to 1966,* ed. Stephen Clissold (New York, 1969), pp.27 ff.

13. Albanian historians contend that the Albanians were descendants of the original population of the Balkan peninsula, the Illyrians, but there can be no absolute clarification of this point. When the Slavs came to the Balkan peninsula, the Albanians fled to the mountains and did not become Slavicized. In following centuries they were ruled alternately by the Bulgarians, Serbs, and Venetians, and finally by the Turks. Under Turkish rule most of them adopted the Islamic faith. See Jens Reuter, *Die Albaner in Jugoslawien* (Munich, 1982), pp.11 ff.

14. Hösch, *Geschichte,* p.262.

15. For Montenegrin history, see Darby, "Montenegro," in Clissold, *Short History,* pp.73 ff., and Bartl, *Grundzüge,* pp.58 ff.

16. Bartl, *Grundzüge,* p.38.

17. See ibid.; Hösch, *Geschichte,* p.74; and Darby, "Bosnia and Herzegovina," in Clissold, *Short History,* pp.63 ff.

18. Language: In the nineteenth century the Serbs, Croats, and Bosnians spoke very similar dialects. In 1818 the Serbian linguist Vuk Stefanovic Karadzic

(1787–1864) wrote a grammar of the most common South Slavic dialect, Stokavian, and cleansed it of Church Slavonic and Russian idioms. Thus he created the basis for modern Serbian and Serbo-Croatian. When the Croatian linguist Ljudevit Gay (1809–72) published a primer of grammar in 1830, he chose Stokavian.

Nevertheless the Serbs and Croats have never been able to develop a unified language. Serbo-Croatian, or Croato-Serbian, which was declared the national language of the Serbs, Croats, Montenegrins, and Bosnians in the treaty of Novi Said in 1954 (Slovenian and Macedonian were also considered official languages in Yugoslavia), comprises the Serbian and the Croatian linguistic variants, and one speaks either one or the other. The differences, however, are minimal: a Serb understands a Croat more or less as an American understands an Englishman. The differences lie in intonation and pronunciation; some alternative expressions and idioms are used, and the grammar is different on certain points (in addition, the Serbs use the Cyrillic alphabet and the Croats the Latin). The most significant differentiating mark is the development of the original Slavic sound *jat*. Whereas the Croats have turned it into *ije* or *je* (i.e., they speak Jekavian Stokavian), in Serbian it is a pure *e* (Ekavian Stokavian). Thus river, for example, is *rijeka* in Croatian and *reka* in Serbian.

Only Serbian Serbs speak Ekavian; Bosnian Serbs, Montenegrins, and Croatian Serbs can be heard speaking Jekavian Stokavian. The Muslims too speak Jekavian Stokavian, enriched by some Turkishisms. Today the Muslims insist that they speak "Bosnian," the Croatians insist on "Croatian," and the Serbs claim "Serbian," and each of the three nationalities cleanses its language of expressions that have been taken over from other nationalities. For the language problem, see Wolf Dietrich Behschnitt, "Nationalismus bei Serben und Kroaten, 1830–1914: Analyse und Typologie der nationalen Ideologie" (Dissertation, University of Cologne, 1976), pp. 86 ff.

19. Behschnitt says that "Yugoslavism" (South Slavism) means the idea of a special community of South Slavic nations. According to the emphasis it can mean linguistic, cultural, familial, or national community, and it calls for a unification of the South Slavs. The concept can also be used, however, to disguise greater Serbian and greater Croatian goals. See Behschnitt, "Nationalismus," p. 65.

20. Ibid., pp. 332 ff.

21. Sugar and Lederer, *Nationalism*, p. 405.

22. The leader of the Croatian Serbs, Milan Babic, in February 1991. Quoted by Roland Hofwiler, "Serbische Großmachtträume bergen Sprengkraft," *TAZ*, February 8, 1991.

23. For the national ideologies of the Serbs and Croats, see also Banac, *National Question*, pp.110 ff.; Josef Matl, *Südslawische Studien* (Munich, 1965), pp.65 ff., and Holm Sundhaussen, *Geschichte Jugoslawiens, 1918–1980* (Stuttgart, 1982), pp.23 ff.

24. For Bosnia-Herzegovina, see Hösch, *Geschichte*, pp.174 ff., and Stadt-müller, *Geschichte*, pp.393 ff.

25. Over the centuries the Macedonian territory had belonged to Byzantium (Greece), Bulgaria, and Serbia, and each of these three states believes that the Macedonians, whose language contains elements of Bulgarian and Serbian, are actually Greeks or Bulgarians or Serbs. After the Balkan wars of 1912–13 Serbia and Greece divided Macedonia, which had been under Turkish rule, between themselves, while Bulgaria received only a tenth of the territory. In socialist Yugoslavia, the "Serbian portion" became a Yugoslavian component republic, and today it is an independent state. For Macedonia, see Darby, "Macedonia," in Clissold, *Short History*, pp.144 ff., and Hösch, *Geschichte*, pp.180 ff.

26. For the founding of the state, cf. H. C. Darby and R. W. Seton-Watson, "The Formation of the Yugoslav State," in Clissold, *Short History*, p.159; Sugar and Lederer, *Nationalism*, p.407; and Sundhaussen, *Geschichte*, pp.36 ff.

27. According to Sugar and Lederer, *Nationalism*, p.397, approximately 12 million people lived in the "Kingdom of the Serbs, Croats and Slovenes": approximately 5.3 million Serbs, Montenegrins, and Macedonians (they were not counted separately; the Serbs alone numbered approximately 4 million), 2.8 million Croats, 1 million Slovenes, 800,000 Bosnian Muslims, and 400,000 Albanians, as well as 1.7 million people of other nationalities. For Serbian self-understanding, see Duncan Wilson, *Tito's Yugoslavia* (Cambridge, 1980), p.9; Banac, *National Question*, pp.141 ff.; and Grothusen, "Historische Voraussetzungen," p.32.

28. Sundhaussen, *Geschichte*, pp.49 ff.

29. According to Sundhaussen, *Geschichte*, pp.71 ff. Bartl gives the number as thirty cabinets (*Grundzüge*, p.101).

30. Sundhaussen, *Geschichte*, p.57.

31. The Macedonians had to change their names to Serbian (Kondovski became Kondovic, for example), and the immigration of Serbs was promoted. See Gustav Chalup, *Unbekannter Nachbar Jugoslawien* (Aarau, Switzerland, 1989), p.29.

32. See Sundhaussen, *Geschichte*, p.458, and Jens Reuter, *Die Albaner in Jugoslawien* (Munich, 1982), p.27.

33. For the dictatorial monarchy, see Bartl, *Grundzüge*, pp.102 ff., and Sundhaussen, *Geschichte*, pp.77 ff.

34. Ustasha: the terrorist Ustasha movement had been founded by Ante Pa-

velic (1889–1959), Croatian lawyer and leader of the right extremist Frankist Party, one day after the announcement of the dictatorial monarchy on January 7, 1929. Pavelic set himself up abroad with a few followers. In April the Ustasha (complete name Ustasa Hrvatska Revolucionarna Organizacija [Rebellious Revolutionary Croatian Organization]) and its Macedonian partner organization IMRO published a manifesto in which they proclaimed the objective of their struggle: the complete liberation and independence of Croatia and Macedonia. They received financial support from Italy and Hungary, where the training camps of the Ustasha were situated. See Bartl, *Grundzüge*, pp.88 and 106 ff., and Sundhaussen, *Geschichte*, pp.75 and 82.

35. For *Sporazum*, see Sundhaussen, *Geschichte*, pp.100 ff., and R. W. Seton-Watson and R. G. D. Laffan, "Yugoslavia between the Wars," in Clissold, *Short History*, pp.199 ff.

36. Hitler in the discussion of the situation on March 27, 1941 (*The Trial against the Chief War Criminals at the International Military Court, XXVIII* [Nuremberg, 1948], p.23), quoted in Bartl, *Grundzüge*, p.126.

37. For the Ustasha state, see Ladislaus Hory and Martin Broszat, *Der kroatische Ustasha-Staat, 1941–1945*, 2d ed. (Stuttgart, 1965).

38. Chetnik, in Serbo-Croatian *cetnik*, from *ceta*, "band, troop, (military) division." Chetniks existed even during the Turkish period, as militialike village patrols who fought against the Turks. See Bartl, *Grundzüge*, p.134.

39. See Hory and Broszat, *Kroatische Ustasha-Staat*, pp.132 ff.

40. For the Chetnik movement, see Sundhaussen, *Geschichte*, pp.125 ff., and Fred Singleton, *Twentieth-Century Yugoslavia* (London, 1976), pp.90 ff.

41. See Bartl, *Grundzüge*, p.138, and Robert Furtak, *Jugoslawien: Politik, Gesellschaft, Wirtschaft* (Hamburg, 1975), p.12. For Tito see also Milovan Djilas, *Tito: Eine kritische Biographie* (New York, 1980).

42. For the numerical statistics, see Bartl, *Grundzüge*, p.140, and Milovan Djilars, *Der Krieg der Partisanen: Memoiren, 1941–1945* (Vienna, 1978), p.570 (American original, 1977).

43. For population numbers (census, 1948) see Othmar Nikola Haberl, *Parteiorganisation und nationale Frage in Jugoslawien*, Osteuropa Institute of the Free University of Berlin (Berlin, 1976), p.182; for the division, Pedro Ramet, *Nationalism and Federalism in Yugoslavia, 1963–1983* (Bloomington, Ind., 1984), p.145, and Milovan Djilas, *Jahre der Macht: Kräftespiel hinter dem Eisernen Vorhang. Memoiren, 1945–1966* (Munich, 1983), pp.111 ff.

44. In 1948 Tito attested: "Our national question has been . . . solved, and solved very well indeed, to the all-round satisfaction of our nations. It has been

solved in the manner taught to us by Lenin and Stalin." Josip Broz Tito, "Über Nationalismus und Internationalismus," speech on November 16, 1948, in Ljubljana, Belgrade, 1948, p.6, quoted by Behschnitt, "Nationalismus," p.1.

45. Paul Lendvai, *Die Grenzen des Wandels: Spielarten des Kommunismus im Donauraum* (Vienna, 1967), p.139.

46. Ramet, *Nationalism,* p.25.

47. For the UDBA see Alexander Graf Razumovsky, *Ein Kampf um Belgrad: Tito und die jugoslawische Wirklichkeit* (Berlin, 1980), p.55.

48. Hans Hartl, *Nationalismus in Rot: Die patriotischen Wandlungen des Kommunismus in Südosteuropa* (Stuttgart, 1968), pp.104 ff.

49. In 1969 Serbs, who made up 15 percent of the population in Croatia, occupied 54 percent of all positions in the police and composed 27 percent of the members of the Croatian party organization. See Felix Niesmann, *Im Spannungsfeld von Zentralismus und Selbstverwaltung: Politische und ökonomische Determinanten des "eigenen Weges" zum Sozialismus und deren Auswirkungen auf die Nationalitäten- und Außenpolitik in der Sozialistischen Föderativen Republik Jugoslawien* (Bochum, 1979), p.235, and Haberl, *Parteiorganisation,* p.210. For the role of the Serbs in 1979 see also Christine Kohl, *Jugoslawien* (Munich, 1990), pp.54 ff., and Ramet, *Nationalism,* pp.146 ff.

50. Kosmet stands for Kosovo-Metohija, originally the official designation of Kosovo.

51. Reuter, *Albaner,* p.44.

52. See Reuter, *Albaner,* p.45, and Erich Rathfelder, "Serbien: Leidenstrauma und Mythos der Geschichte," *TAZ,* August 6, 1991.

53. See table 1 for Yugoslavian demographics.

54. In 1961 the Serbs made up 42 percent and the Montenegrins 3 percent of the population of Yugoslavia, but they represented 84 percent of the ministers, officials, and functionaries active in federal institutions, 8 percent of federal judges, 70 percent of officers, and 65 percent of generals in the Yugoslavian Federal Army, as well as 57 percent of all party members. For these figures, see Furtak, *Jugoslawien,* p.153, and Haberl, *Parteiorganisation,* p.190; for the economic and political discussions in the sixties, see Ramet, *Nationalism,* pp.87 ff.; Haberl, *Parteiorganisation,* pp.21 ff. and 174; Sundhaussen, *Geschichte,* pp.169 ff.; and Wilson, *Tito's Yugoslavia,* pp.138 ff.

55. For national demands, see Ramet, *Nationalism,* pp.61 ff., 105 ff., 236, 146 ff., and 233 ff.; Reuter, *Albaner,* pp.46 ff.; Sundhaussen, *Geschichte,* pp.192 ff.; Kohl, *Jugoslawien,* p.152; and Behschnitt, "Nationalismus," p.56.

56. The authority of the component republics now went so far that some po-

Table 1. Yugoslavian demographics.

	A			b		c		d	e
	1947	1962	1981	1970	1980	1966	1981	1971	1971–81
Slovenia	175	199	198	16.3	16.9	2.6	1.5	1.2	0.95
Croatia	107	121	125	27.1	25.9	6.1	5.6	9.0	0.49
Vojvodina	109	103	117	10.5	10.3	5.4	12.5	9.0	0.49
Serbia	96	96	98	24.8	25.1	7.0	14.9	17.6	0.95
Montenegro	71	66	75	2.0	2.1	7.6	15.0	16.7	1.0
Bosnia-H.	83	73	67	12.2	12.1	5.3	14.1	23.2	1.0
Macedonia	62	57	67	5.1	5.6	16.4	22.3	18.1	1.61
Kosovo	53	34	30	2.0	2.0	21.0	27.7	31.5	2.75
Yugoslavia	100	100	100	100	100	6.9	14.9	15.1	0.61

A. Yearly index of per capita income.
B. Share of gross national product in %.
C. Unemployment figures in %.
D. Illiteracy figures in %.
E. Average yearly gain in population in %.

For per capita income in 1947 and 1952 see F. B. Singleton, "Regionale ökonomische Ungleichheiten in Jugoslawien," in *Jugoslawien am Ende der Ära Tito,* vol. 2, *Innenpolitik,* ed. Klaus-Detlev Grothusen, Othmar Nikola Haberl, and Wolfgang Höpken (Munich, 1986), pp.148 and 151. For the illiteracy figures, see Niesmann, *Spannungsfeld,* p.201; for GNP share, see Ramet, *Nationalism,* p.214; and for the other numbers, see Thomas Eger, "Probleme bei der Überwindung des regionalen Entwicklungsgefälles," in Grothusen, Haberl, and Höpken, *Jugoslawien,* p.29.

litical scientists speak of a confederation, such as Dennison Rusinow, "Nationalities Policy and the 'National Question,'" in *Yugoslavia in the 1980s,* ed. Pedro Ramet (Boulder, Colo., 1985), p.136.

57. See Ivo Bicanic, "Fractured Economy," in *Yugoslavia: A Fractured Federalism,* ed. Dennison Rusinow (Washington, D.C., 1988), pp.121 ff., and Dennison Rusinow, "Nationalities Policy," in Ramet, *Yugoslavia,* p.141.

58. Figures of the Yugoslavian prime minister at the first Central Committee session after Tito's death in June 1980 (according to Werner Zürrer, *Weltgeschehen: Analysen und Berichte zur Weltpolitik für Unterricht und Studium. Jugoslawien von 1980 bis 1989* (Sankt Augustin, 1989), p.8, and Hans Peter Rullmann, *Krisenherd Balkan: Jugoslawien zerbricht* (Hamburg, 1989), p.463.

59. See Zürrer, *Weltgeschehen,* p.47.

60. Between 1980 and 1988, 134 rapes were reported in Kosovo. That is fewer rapes than were registered in one year in Slovenia, with its higher number of inhabitants (1.9 million to 1.6 million in Kosovo). And in only 17 of these 134 rapes was the perpetrator an Albanian and the victim a Serb or Montenegrin. See University Conference in Ljubljana, ed., *Kosovo-Serbien-Jugoslawien* (Ljubljana, 1989), quoted in "Serben und Albaner im Kosovo," *Osteuropa,* 1/90, S.A. (1990): pp. A56ff.

61. According to figures of the *Süddeutsche Zeitung,* 8,000 Serbs and Montenegrins had emigrated from Kosovo between April 1981 and September 1982. The *Frankfurter Allgemeine Zeitung* spoke of 55,000 to 100,000 emigrants in the past fifteen years. A Yugoslavian commission, which examined every case of Serbian migration, came to the conclusion that there were in fact isolated cases of violence and anti-Serbian slogans, but that the migration was happening primarily for economic reasons. See Zürrer, *Weltgeschehen,* pp.52ff., and for the accusations of Serbian propaganda, ibid., pp.51ff. and 158ff.

62. For Milosevic's rise to power, see Jens Reuter, "Jugoslawien im Umbruch," in "Aus Politik und Zeitgeschichte," supplement to *Das Parlament,* vol. 45/90 (November 2, 1990).

63. Old Yugoslavia consisted of the republics of Serbia (5.7 million inhabitants), Croatia (4.6 million), Bosnia-Herzegovina (4.1 million), Slovenia (1.9 million), Macedonia (1.9 million), Montenegro (600,000), and the two "autonomous provinces" of Kosovo (1.6 million) and Vojvodina (2 million), which belonged to Serbia. The figures are from the census of 1981, the last one to be taken in the whole of Yugoslavia.

64. Quoted in "Der Bruch unter Jugoslawiens Kommunisten," *Neue Zürcher Zeitung,* February 7, 1990.

65. The four S's (Cyrillic C's) stand for *Samo sloga Srbina spasava* (Unity alone will save the Serb) and are the national symbol and motto of the Serbs.

66. Milosevic said this at the end of June 1990, for example, when the outline of a new Serbian constitution was passed. See Reuter, *Albaner,* p.12.

67. For figures, see "Wenn Generälen das Wasser bis zum Halse steht," *Deutsches Allgemeines Sonntagsblatt,* July 5, 1992.

68. There are several reasons why the war in Slovenia lasted only a few days. The Yugoslavian Federal Army met a well-organized resistance in Slovenia. Their attack did not turn out to be the little stroll it was conceived to be, and waging a double-front war seemed risky. In addition, for Serbia, on whose orders the Yugoslavian army was in essence acting, Slovenia is not as interesting as Croatia. It is too far away from Serbia and has only a small coastline. Furthermore, there is no

Serbian minority in Slovenia; such a presence is important in waging a war, because it supplies a propaganda rationale – the minority has to be "protected" – and offers the military logistic bases in Serbian-inhabited villages.

69. See Carl E. Buchalla, "Allianz des serbischen Riesen mit einem Zwerg," *Süddeutsche Zeitung,* February 29, 1992.

70. See Viktor Meier, "Kaum Behinderungen durch die Serben beim Referendum in Bosnien-Herzegowina," *Frankfurter Allgemeine Zeitung,* March 2, 1992.

71. This information comes from the Serbian journalist Petar Lukovic, deputy editor-in-chief of the independent Belgrade weekly *Vreme.* According to him, Belgrade television is "Milosevic's main weapon. Without television, there would be no Milosevic, and if television falls, he falls too" (interview on September 3, 1992, in Belgrade).

72. After Serbia and Montenegro announced that their two nations were forming the "Third Yugoslavia" on April 27, it was no longer appropriate to have an army in Bosnia-Herzegovina fight with this same name, so it was abruptly renamed the "Serbian army" of Bosnia-Herzegovina. Officially neither Serbia nor the new Yugoslavia has anything to do with the war in Bosnia-Herzegovina.

73. George Kenney, "See No Evil, Make No Policy," *Washington Monthly,* November 1992, pp.33 ff.

74. Interview on November 30, 1991, in Zagreb.

75. See Roy Gutman, "Mass Rape – Muslims Recall Serb Attacks," *Newsday,* August 23, 1992.

Open Wounds:
Ethnopsychoanalytic Reflections on
the Wars in the Former Yugoslavia

Paul Parin

I am frequently asked whether ethnopsychoanalysis[1] can offer an explanation for the terrible acts of war unleashed by the political conflict in Yugoslavia. Because the hatred and other irrational emotions of the warring parties, the Croats and the Serbs, contribute to the acts of war, and because Croat and Serb politicians refuse to enter into rational compromises but instead pursue unreachable goals, we expect that the field of psychology can enlighten us: it is the only science capable of explaining an event that is governed by feelings. This is an expectation I must disappoint.

Psychoanalysis is not in a position to deliver causal explanations for every collective phenomenon. Of course there is no doubt that every political movement, especially every warlike or otherwise violent conflict, is determined in part by the psychology of the active parties, and that such conflicts in return call forth emotional reactions in individuals, groups, peoples, nations, and organized institutions, reactions that can be understood psychologically. But the psychology of the contending parties can never be deemed a cause. Let us consider the well-known historical example of the Yugoslavian people's struggle for liberation from the brutal suppression by two forces of occupation, the German and the Italian, in World War II. One might exclaim rhetorically: The Yugoslavian people's love of freedom caused the *ustanak,* the revolutionary uprising, and sustained the Partisans' war for four years until they achieved victory. But other questions immediately arise: Where was this love of freedom when the Royal Yugoslavian Army collapsed in ten days without offering serious resistance to the invading armies? Where was it when the occupiers set up dictatorial regimes that depended on that army? And where was it residing during the forty-five years when a party apparatus whose power monopoly was based on the UDBA (secret police) dictated to a great degree all official politics and even civilian society?

Clearly one has to employ historical, political, and economic arguments in order to get to the bottom of the present crisis in Yugoslavia. If presented in isolation without their sociohistorical context, psychoanalytical interpretations, I believe, can suggest a false picture. Emotions – anxiety, hatred, impotence, hope, and the like – already obscure our view of historical processes: if we isolate this psychological aspect, our seemingly scientific assessment is likely to be incorrect.

Even worse errors come about if the ethnologically understood unique character of a people, based on its recorded historical experiences and traditional mentalities, is deemed the determining cause of conflicts. Pseudopsychologists have tried to do this, attributing a "phallic-aggressive," warlike character to the Serbs, for example, and an "anal-passive," deceitful nature to the Croats. Such views are nothing other than psychologically disguised prejudices and projected fantasies. Simple historical analogies demonstrate the absurdity of such arguments. Western Europeans like to think of the Britons as constituting a civilized, rational nation, mature in its old democratic form of government. In Germany and Austria at the beginning of World War I, "perfidious Albion" was styled as a particularly barbaric nation within a few weeks. Since then history has provided us with many experiences to challenge both stereotypes: to support the "barbaric" thesis one can refer to numerous colonial wars and other "typically British" collective horrors right up to the Manchester football rowdies' vandalism and racist excesses in the late 1980s; to support the opposite thesis one can refer to England's rational and conciliatory dismantling of its colonial empire and its reshaping after the victory over Nazism into a humane social state and a peaceable civilian society.

I might add that the current situation in Yugoslavia does not permit us to submit individuals or groups to ethnopsychoanalytic investigations. The tested methods of ethnopsychoanalysis demand time, a certain amount of political stability, and social tranquillity. To my knowledge there are no sociological or psychological studies coming out of present-day Yugoslavia. And yet I do not mean to shirk my responsibility or suggest that ethnopsychoanalysis has nothing to say about the war in Yugoslavia. There are some speculations, hypotheses, and interpretations about psychological factors, partially derived from similar situations and supported by this or that sign or symbol. I will cite a few, but I cannot determine the chronological sequence or the importance of these phenomena, let alone their causal role in the origin and evolution of the conflicts.

The "Unresolved" Past

The hatred between Serbs and Croats was ignited by an especially repellent "unresolved past." For forty-five years the mass murders of Serbs by the Ustasha guards (soon after the Ustasha state was founded in 1941, in many locations and then in the death camp of Jasenovac), the mass murders of Ustasha supporters by Serbian Chetniks, and the murders of war prisoners of the Ustasha state by the victorious Partisan army were never elucidated and put in order, either in publications or within the context of parliamentary or legal discussions. By no means have these events been repressed – that is, forgotten. They have not been extinguished in the memory of the survivors. (At the moment it is dawning on everyone that the Yugoslavian army's general chief-of-staff, the former defense minister Adzic, "has to" feel hatred toward everything Croatian, because at the age of twelve he was the only one in his large family to escape a Ustasha massacre in Bosnia.) Yet these massacres played no part in the constitutional, legal, or juridical development of the federation. Private and intimate relationships seem to have developed undisturbed by the horrors of the past.

In the first years after victory (1945) the stern party leaders conducted spectacular war-crimes trials against the commandant of the Chetniks, Colonel Draza Mihajovic, and against the few Ustasha leaders who could be apprehended. Nor did they spare the Catholic Church, which had organized official forced conversions, expulsions, and massacres of Serbs of the Orthodox faith through the Zagreb archbishop Alojzije Stepinac and with the active participation of priests and monks. To my knowledge there were no similar trials against members of the victorious federal army who had killed thousands of defenseless prisoners of war. (For example, there was a British internment camp in Bleiburg for approximately 150,000 Croats and more than 10,000 Slovenian home defense force members who had fought on the side of Nazi Germany. British occupation troops turned them over to Yugoslavia; those Croats and Slovenes who did not escape their fate by mass suicide were brutally murdered in large numbers by the federal army.)

After this first phase of settling accounts, there was no more. People said "let bygones be bygones, no need to open up closed wounds, let sleeping dogs lie." The public media were under the control of the party, which took care that these horrible events would remain undisturbed while filling the media instead with heroicized and pseudorealistic memories of the war and the struggle for "the people's" liberation, for the entertainment, edification, and indoctrination of the "masses." Especially important psychologically is that in Yugoslavia the newspapers, magazines, film, radio, and television were much freer in reporting than in the satellite states; the massacres remained the exception. It is true that trials of individual journalists took place because of infractions against national security laws, but one cannot speak of an absolute censor. Daily newspapers uncovered the scandalous practices of highly placed members of the establishment and were not punished, but neither did they have much effect. After Tito's death (1980) countless literary works also appeared revealing grievances of every kind, including the terrible violent and repressive measures of the UDBA and conditions in Goli Otok, the torture camp of the secret police (a barren little island off the Dalmatian coast). Psychologically, the silence about the fascist mass murders on both sides functioned as a taboo that could not be violated. My informants told me of only one significant attempt to open up a public discussion: a 1984 play titled *Jama* (The hole). Near a chalk cave, into which the bodies of Croatian and Serbian victims of the massacres were thrown during the war, young people – Croats and Serbs – discuss the gruesome events of their fathers' time. The play was banned in Belgrade before its premiere and was then performed in a little theater in Novisad (Vojvodina) but banned after the first two performances. The taboo remained unbroken.

It seems likely that a certain self-censorship about this topic on the part of historians, journalists, and writers came to the aid of the authorities. Precisely because the memories were still relatively fresh, the unimaginable horrors still a sensually apparent reality, research and written portrayals were bound to produce an ambivalent tension in the authors: "All of this really ought to be written about and revealed," they seemed to think, "yet I cannot believe anyone capable of such horrors." Because in Germany a certain pressure from the victorious powers and strong political groups (international Jewish organizations, victims' associations) forced the revelation of Nazi crimes, authors could expect at least a moral reward; but in Yugoslavia there was no public encouragement to help authors conquer their inner inhibitions and concern themselves with this material. Their work would have no effect: rather than a moral affirmation, they could expect only national repression and even revenge from the ranks of the denounced murderers. The memory of the mass murders was preserved in the icebox of history.

The rise of the Serbian party ruler Slobodan Milosevic was accompanied by an intensive propaganda campaign. Alleged "atrocities" of the Kosovo Albanians were soon supplemented in the Serbian press and in Serbian politicians' speeches by the atrocities of the Croatian Ustasha. Present-day Croatia was compared to the Ustasha state and all contemporary Croatians to the cruel Ustasha guards. Serbs living in Croatia were said to be threatened by fascist genocide. After the former general Franjo Tudjman and the HDZ, his right-wing party, won the election in 1990, they were supported by those former Communists who had been removed from office and replaced by Serbian comrades in 1971. The Croatian government and parliament did much to confirm the propaganda. They changed the constitution and demoted Serbs living in Croatia from a national people to a minority; they revitalized Catholic Croatia's "great" past with all its emblems, symbols, and symbolic characters, which the fascist Ustasha state had also used, without clearly distancing themselves from the crimes of fascism.

The occasion for war – at first for the local, ultranational Serbian groups and soon after for the army, which supported and organized the war of aggression and soon directed it in its own interest – was the Croatian massacres of the Serbs, more precisely the massacres "before 1945." There had been no more recent ones, despite occasional chauvinist rhetoric, when the bloody war began. The "unresolved past" legitimized the war of aggression. Large groups of Serbs, in the Serbian republic and in areas of the Krajina, Slavonia, and so forth, were apparently in emotional agreement. And yet not all Serbs were susceptible to this propaganda, particularly not all who had until then lived peaceably in Croatia. But resistance against the policy of conquest and annihilation could hardly be formed among the Serbs. Who could take the part of the notorious mass murderers? All of this happened before the Croatian state drew on financial and material support from nationally minded Croat emigrants abroad, often descendants of the Ustasha who had sought foreign shores in 1945.

Constructing National Enemies

All nationalistic propaganda is based on projections: we are the just ones, the good ones, the threatened ones – those people over there are unjust, bad, dangerous. These projections attain an almost unalterable independence, political effectiveness, and endurance because of a typical change in the deliberately generated image of the enemy. Real experiences contribute to this change. One of the two emotive realities stems from the unprocessed feelings of impotence, grief, and rage in families whose fathers, brothers, and grandfathers were victims of unexpiated mass murders. The other real experience has been furnished since hostilities broke out in Croatia, where bellicose armed bands and their leaders, inadequately controlled by the authorities, have committed atrocities that need not take a back seat to the crimes of the Chetniks.

Both in collectives and in individuals the syndrome functions blindly: that is, it cannot be corrected by current reality or critical reflection. The "production of unconsciousness" supplies the emotional content of a reality, a "new reality." Because arguments and experiences that contradict this reality are not supported by feelings, they are shoved aside or reinterpreted. Well-informed and critically inclined people with a different or opposing view of reality, often intellectuals (or children), cannot prevail in the community; they are seen as ignorant, naive, or crazy and lose all influence on the public consciousness.

The deliberate production of the "image of the enemy," made up of the revitalization of a long-latent, unforgotten experience and a new "real experience," derives from many irreconcilable national feuds. In this case the production of the distorted "national" reality is furthered by a particular modern kind of propaganda, which the British journalist Ian Traynor calls the "television war in Yugoslavia."[2] He describes recent television in Serbia or Croatia:

Contorted corpses, maimed bodies of children or old peasants, singed limbs and faces with bloody holes in place of eyes – this was the everyday fare in the time before the cease-fire. The perpetrators and victims of this kind of slaughter are not invented characters in an imported horror film. The scenes come from Yugoslavia's television war; they were snapshots of the atrocities being committed on both sides in the Croatian war zones. The continual presentation of the massacre victims incited fear, hatred, hysteria, and blood lust on both sides of the ethnic border.

Television was a key element, perhaps *the* key element fanning the flames of the Serbo-Croatian war that has swallowed up postwar Yugoslavia. You cannot wage war in Croatia or Serbia without television, explains Nenad Pejic, the television director in Bosnia. "If you want a war, then you need television, you need an instrument of influence." The regimes in both Belgrade and Zagreb were immediately aware of the value of television in a war. They exercised total control over radio and television and gained public support by serving the populace a diet of lies, inventions, and propaganda, sometimes horrifying, sometimes sentimental.

The intensity and duration of the television war has astonished even experienced foreign observers like Marco Altherr, head of the International Red Cross delegation in Yugoslavia. Altherr has experienced the Lebanese, the Afghan, and the Angolan civil wars. He believes the conflict in Croatia differs fundamentally from the others because of the intensity and effectiveness of the rival propaganda machines. Never has he seen such effective propaganda in both warring parties, he declared. "If you talk to them, the people on both sides are absolutely convinced that the other side is intent on killing them. And it's all the result of propaganda." In the past months there have undoubtedly been numerous atrocities on both sides. Altherr is convinced that television is in large measure responsible for them by having aroused instincts of revenge and unleashed reciprocal acts of retribution.

In Croatia, television has been manipulated by a strict censor, and in Serbia this has been done above all by setting terrorist rowdies against those in the media who wanted to report in a more objective fashion. Both sides have exclusively shown pictures of crimes on the other side and supplemented them by fictional, cleverly staged reports of atrocities. Traynor goes on to write:

The power of television as the driving force of the conflict was illustrated negatively by the fact that Bosnia was able to avoid a blood bath for a while. . . . This fact is attributable in some measure to the stance of Bosnian television under Nenad Pejic, whose reporting was sober and without inflammatory propaganda. In December 1991 the three rival parties in Bosnia tried to divide up radio and television along ethnic lines. Pejic and his staff protested and resisted. Telephone surveys showed support for them by ten to one. . . . Bosnia would broadcast the Belgrade and the Zagreb programs alternately and without commentary, thus revealing by simple juxtaposition the one-sidedness of the portrayals in the rival capitals. Thus the Bosnians were given an opportunity to decide for themselves whom they wanted to believe. (February 1992)

In this way the social production of fear and vengefulness was charged with intense emotions. The terrible reality, affecting the sensibilities of viewers in front of the television screen every evening, resulted from an intentional construct that warded off all criticism by excluding any opposing portrayal. The falsified image – in psychological terms – had reality value.

Shame and Retribution

Again and again, historians have underlined that a nation violently shaken in its self-esteem by military defeats will in the next generation experience a need for reparation and retribution. We connect the rise of National Socialism and Hitler's triggering of World War II with Germany's need to make up for the "shame" of the Treaty of Versailles. Many people, in fact, not only soldiers, experience a defeat and the fall of an admired ideal (an emperor, a leader, etc.) as a deep personal affront. This "narcissistic wound" is incorporated into the family mythos, whether the defeated father maintains a depressive silence or laments his lot or calls for revenge. Certainly the Serbian rule during the royal period (1918–41) marked many Croats with this type of narcissistic wound.

History seems to have been kinder to the Serbs, who emerged victorious from the Balkan wars and World Wars I and II. But they too were easily able to mobilize the gnawing feeling of finally having to seek satisfaction. Apparently this is always possible when a nation finds itself in economic distress or some other kind of trouble. Within a short time, the "trauma" of the battle on the Field of the Blackbirds, fought against the Turks six hundred years earlier, and the Albanians' subsequent settlement of the "holy earth" of Kosovo took on the character of a festering wound in the nation's self-esteem. It seems almost grotesque that Marshal Tito, the undisputed victor in the people's struggle for liberation, who brought the Communist Party to power and led it unopposed for decades, was at first honored by the Serbian party as charismatic leader but, because he was a Croat, could soon be successfully reinterpreted as the symbol of a national disgrace. Because he was the son of a Croatian smallholder and a mother from Slovenia, it suddenly did not matter that his wartime cabinet contained only Serbs and Montenegrins and not a single Croat, and that he scrupulously avoided any injury to the notorious Serbian national pride. For the unconscious levels of a nation's feelings of self-worth, it is almost as injurious to be led to victory by a stranger as to be defeated by one.

When Tito died there was confusion and grief, as when the authoritarian father of a family dies. But Sigmund Freud's view that an organized mass falls apart when the beloved and secretly hated leader dies does not fit the Yugoslavia of the 1980s. For a long time, and by no means unremarked, state power had devolved to the greater and lesser party bosses. Out of the "new class" (the concept of Milovan Djilas, 1954), a caste of politicians (nomenclatura) with its fellow travelers and profiteers had developed. The last time Tito had personally suppressed antiauthoritarian impulses was during the student protests in 1968. Later the hand of the party is clearly recognizable, a political-military apparatus acting as the establishment yet gradually becoming uncertain.

Anomie and Regression

What was lacking was a counterweight, a political opposition emerging against the ever more untrustworthy ruling class. It was not lacking everywhere. In Slovenia, antiauthoritarian impulses came from the younger generation (students) and the intellectuals, in forms familiar to us from the Soviet satellite states, leading to pluralism and the formation of opposition groups and structures. Most likely they are responsible for Slovenia's relatively painless transition to a civilian society and to a democratic changeover.

In the remaining provinces the nearly complete absence of a political opposition is attributable to a psychological condition (also prevalent in Western countries), the political abstinence of the citizens, especially the younger generation. The hegemony of the party is responsible for this, I believe, to the extent that nothing could shake or influence it. Yet it was not the overall oppression, but rather the many civil liberties of relative prosperity, especially that of the urban population in every province with the exception of the extreme south, that spoke for a "life without politics": freedom to travel, combating unemployment by encouraging workers to emigrate, relative openness in the media, tourism, and massive improvements in the service sector of the economy, financed with borrowed wherewithal and the export of products and wares to East and West.

When the worsening economy began to affect their living standard, the disadvantaged who were unable to emigrate began to feel rage and hatred, and profiteers feared for their privileges. At the same time the Communist ideology, internally already long atrophied, was externally questioned by *perestroika* and the ever clearer collapse of the Soviet empire. Political structures were not up to the challenge: they dissolved piece by piece, and in none of the republics but Slovenia were they supplanted by "more democratic" structures. And thus – as others have written – there was nothing left but a return to old national and religious ideas, which now perniciously came into their own.

From a psychological perspective, I believe the development was different, more complicated. The creeping loss of ideal values, the dissolution of structures, the loss of social certainties and of economic efficiency and integrity, led to anomie, to the cessation of all rules that had heretofore been valid. It was no longer possible to find a place in society, to plan one's own life, to ensure the continuation of one's family. Such anomie is always accompanied by individual regression. It is not the society that regresses, it is men and women who no longer know what to do with their civil freedom – or lack of freedom. They demand a refuge – a spiritual one – security, safety, or at least the symbols and symbolic figures that convey those affect-laden, emotionally meaningful values and hopes. In such a mood it is hard to wait for the economy to be reorganized, for confusion to yield to discourse, for the testing of interests and their social structures to produce a new civilian society, and it is certainly hard to wait for new political structures to improve on the old ones.

This is also the time when those who used to be powerful – party cadres, the army, state police – try to preserve their power. The developments in the former Soviet Union have taught us to fear these yearnings for reactionary coups or dictatorships. We still fear it today. On the other hand, this time is decidedly favorable for any politician, whether from the former ruling elite or a new rising group, who can exploit the citizens' regressive needs to establish his own position of power. To do so he must be a good demagogue, propagating "populist" politics, and he must bring with him or organize a group of supporters who, although they will not share in his power, can look forward to advantages if they follow him unconditionally.

This is exactly what has happened in Yugoslavia. But no one in Yugoslavia or in the West saw it clearly, because the process began not suddenly but gradually, at a rather remote location in the autonomous region of Kosovo and in connection with a seemingly unimportant national problem. When Slobodan Milosevic, a banker educated in the West, worked his way up to Serbian party strongman, his rise was similar to Hitler's in the Weimar Republic. It took Hitler approximately ten years to be legally named Germany's chancellor. It took Milosevic about the same amount of time, if you mark the beginning of his populist career with the repeated suppression of the Kosovo Albanians in 1981. We know well the tools of chauvinistic power politics: media takeover, ruthless imposition of party forces (police, military), the whole arsenal of ancient national pretensions to greatness, and to support it all emotionally, the hatred of an inferior, unworthy, politically and sexually unprincipled, traditionally despised people: the Albanians.

The Yugoslavian situation – widespread regressive tendencies triggered by anomie – is special in that a similar development can be noted in Croatia, although with a power politician of less talent, Franjo Tudjman. One can find exceptions in provinces where new political groupings and structures (parties, unions) were able to form, as in Slovenia, or where the rulers are more reasonable, perhaps less corrupt, or at least not so obsessed with preserving and expanding their power and privileges as were the central political power and army in Serbia.

Groups predisposed to fanaticism also exist in Western countries: the New Right in France, Germany, Italy, and Switzerland would be just as susceptible to collective hatred (also called "racial hatred") if the other conditions (collapse of political structures, anomie) were similar to those in present-day Serbia and Croatia.

But I seem to have strayed from the ethnological point of view. There must indeed be differences, "Balkan" particularities that make up the special psychology of this belligerent madness. We can discover nothing specifically Balkan in the Yugoslavian Federal Army's declared grounds for war. They are part of the classic arsenal of European ultranational parties. The Serbian-oriented army leadership claims it must protect threatened minorities beyond the borders of the republic; Hitler proclaimed this as his reason for occupying great portions of Czechoslovakia and for invading Poland in 1939. The conquest of neighboring territories, the expulsion of Croatian inhabitants, and the plan to send in settlers of Serbian nationality reminds us of Nazi Germany's need for *Lebensraum*. That churches and cultural monuments are destroyed is attributed to the Catholic Church and its spiritual leaders' active support of the fascist Ustasha state with its accompanying atrocities. However, the military actions against all cultural monuments are aimed at destroying Croatian culture. That reminds us of *Kristallnacht,* when the destruction of the Jews' synagogues was meant to destroy their culture.

The Causes of Brutality

Recently *Helsinki Watch* published two lists of war crimes committed by both parties to the conflict. In their savage brutality the crimes strike us as strange, specific somehow to the Balkan people. Before I enter into ethnopsychological speculations, let me offer three observations. Reports of collective crimes in their linguistic form alone already contain culture-specific prejudices. In the *Neue Zürcher Zeitung* the killing of three Israeli soldiers with axes and sharp instruments was recently described as an unimaginably gruesome murder. According to the same newspaper, a Hezbollah leader who was shot down (along with his wife and infant child) by the guided missiles of a military helicopter outside its national borders had been "eliminated." It described the civilians, women and children, who were victims of a bombing on Lebanese territory as victims of a "retaliatory strike." Certainly a Palestinian or Lebanese newspaper would have described the incidents in other terms.

Second, every collective deed or misdeed demonstrates culture-specific characteristics. We are used to thinking of the annihilation of the Jews in the Third Reich as bureaucratically organized mass murder, and of the 1991 Gulf War as typical of the highly developed, electronically guided technology of Western industrialized nations, especially the United States. Less structured fanatical gangs are more characteristic of a dissolving societal structure than of the Balkans.

Finally, I have not investigated any officer or soldier who committed crimes; I have not even read the notes of interrogations or interviews. What follows is therefore no more than extrapolation, speculation, or hypothesis.

During a child's socialization from birth to the point at which one is considered an adult, the inhibition of affect is thought to be the most important educational means of ensuring that aggressive actions against fellow human beings or against enemies are less crass and sadistic or are even blocked or diverted before they are carried out. The Eskimos (Inuit) of Hudson Bay and the "gentle" Sakuday (inhabiting an island near Sumatra) are examples of peoples for whom any physical aggression against their fellow humans is impossible. Yet in our eyes, both peoples seem more brutal than we are toward the animals they hunt.

My experiences with typical child-raising practices in rural families in different areas of Yugoslavia have led me to a hypothesis. In these thoroughly patriarchal families there is much tenderness and concern for children, but also strictness and severe corporal punishment. Neither mother nor father seems to "know" that one can or should mute the emotions through reassurance, distraction, or constant monitoring of emotional expression. To this I attribute the open, direct expression of positive feelings and sexual desires of men and women from many areas of the former Yugoslavia. Perhaps the same thing is true of aggressive deeds: they happen spontaneously, are uninhibited, and are often sustained by sadistic pleasure.

My explanations may seem superfluous to those experts who assume that the Yugoslavs' urgent need for identity is the key factor. After the dissolution of Yugoslavia as a whole, Serbs, Croats, Slovenes, and all the others are in the process of regressing back to their national histories and respective ancestral religions in order to find a new identity. Fights are inevitable, therefore, as each group's new borders are drawn and solidified.

Although it seems at first to be insightful, I must challenge this explanation. There are peoples who have adequately solidified their identity without complete political independence – the French-speaking Swiss, for example, or the Swedish minority in Finland. Others are fighting for their identity and expect to gain it with their complete political independence, even though this may bring with it other disadvantages, such as economic ones: the Basques and the Corsicans are examples. But Croatia and Serbia are at war.

Let me add one more observation. In individual psychology one regularly observes that self-esteem and the need for identity are polar opposites. The higher the self-esteem, the less the need to define oneself against the outside world and to feel identical to those who share the same traditions, origin, religion, and so on. The more unstable and uncertain the sense of self, the more important becomes an identity as a group member.

Similar things are happening in some large, politically well structured, democratically organized states. Propaganda is used to construct a new "enemy" when the old one has become obsolete. After the United States lost the Communist "evil empire" as an enemy, a whole series of new enemies was constructed, some of them combated and some of them dropped: Grenada, Panama, gays, drugs, AIDS, Iran, Mu'ammar Gadhafi, Saddam Hussein. This has led us to conclude that the nation's self-esteem is shaken.

We should ponder whether the aggressive and belligerent search for a new identity can really be attributed to a historically inherited deficiency and to a lack of historical experience and uniqueness. The Slovenes never had their own state and did not even have their own state coat of arms until 1991, but they were more fortunate than the Croats in defending against military invasion and now, despite their great economic problems, seem not to need to confirm their identity through aggression. Perhaps the search for identity by waging war against an evil enemy is not the cause, but rather is simply the result of the collapse of the People's Republic of Yugoslavia, so long held together by an artificial ideology and police power, the result of anxiety, uncertainty, and confusion about a gloomy future.

Projection, Paranoia, and Narcissism

At the bottom of collective political, historical, or ethnic-religious attitudes that make belligerent conflicts seem self-evident or "logical" is the mechanism of projection: "Projection means that one's own impulses, fears, aggressions, wishes are displaced outside, onto another people. The analogy with optics expresses the fact that what is perceived outside is taking place inside oneself. The projective surface is empty, or its composition is of no importance, but without a projective surface no image appears. As soon as the inner economy of the one projecting changes, the projected image also changes."[3] In other essays I have described the traditional and propagandistic factors that cause projections about "the Croats" to be retained uncorrected by "the Serbs" in wide circles of the population. Even people with enough intelligence and information to test propaganda critically tend to identify with the projected image of the enemy, that is, to assimilate it uncritically. Ignorant people, cut off from the flow of news, isolated in villages, are particularly inclined to misconstrue the unknown "enemies" through projection. What the admired (or feared) political or spiritual leaders say and repeat becomes an emotionally charged possession, "faith." The common "faith," acquired by identification, strengthens the feeling of belonging, identity, and group cohesiveness.

Melanie Klein was the first to describe a psychological mechanism that originates in a regularly occurring split in the ego of infants. In this "paranoid position" one's own person is perceived as good and correct but threatened, while the outside world is threatening, and other people are dangerous persecutors. This position must later be overcome if development is to occur normally. The mechanism of this split has been called "projective identification." At later stages it can be regressively reactivated, that is, in certain circumstances adults can react in a similar fashion: they misconstrue others in a delusional way. The result is similar to persecution mania in the mentally ill. For that reason the mechanism was originally attributed only to the mentally ill. Only recently has it been recognized that projective identifications often occur in the inner life of every normal human being and that they take on great and pernicious meaning in the lives of peoples. Constructions of the enemy usually stem from projective identifications, and these can be produced and manipulated in a society.

Even a projective identification demands a surface, a screen, without which no image can take shape. But our perceptions of the other, of the antagonist's structures and ways of relating, are much more important. They are part of the image we construct "externally." In other words, projective identifications do not come about with any arbitrary antagonist, but occur only with one who is well suited for the formation of a new image, composed of what we project plus what we perceive. It is this that makes the projective image relatively constant, so that it seems to take on a life of its own. True, it bears above all the characteristics we have given it. But neither the antagonist's behavior nor changes in our own psychological economy effect a correction. Both are reinterpreted. In the history of many European countries anti-Semitism is the best-known example of enduring projective identification. Anyone who knows a "good Jew" knows he is the exception that proves the rule. Anti-Semitic groups and crowds are easily persuaded that the real harmlessness and powerlessness of the Jews are products of disastrous self-deception. "Our" image (the projection we identify with) is the only true one: "Jews are evil, dangerous, and full of secret power."

Projective identifications that distinguish the ideology of a nation or some other community do not arise spontaneously. They are produced, even where it seems that they are developing out of a tradition and growing strong again under special conditions. Projective identification in turn has produced a "syndrome of evil ethnocentrism" that functions along with a "paranoid collective consciousness and a paranoid political culture."

> Paranoid structures make notably clever and successful use of other mechanisms, namely intellectualization and rationalization, to the end of logical self-affirmation. This is in part the reason that paranoid ideas and explanations seem to be insightful, convincing, quite logical and well organized, in such a way that those who are not familiar with the situation are not easily able to see through the distortion of reality. . . . in this process, people who were normal – in psychiatric terms – develop a political persecution mania or megalomania. Shared paranoid disorder spreads very quickly, reaching large masses in times of economic or political crisis and collective tension, when their critical consciousness is reduced and their realistic observation of reality obscured.[4]

Thus political statements like the following are able to win believers: "The truth is that all non-Serbian ethnic groups, especially the Croats, are at this very minute preparing the genocide of all Serbs," or "The Croats hate us, the Slovenes don't like us, we are despised by the Muslims and Macedonians."[5]

The "cultural conflict" theory attempts to define the war between Croats and Serbs as a conflict between a narcissistic and a paranoid political culture: "Political culture is expressed by a definite structuring and formation of the social and political relationships in a community (a nation or state, for example) and also means the special way in which these relationships are experienced, understood, interpreted. By virtue of the political culture, a person becomes a political individual (*zoon politikon*), part of a political group, party, or nation."[6] Thus traditional national attitudes and symbols, current economic and political interests, are not denied; rather, their cultural content is condensed and pursued in its psychological effect.

According to this theory, the political culture in Serbia has taken on a paranoid form: We are the eternal victims, therefore we must defend ourselves and all Serbs against enemies lurking everywhere who want to annihilate us, and we have every right – and even (magical) power – on our side. This existential need justifies every act of aggression and cruelty as self-defense against a mortal danger.

A "narcissistic political culture" would characterize the Croats. "Here narcissism, as a metaphor, means all forms of vanity, self-admiration and self-elevation by a political group or community, to such an extent that ethnic or racist prejudices impede cooperative work with others. . . . We know that our/my truth and your truth exist, but for us only our/my truth counts."[7] The highly charged, illusionary inner image of a grandiose supreme self protects the collective narcissistic self. The collective and its partners are spared negative experiences and feelings such as anxiety, guilt, inferiority, and impotence.

The reckless and inconsiderate self-centeredness of the political world of Croatia has in fact contributed much to enabling the political class of Belgrade to project its delusional projections undisturbed onto "the Croats." In its self-righteousness, the ruling party of Croatia has taken itself to be morally and legally unimpeachable; in its overestimation it did not bother to organize its material defense in any rational manner. In the pride of its own political and moral superiority, it did not even deem it necessary to distance itself clearly from the atrocities of the fascist Ustasha state. This attitude was taken by potential opponents as arrogant provocation.

Some of the population, especially in Croatia's cities, proved immune to narcissistic acculturation. These people are psychologically distanced from events. They believe the policies of their government are absurd or downright mad. In the course of the war, monomaniacal ideas have been transformed into unrealistic fantasies of national salvation through powerful friends – the Germans, the European Community, or the United Nations. Various fighting units seem to have left the "narcissistic position" and slipped over to the "paranoid position."

Conclusion

No culture can respond in a rational way to a warlike invasion like the one in Croatia and Bosnia-Herzegovina, aggression that aims to destroy a culture and expel or murder its population. All too easily the struggling victims of warlike violence create a "political culture" that takes on the same shape as the aggressors' "paranoid political culture." The aggressors feel that they are victims, and in delusional persecution of their supposed persecutors they fight "to the death" of the enemy or of their own nation. Many of the real victims of aggression, especially (but not exclusively) the ruling authorities and the fighting troops, react with a hatred that helps defend them against their feelings of impotence and fear. This psychological release greatly assists them in warding off the danger of an annihilating defeat as if it were unreal, a delusion. But the opponent, in this case everything "Serbian" – that is to say, also harmless, peaceable men, women, and children, Serbs whom one has heretofore respected, one's friends or relatives – are now likewise delusionally, paranoically identical to the real persecutors. Everything "Serbian" has become the enemy and must somehow be eliminated.

As I mentioned above, any rational judgment of the situation is severely reduced in such a political culture. Rational compromises find no support. People and political groups that strive for peace are discriminated against, branded as parasites or "traitors," or at the very least as naive idiots, because they will not or cannot follow the paranoid reasoning of the situation.

Notes

Paul Parin's essay originally appeared in *Aufrisse* 13, no. 3 (1992), and refers to the ethnic conflicts between Serbs and Croats.

1. Ethnopsychoanalysis, a combination of ethnography and Freudian psycho-analysis, serves the study of human beings' relation to the social structure in which they grow up and live.

2. *Neue Zürcher Zeitung* 54 (1992): 4, according to the monthly bulletin of the International Press Institute.

3. Miro Jakovljevic, "Psychiatric Perspectives of the War against Croatia," *Croatian Medical Journal,* war supply 2, 1992.

4. Ibid.

5. Batric Jovanovic in Serbia's parliament, June 2, 1991.

6. Jakovljevic, "Psychiatric Perspectives."

7. Ibid.

War and Rape:
A Preliminary Analysis

Ruth Seifert

When Helke Sander and Barbara Johr filmed *BeFreier und Befreite* (Liberators take liberties) about mass rapes in the vicinity of Berlin at the end of World War II in spring 1945, it appeared that this would be a film about the past. During the preceding forty years these rapes had become neither a topic for research nor a political issue, despite their scale, their aftereffects, and the sociopolitical significance of sexual violence against women.[1] According to cautious estimates, 110,000 women were raped in the Berlin area after the war. Less conservative estimates cite the number as 900,000 raped and abused women.[2]

By 1992, civilizing influences in Europe had become so widespread that many people considered the barbarities of the past war unthinkable in the present. Improvements in women's social status also seemed to guarantee that women could no longer be the victims of mass violence directed explicitly against them. The events of 1992 have taught us otherwise. With camps in the middle of Europe constructed expressly for the purpose of rape or sexual torture, the violence against women has reached a new level. According to information from an investigative committee of the European Community, the mass rapes and sadistic torture of women in Bosnia-Herzegovina can be regarded as a systematic and mandated procedure. There are also sufficient statements from witnesses to verify that the rapes are considered an important element of Serbian war strategy. Aside from the unreported cases, the number of raped women is currently estimated to be 20,000 to 50,000.[3]

In what follows I will attempt to analyze these events. The first step will be to inquire into the function of rape in a general sense. The second will be to develop five explanations of the function of rape in war. Finally, I will try to throw some light on the logic of silence that continues to be characteristic of war crimes against women.

On the Function of Rapes

Those who inquire about the reasons for rape run up against a confusion of myths and ideologies. The most popular and effective myth is that rape has to do with an uncontrollable male drive that, insofar as it is not restrained by culture, has to run its course in a manner that is unfortunate, to be sure, but also unavoidable. This is predicated on the "pressure-cooker" theory of male nature. According to this idea men are finally not the lords of their own manor. They are seen as involuntary victims of their violent and instinctive nature. The advantage of this theory is that it relieves the individual of responsibility for his actions and exculpates him for the use of sexual violence. In fact, there are good reasons to assume that rapes do not have much to do either with nature or with sexuality. Rather, they are acts of extreme violence implemented, of course, by sexual means. Studies show that rape is not an aggressive manifestation of sexuality, but rather a sexual manifestation of aggression. In the perpetrator's psyche it serves no sexual purpose but is the expression of rage, violence, and dominance over a woman. At issue is her degradation, humiliation, and submission. To be sure, this violent act is carried out by sexual means.[4]

A violent invasion into the interior of one's body represents the most severe attack imaginable upon the intimate self and the dignity of a human being: by any measure it is a mark of severe torture. When a woman's inner space is violently invaded, it affects her in the same way torture does. It results in physical pain, loss of dignity, an attack on her identity, and a loss of self-determination over her own body. Andrea Dworkin notes that any human being's "struggle for dignity and self-determination is rooted in the struggle for actual control of one's own body, especially control over physical access to one's own body."[5] Because personal identity is so tightly intertwined with sexual identity, the personal self is also touched to the quick when the sexual form of violence is applied.[6] Investigations of rapes in a civilian context have also shown that the violence employed in the form of blows, choking, and other abuse often goes far beyond what would have been necessary to achieve the rape. In most cases the rape victims themselves experience the act not as a sexual one, but as an extreme and humiliating form of violence against person and body, accompanied by an intense fear of dying. Even the rapists themselves hardly ever speak about a sexual experience: one out of three has trouble performing sexually during the act. The perpetrators themselves articulate feelings of hostility, aggression, power, and dominance.[7]

Additional motives come into play with gang rapes: here the first order of business seems to be a mutual demonstration of masculinity. Gang rapes are often distinguished by a ritualized procedure, that is, the order of the rape is determined by the status of the men within the group. It has also been proved that rapists tend to depersonalize their victim. They hardly perceive her as a real person, and if they did not know their victim previously they are almost unable to describe her later. For the perpetrator the victim is a proxy for "woman" pure and simple, not a real person. To summarize, one can say that the rapist's sexuality is not at the center of his act; it is placed instrumentally at the service of the violent act.[8] For this reason some studies designate rape as a "pseudosexual" or even "antisexual" act. Sexual attacks on women have their origins not in sexual passion, but in hate and the wish to exercise power.

Ethnological research offers a further argument against considering rape in any biologistic or "naturalizing" way, for some societies have a high incidence of rape and others a low one. The prominence of rape in various societies can be traced in the following manner: societies with few rapes are those in which (a) male supremacy is completely assured (an example would be most Muslim societies, which are considered to have a low incidence of rape) or else (b) women enjoy respect and an honored status in the culture (certain tribal societies can be mentioned as examples). In contrast, societies with a high incidence of rape are those in which (a) male power has become unstable, (b) women have a subordinate status and low esteem, and (c) rigid definitions of "masculine" and "feminine" prevail and are connected to strong hegemonies or hierarchies of value. Virtually all modern Western societies are counted among those with a high incidence of rape. The United States with its historically strong women's movement and correspondingly weak male dominance is a good example. In the United States the number of rapes is continuously increasing. At the moment rape is the most common felony.[9]

Thus we must conclude that rape can by no means be explained by nature or against a background of human sexuality. For the most part, rather, it is an act that must be understood within the social and cultural context. In seeking the societal function of rape, everything points to the conclusion that it regulates unequal power relationships between the sexes: it serves to maintain a certain cultural order between the sexes or – when this order becomes fragile – to restore it. If women want a clear demonstration of the effect of rape on society, they need only think of themselves. In rape cultures the mere danger of rape and the frequency of sexual violence contribute to women's (and men's) identity formation. We know that women's everyday behavior is influenced by the knowledge that they might become prey to a massive attack on body and mind because of their gender. The terror growing out of the danger of rape shows that rape has the symbolic power to shape a society even when no direct rape is occurring. The mass rapes of World War II and those in Yugoslavia determine and influence women's social position, their identity, and their self-esteem in a way that transcends historical eras or national borders.

On the Meaning of Rape in and after Wars

Before developing a few explanations of the meaning of rape in the context of war, I must first set forth three limitations: first, we must assume that rape has no function that is necessarily common to all times and all societies. Its functions depend on the historical and cultural context and must ultimately be discussed with reference to concrete cases. Second, the following attempts at explanation are not primarily of a psychological nature and thus do not try to determine what is going on in the mind of the rapist. Rather, the main concern is the cultural models that operate more or less behind the backs of individuals and have not necessarily found their way into their waking consciousness. Finally, we must remember that these attempts at an explanation are by no means exhaustive. They are meant to single out certain aspects of rape in war and make them accessible to analysis.

THESIS I:

RAPES ARE PART OF THE "RULES" OF WAR

As Sander and Johr have noted, some evidence suggests that rapes have always taken place in the wars we are familiar with – that is, even in societies that presumably had a "low incidence of rape" as defined above.[10] Historical sources tell us that this was true before the beginning of the early modern period. We assume for one thing that there was a lower incidence of rape in this period than in ours, and in addition we are rather certain that the division of the sexes – that is, the established definition of "masculine" and "feminine" – was even looser then and not so rigidly overdetermined, so that a borderline existence was rather more possible than it would be today. In times of crisis, especially, the "boundary between the sexes was temporarily erased or drawn less rigorously."[11]

If this changed in time of war, however – if mass rapes were always part of wars – a glance at the highly ritualized process of war may help us understand the reasons. War is a ritualized, finely regulated game. I use the word "game" – a strange word given the lethal context – because behavior in war follows specific "rules of the game" (one of the reasons the military hesitates to intervene in Yugoslavia is that it would be dealing with an enemy that is not prepared to recognize these rules). In war well-defined armies are present, the enemy is clearly identifiable, and there are recognizable procedures at the front, with a clear order of command.[12] When looking back through history we find much to suggest that within this ritual one rule of the game has always been that violence against women in the conquered territory is conceded to the victor during the immediate postwar period. We have no evidence that any negotiations have ever been carried out to halt this outrage against women. It also seems to have made no difference whether women's bodies were at soldiers' disposal in other quarters – in brothels, for example. As a member of the highest military court in the United States explained, a rape in a war zone has no relation to available women or prostitutes.[13] That means that in the "open space" of war, many men simply prefer to rape: it has nothing to do with sexuality, but rather reflects the exercise of sexual, gender-specific violence. Normally the orgies of violence toward women last from one to two months after a war and then abate (as in Berlin in 1945 and Nanking in 1937).

IN BELLIGERENT DISPUTES THE ABUSE OF WOMEN IS AN ELEMENT OF MALE COMMUNICATION

In the context of war, rape can be considered the final symbolic expression of the humiliation of the male opponent. As experience teaches us, the myth of man as protector that is mobilized in most wars is really nothing more than a myth. There is by no means a cultural imperative to protect women from war and its consequences. This is not to say that this myth has no social effect and possesses no psychological reality for many men (and women). Neither do I mean to deny the possibility that isolated men do protect isolated women (just as isolated women protect isolated men). But in principle women are always laid open to the consequences of war. Furthermore, the rape of women carries an additional message: it communicates from man to man, so to speak, that the men around the women in question are not able to protect "their" women. They are thus wounded in their masculinity and marked as incompetent. In the former Yugoslavia, this communicative function from man to man is clearly evident when buses filled with women in their sixth, seventh, or later month of pregnancy are sent back over enemy lines, usually with cynical inscriptions on the vehicles regarding the children about to be born. Sander and Johr's studies also throw light on this aspect: in spring 1945, they report, wartime rape victims' husbands held their wives responsible for the deed or ended their relationships because of the rape. For this reason many women kept silent about having been raped.[14] So we see that many men regard their masculinity as compromised by the abuse of "their" women. At heart is the outcome for the men, not the suffering of the women.

THESIS 3:

RAPES ALSO RESULT FROM THE OFFERS OF MASCULINITY THAT ARMIES MAKE TO THEIR SOLDIERS, OR FROM THE ELEVATION OF MASCULINITY THAT ACCOMPANIES WAR IN WESTERN CULTURES

One of the reasons men find it attractive to become soldiers is that their masculinity is thereby confirmed and reinforced.[15] For many years military service served a symbolic function as a young man's rite of passage on his way to the final acquisition of a specific gender identity or as his "graduation to manhood."[16]

Despite the changes in relations between the sexes that have taken place in recent decades, ideas of masculinity are still significant both for armies and for the relation of army to society. The military profession provides subjective identities that are connected to ideas of masculinity in different ways depending on the country and that have connotations of power and dominance as well as eroticism and sexuality. Thus the military is also dependent on those ideas of masculinity and femininity that are valid in a particular society or on the relations between the sexes that are prevalent there. The attractiveness, status, and social privilege of a profession also depend on these constructions. Certain aspects of the military are scarcely understandable without their more or less subtle implications for the arrangement of the sexes. If we try to "ignore gender – the social constructions of 'femininity' and 'masculinity' and the relations between them," writes Cynthia Enloe, "it becomes impossible adequately to explain how military forces have managed to capture and control so much of society's imagination and resources."[17]

The significance of constructions of "masculinity" in armies is also shown by the way the increasingly strong position of women in the American army has shaken the image and professional self-understanding of the soldier, which is currently having to be redefined.[18]

If one examines the ideas of masculinity that still apply in Western societies, the definition of masculinity is usually linked almost inextricably to heterosexuality and the monopoly of power: in our culture a homosexual man is perceived as less masculine than a heterosexual one, a gentle, fearful man as less masculine than an aggressive one. Armies make offers of masculinity on both accounts: by excluding women, they associate the monopoly of power with masculinity, homosexuality being outlawed in (almost) all modern armies;[19] dealing lewdly with heterosexuality is a component of everyday life in many units. All this is overlaid with feelings of male superiority.[20]

Furthermore, Western culture is characterized by its mixture of violence with eroticism or sexuality. Language is revealing here: a "conquest" is made both on the battlefield and in the bedroom; the Germans' invasion of Belgium at the beginning of World War I was described in the English press as the "rape of Belgium," just as the Iraqi invasion of Kuwait was described as the "rape of Kuwait"; a weapon is called the "soldier's bride." The list of images that link power and masculine sexuality could be continued indefinitely.[21]

To this extent the construction of armies and the ideal of masculinity they cultivate, which stylizes masculinity and links it to power in a particular, heterosexual way, results in an inclination (not a predetermination) to rape. This is supported by the observations of David Marlowe, a military psychiatrist, who determined that there is hardly any army in which sexual symbolism plays no role. According to Marlowe, male bonding – the collegiality among men that is required and promoted in the military – is produced by means of the shared language of male sexual identity, in which the metaphor of "soldierly masculinity" produces a strong and superior self-image.[22] At the end of World War II, a military sociologist determined that in the purely masculine context of an army the values "that are connected with the ideal of virility play a decisive role in the formation of the soldierly self-image, in the creation of inner tensions and of possibilities for releasing those tensions."[23]

> That does not mean that every soldier rapes. But it does mean that the construction of the soldier – or to express it differently, the subjective identity that armies make available, by fusing certain cultural ideas of masculinity with a soldier's essence – is more conducive to certain ways of behavior rather than others. For in a stress situation like war, how one reacts depends not only on the specifics of the stressful situation, but beyond that also "on the individual and sociocultural availability of certain coping strategies. Part of coping is also the culturally coded manner of dealing with emotions."[24] Whether or not one reacts violently in a certain situation, then, also depends for example on which alternatives are available for the channeling of feelings in a cultural context (and in various cultures and also in various armies that includes varying ideas of masculinity and femininity).[25]

Reports about gang rapes by Americans in Vietnam also reveal how important the amalgamation of power and masculinity can be in cultural representations. We know that in that war gratuitous atrocities to the victim were taken as a competition for greater masculinity. A very few acts of this kind were reported by soldiers who had witnessed them but had not taken part in the rapes or sexual torture. In subsequent court-martial proceedings, the rapists typically questioned the masculinity of the soldier who had accused them. In a case that became well known, a soldier who had refused to take part in a rape was derided by his patrol leader as a queer and a chicken.[26]

A further explanation for outbreaks of sexual violence in wars is shown by the interplay between male psychology and society's construction of masculinity. Joan Smith argues that the military's characteristic denial and suppression of gentle, sensitive, and anxious feelings calls forth a situation in which men must continually hold their masculine identity up for inspection. This happens when "feminine" characteristics such as empathy, sympathy, and gentleness are valued less highly, at least in the organizational context. Entrenched in such a defense of masculinity, she believes, it is hardly possible to deal reflectively with emotions like sympathy, desire, fear, or rage.[27] Such feelings are a threat to the carefully constructed masculine existence. If feelings are released in extreme situations, however, the affect they evoke is antifeminine. Subsequently many soldiers have recourse to the "masculine" solution offered by their culture, for which they also have been trained as experts: to violence, which then becomes a specifically sexual violence against women.[28]

THESIS 4:
RAPES IN WARTIME AIM AT DESTROYING
THE OPPONENTS' CULTURE

To clarify what is involved, we must look briefly at what could be called the inside of war, that is to say, what goes on in war. Current opinion, from the military especially, contends that civilians (and in wartime that is for the most part women) must unfortunately, but sometimes unavoidably, be affected by the actions of war. The armed dispute between soldiers is termed the "actual" action of war. But the results of a research project about the position of women in the civil war zones of Mozambique and Sri Lanka challenge this ideal definition of war.[29] These results showed that civilians were greatly affected by war actions. Women in the affected regions perceived the war as anything but men's business. Analysis showed that it was civilians, not soldiers, who stood in the middle of these wars. Furthermore, as tactical objectives, women were of special importance: if the aim is to destroy a culture, they are prime targets because of their cultural position and their importance in the family structure. In "dirty wars" it is not necessarily the conquest of the foreign army, but rather the deconstruction of a culture that can be seen as a central objective of war actions, for only by destroying it – and that means by destroying people – can a decision be forced. We must remember that "the obsessive nature of war is the mutual infliction of harm, and that we often lose sight of the central meaning of this fact,"[30] since we so often act as if civilian victims stood outside the target of attack. Terms such as "unintentional" or "unexpected" are bound up with the idea that civilian victims are "by-products" of war. "The latter meaning is especially awkward, for while the others seem only to be disavowing responsibility, the latter term reduces victims on both sides to nullities, whatever the objective of the belligerent dispute might have been."[31] Military history shows that dead and wounded people, civilians especially, constitute the path to military victory.

That the civilian population is systematically drawn into war strategy is confirmed by the following numbers: In World War I a disproportionately greater number of civilians than soldiers were killed. The former Soviet Union cites the number of 9 million soldiers of both sexes killed in World War II compared with more than 16 million civilians. Official statements about the Korean War quote a proportion of 1:5, and for the Vietnam War it is 1:13. According to 1989 UNICEF data, in the wars fought since World War II 90 percent of all victims are found in the civilian population, a large share of them women and children. For future wars, a study from 1979 anticipates a proportion of 1:100.[32]

Within the context of this systematic involvement of the civilian population, indications are that the attack on women is a conscious military tactic. This thesis was under discussion even before the events in Bosnia and Croatia. The question was posed in 1971, in connection with the mass rapes in Bangladesh. The number of raped women in Bangladesh was estimated at 200,000. At the time an Indian writer was already convinced "that it had to do with a planned crime. The rapes were so systematic and all-inclusive that only a conscious military strategy can have been behind them."[33] He suspected that the objective was to create a new race and extinguish Bengali national feeling.

We see an additional aspect of cultural destruction in the fact that the female body functions as a symbolic representation of the body politic. Thus artistic portrayals also show that in many cultures a group's system of meaning is denoted by the female gender, "on whose person, body, and life the construction of the community . . . is created and brought to completion."[34] That also means the violence inflicted on women is aimed at the physical and personal integrity of a group. This in turn is particularly significant for the construction of the community. Thus the rape of the women in a community can be regarded as the symbolic rape of the body of this community.[35] Against this background, the mass rapes that accompany all wars take on new meaning: by no means acts of senseless brutality, they are rather culture-destroying actions with a strategic rationale. A few more examples:

The area around Berlin is not the only one to have reported mass rapes in World War II. In this war they were a mass phenomenon, occurring as a matter of principle in the military conflicts. When Japanese forces captured the Chinese city of Nanking in December 1937, approximately 20,000 women were raped, sexually tortured, and murdered in the first month of the occupation. Foreign missionaries reported at least ten gang rapes a day. The rapes took on such dimensions that the press in response started to speak not of the capture, but of the rape of Nanking.[36]

In 1943 Moroccan mercenaries fighting with what was left of the Free French Army were given explicit license to plunder enemy territory and to rape. As a result there were widespread mass rapes in Italy resulting, as they do everywhere, in pregnancies. The Italian government later offered these women a modest pension.[37]

The soldiers of Nazi Germany also committed mass rapes. We know that the German army also ran brothels that were forcibly supplied with women. According to witnesses' statements, the German army command in Smolensk opened a brothel for officers in a hotel, into which Russian women and girls were driven.[38] That the army that ostentatiously cultivated the lofty ideology of man as hero and protector also contained rapists is of course hardly surprising if one considers the misogyny of the National Socialist ideology, which in essence defined women as tools for men. Thus Goebbels openly declared: "Man should be trained as a warrior and woman as recreation for the warrior: anything else is foolishness," thereby providing the ideological legitimation for defining the female body as a tool for men.[39]

These examples of systematic wartime rapes could be extended by many others. In every case women in war zones are in a more precarious situation than men. As civilians they, like children and old men, are the stuff of war. This is corroborated by the stories of Bosnian refugees: "Women, children, and old people hoisted white flags and remained behind, hoping they would enjoy special status as the unarmed civilian population. In isolated cases their naive calculation came out right. In general, however, a person without a weapon is especially open to attack."[40]

THE BACKGROUND TO RAPE ORGIES IS A CULTURALLY ROOTED CONTEMPT FOR WOMEN THAT IS LIVED OUT IN TIMES OF CRISIS

Along with all the other motives, rape remains an act of extreme violence by men against women that would not be possible without hostility toward women. In her "Report from Zagreb," the Croatian journalist Ines Sabalic pointed out the dimension of rage and hatred toward women that is crucial to explaining specific acts of sexual violence. She mentioned especially atrocities of a quasi-ritualistic character, whose core was the femaleness of the body. Thus, after being raped, women had their breasts cut off and their stomachs slit open. Because of the specific way it was carried out, she interprets this violence as a special expression of hatred toward women.[41]

The thesis that rape is primarily a matter of revenge against the enemy, recurring continually in the discussion, acknowledges on the one hand women's condition as "the stuff of war." On the other hand, however, reality carries the thesis ad absurdum. In May and June 1945 not only German women were raped, but also Jewish women who had survived the Nazi regime, and forced laborers who likewise had been victims of the Nazis. It was not exclusively native women who were raped in Kuwait, but in equal measure foreign workers from the Philippines, Egypt, and other countries. In Brownmiller's assessment, women in war are raped not because they "belong to the enemy camp, but because they are women and therefore enemies."[42]

To be sure, the term "enemy" presents problems in this context. For enemies usually know they are enemies and have theories about why that is so. If one is attacked by an enemy, one usually fights back. But none of these points applies to the gender relationship. Usually women neither expect to be treated with hostility as a group nor know why it is being done. They felt secure – as the women from the former Yugoslavia also report – until the madness broke upon them.[43] Getting to the bottom of this definition, we have to say that women are raped not because they are enemies, but because they are the objects of a fundamental hatred that characterizes the cultural unconscious and is actualized in times of crisis. "Times of war and crisis are the external conditions that permit those thresholds that inhibit direct sexual violence, fragile and porous from the outset, to subside."[44] This applies not only to the direct arena of a war.

Thus during the Gulf War in 1991 the number of rapes in Israel grew noticeably.[45] Similar changes are reported from Croatia. Since the beginning of the war, the general violence against women has been intensifying there in a frightening way. Thus the "threats to women's lives and rapes under threat of weapons have also increased within the family by nearly 30 percent. The violence against women increases especially after nationalistically tinged television programs."[46]

Apparently we cannot escape the knowledge that a virulent misogyny exists to varying degrees beneath the fragile surface of our societies.[47] And these feelings of hatred and contempt are already evident in peacetime. Hatred is cultivated, for example, in socially accepted pornography, which is a peacetime celebration of the physical power of men over women, offering a system of hate-filled values consistent within itself. With the help of a specific definition or construction of aggressive sexuality (which is described as "normal"), these values are "naturalized" and therefore legitimized. Consequently these hate-filled images seem to most men and also to many women as "normal" and neutral or at least not especially worth mentioning.[48] A glance at the cultural production of the Western world (which is almost entirely a reflection of male experience) reveals a cultivation or aestheticization of rape, ranging from the rape of the Sabine women to *A Clockwork Orange*. Against this background war becomes among other things "an adventure that affirms and acts out unconscious destructive fantasies against women."[49]

The Logic of Silence

Until now widespread silence has historically cloaked this cruelty toward women. Sander and Johr also have addressed this silence.[50] During their research on the mass rapes at the end of World War II, they were astonished to discover that no one had taken up this topic in more than forty years. This silence, too, has a deep-seated cultural meaning and can in no way be attributed to coincidence, embarrassment, or the pain of the women in question. Although it is a mass occurrence in wars and pogroms, rape is also treated historiographically as an isolated phenomenon. Male historians mention rapes in a footnote or use portrayals of sexual violence against women if they want to suggest the particular drama of a situation. By doing this they deny that rapes have a historical or a structural significance in gender relations.[51]

At the beginning of this essay I asserted that rape is a massive attack on female subjectivity that goes so far as to destroy it. If one suppresses and silences this experience, it means that in a cultural context women's experience and therefore women's subjectivity is being extinguished. After that there is only the female body, with which men have experiences, interpreting those experiences according to criteria that leave their social position of power intact. For those who have hegemony in a culture also have the power to name things. "This power of naming enables men to define experience, to articulate boundaries and values, to designate to each thing its realm and qualities, to determine what can and cannot be expressed, to control perception itself."[52]

By being marginalized, suppressed, or even "naturalized," rape as an extreme and structural act of violence against women disappears from the cultural memory (when rape is seen as an unfortunate but "natural" by-product of war, for example, beyond further analysis, or when, despite the innumerable instances of it, it is interpreted as an atypical "slip" on the part of insane hordes). The experiences, the reality, and thereby the subjectivity of women are being denied. Besides rapes, there are other examples of the silencing of women's experience, particularly in wartime.

Thus during World War II 450,000 women – not counting medical personnel – worked in the German army. If at the end of the War they were stationed near the front – and this could be the case nearly everywhere – a terrible fate usually awaited them: here too rapes and torture were the order of the day. For example, at the beginning of January, air force aides who were stationed in eastern Prussia – a total of approximately 1,000 young women about twenty years of age – were ordered west from their mobilization camp in Königsberg. They never arrived. It is presumed that approximately 25,000 aides disappeared in the East. In southeastern Europe and in southern France a large number of army aides also disappeared. There was never any systematic search for these women.[53] There are no statistics about the losses among the so-called army aides. War diaries, like the other portrayals of World War II, remain silent on the topic of "women."[54]

This silence also applies to the current situation in the former Yugoslavia. The Red Cross and other humanitarian organizations had apparently been informed about the rape camps for a long time without objecting especially strenuously or bringing it to public attention. Allegedly the United Nations also had long possessed similar information. Nevertheless the UN Commission on Refugees asserted as late as October 1992 that "there is no indication of systematic rapes; it is a matter of wandering gangs."[55] Ines Sabalic has expressed the fear that the female experience with war may repeat itself in Croatia and Bosnia in that the war crimes against women could go unpunished despite the widespread publicity the mass rapes have received.[56]

For a long time international politics did not react to the rape camps in Bosnia either, although as early as August 1992 an article about the camps appeared in the New York newspaper *Newsday*. Only very recently have there been attempts to restore rape to cultural memory as a systematic historical and political event, to broadcast and problematize it. Only when violence is brought up in this way and made public can there be any change. For only when sexual violence is perceived as a political event, when it is made public and analyzed, can its causes and contexts be probed and strategies to overcome it be considered.

Mobilizing a sympathetic public might have a further effect: it can offer the victims of sexual violence an opportunity to discuss it so that the experience itself can be articulated. According to Sander and Johr, the rapes at the end of World War II are characterized not only by their vast numbers, but also by the fact that the victims do not speak.[57] That may also be because there was no discourse available to them within which the women could have revealed their experiences while preserving their dignity.

The dominant way of thought included no female perspective and conceded neither women's experience nor their dignity. Essentially it asserted that rape was natural in war and that women were its natural objects. Governments too tended either to tolerate the brutalities in silence or else to use them for propaganda purposes. If the propaganda purposes vanished, the rapes as crimes against women sank back into oblivion. Thus during the war crimes trials in Nuremberg and Tokyo, rapes were not treated separately.

In 1949, in reaction to war brutality on all sides, international law – an institution that sets norms and therefore also steers our perceptions – did order the special protection of women. This notwithstanding, sexual torture of women and mass rapes have taken place in all wars since World

War II without being given any special publicity. Rape has become a forgotten war crime.[58] That is to say, until now this central cultural experience of women has been stifled, erased from cultural memory, or else placed on the inevitable margin in the form of biologism or naturalization, in the last analysis natural and historically not very important. It must be brought back to the center of the historical and political discourse.

Notes

1. Helke Sander and Barbara Johr, *BeFreier und Befreite: Krieg, Vergewaltigung, Kinder* (Munich, 1992), p.21.

2. Ibid, pp.46 ff.

3. *Frankfurter Rundschau,* March 3, 1993.

4. See Nicolas Groth and William Hobson, "Die Dynamik sexueller Gewalt," in *Vergewaltigung: Die Opfer und die Täter,* ed. Jürgen Heinrichs (Braunschweig, 1986), p.88.

5. Andrea Dworkin, *Pornography. Men Possessing Women* (New York, 1989), p.243. Page references in this chapter are to the German edition: *Pornographie: Männer beherrschen Frauen* (Frankfurt, 1990).

6. Harry Feldmann, *Vergewaltigung und ihre psychischen Folgen: Ein Beitrag zur post-traumatischen Belastungsreaktion* (Stuttgart, 1992), p.6.

7. Ibid., p.7.

8. Ibid.; Groth and Hobson, *Dynamik.*

9. Roy Porter, "Rape – Does It Have a Historical Meaning?" in *Rape,* ed. Sylvana Tomaselli and Roy Porter (London, 1986).

10. Sander and Johr, *BeFreier und Befreite.*

11. Rudolf Dekker and Lotte van de Pol, *Frauen in Männerkleidern: Weibliche Transvestiten und ihre Geschichte* (Berlin, 1990), p.47; see also Porter, "Rape," and Ruth Seifert, "Männlichkeitskonstruktionen: Die diskursive Macht des Militärs," *Das Argument,* no.196 (1992).

12. International military law likewise requires a clear order of command with accountability for orders. Weapons must be carried openly and insignia must be worn to identify the people fighting as members of a definite combatant group.

13. Susan Brownmiller, *Against Our Will: Women and Rape* (New York, 1975), p.80. Page references in this chapter are to the German edition: *Gegen unseren Willen: Vergewaltigung und Männerherrschaft* (Frankfurt am Main, 1978).

14. Sander and Johr, *BeFreier und Befreite.*

15. See Ruth Seifert, "Feministische Theorie und Militärsoziologie," *Das Argument: Zeitschrift für Philosophie und Sozialwissenschaften,* no.190 (1991).

16. Karl W. Haltiner, *Milizarmee – Bürgerleitbild oder angeschlagenes Ideal?* (Frauenfeld, 1985), p.37.

17. Cynthia Enloe, *Does Khaki Become You? The Militarisation of Women's Lives* (London, 1983), p.212.

18. See Cynthia Enloe, "The Politics of Constructing the American Woman Soldier as a Professionalized 'First Class Citizen': Some Lessons from the Gulf War," *Minerva: Quarterly Report on Women and the Military* 14 (1992); *Time Magazine,* November 30, 1992.

19. President Clinton has attempted to change this in a legal sense, at least. Of course no one expects that everyday life in the army will change for a while (see *Time magazine,* November 11, 1992).

20. See Cynthia Enloe, "Beyond Steve Canyon and Rambo: Feminist Histories of Militarized Masculinity," in *The Militarization of the Western World,* ed. John R. Gillis (New Brunswick, N.J., 1989); Seifert, *Feministische Theorie.*

21. See also Klaus Theweleit, *Männerphantasien,* vols. 1 and 2 (Reinbek, 1972); Rolf Pohl, "Männlichkeit, Destruktivität und Kriegsbereitschaft," in *Logik der Destruktion: Der zweite Golfkrieg als erster elektronischer Krieg und die Möglichkeiten seiner Verarbeitung im Bewußtsein,* Reihe des Instituts für Politische Wissenschaften (Uni Hannover, 1992).

22. David H. Marlowe, "The Manning of the Force and the Structure of Battle: Part 2, Men and Women," in *Conscripts and Volunteers: Military Requirements, Social Justice and the All-Volunteer Force,* ed. Robert K. Fullinwider (Totowa, N.J., 1983), p.192.

23. Henry Elkin, "Aggressive and Erotic Tendencies in Army Life," *American Journal of Sociology* 51 (1946): 410.

24. Hans-Günther Vester, *Emotion: Gesellschaft und Kultur. Grundzüge einer soziologischen Theorie der Emotionen* (Opladen, 1990), p.144.

25. Ibid.

26. Brownmiller, *Against Our Will,* pp.105 ff.

27. The differing ways men and women deal with fear are also illuminated in Frigga Haug and Kornelia Hauser, eds., *Die andere Angst: Frauenformen,* Argument-Sonderband 184 (Berlin, 1991), pp.250 ff.

28. Joan Smith, *Misogynies* (New York, 1990), pp.135 ff. Page references in this chapter are to the German edition: *Misogynies: Frauenhaß in der Gesellschaft* (Munich, 1992).

29. Carolyn Nordstrom, "Women and War: Observations from the Field," *Minerva: Quarterly Report on Women and the Military* 9, no.1 (1991).

30. Elaine Scarry, *The Body in Pain: The Making and Unmaking of the World* (New York, 1985), p.102. Page references in this chapter are to the German edition: *Der Körper im Schmerz: Die Chiffren der Verletzlichkeit und die Erfindung der Kultur* (Frankfurt, 1992). This insight had also occurred to the military theorist Clausewitz, who described military invasions as follows: "The immediate purpose is neither the conquest of enemy land nor the defeat of enemy forces, but quite simply to inflict general harm on the enemy" (Carl von Clausewitz, *Vom Kriege,* 18th ed. [Bonn, 1973], p.219).

31. Scarry, *Body in Pain,* pp.109 ff.

32. See Richard Gabriel, *The Culture of War: Invention and Early Development* (New York, 1990), p.14; Nordstrom, *Women and War,* p.191.

33. Brownmiller, *Against Our Will,* p.89.

34. Theresa Wobbe, "Die Grenzen des Geschlechts: Konstruktionen von Gemeinschaft und Rassismus," in *Mitteilungen des Instituts für Sozialforschung,* vol. 2 (Frankfurt, 1993), p.106.

35. Ibid.

36. Brownmiller, *Against Our Will,* p.65; see also Leon Friedmann, *The Law of War: A Documentary History,* vol. 11 (New York, 1972), pp.1060 ff.

37. Michael Walzer, *Just and Unjust Wars: A Moral Argument with Historical Illustrations* (New York, 1977), pp.133 ff.

38. Statement on January 31, 1946, in *Trial of the Major War Criminals before the International Military Tribunal* (Nuremberg, 1947), 6:404 ff.; 7:456 ff.; Brownmiller, *Against Our Will,* pp.55 ff.; see also Raul Hilberg, *The Destruction of the European Jews* (Chicago, 1961), pp.126 ff.

39. In this connection it is worth mentioning that virtually no rapes took place among the Vietcong during the Vietnam War. Although the Vietcong practiced terrorism, rape was not part of their standard repertoire. Aside from possible ethnological peculiarities (many Vietcong had a Buddhist background, and in Buddhism rape is held to be a serious crime), another possible explanation is that the Vietcong had women among their ranks and for this reason depersonalization and contempt for women could not take on great dimensions (see Brownmiller, *Against Our Will,* pp.94 ff.).

40. Cheryl Benard and Edit Schlaffer, eds., "Kleiner als ein Stück Dreck," *Der Spiegel* (Hamburg) no.50 (December 7, 1992): 186.

41. Ines Sabalic, *Nirgends erwähnt – doch überall geschehen: Ein Bericht aus Zagreb,* Publikation der Gleichstellungsstelle der Landeshauptstadt (Munich, 1992).

42. Brownmiller, *Against Our Will,* p.69.

43. Benard and Schlaffer, *Kleiner,* p.190.

44. Pohl, "Männlichkeit," p.111.

45. Ibid.

46. Elisabeth Raiser, "Vergewaltigungen als Kriegsstrategie," *Junge Kirche: Zeitschrift Europäischer Christinnen und Christen* 1(1993): 6.

47. The psychoanalytical side of this process, which must be taken into consideration along with everything else, has been articulated by Pohl, among others. See Pohl, "Männlichkeit," pp.157 ff.

48. See Dworkin, *Pornography*, p.35. Data from various countries confirm that easy access to pornographic material is accompanied everywhere by a considerable increase in rapes (Lee Ellis, *Theories of Rape: Inquiries into the Causes of Sexual Aggression* [New York, 1989], p.25).

49. Pohl, "Männlichkeit," p.161.

50. Sander and Johr, *BeFreier und Befreite*.

51. See Porter, "Rape."

52. Dworkin, *Pornography*, p.26.

53. Another reason for this omission lies in the male bias of international treaties. Thus one of the primary tasks of the International Red Cross was to look for prisoners of war, but not for "civilian displacees." Since the women in question were not given combatant status, they were not considered prisoners of war and therefore fell through the cracks of international regulations. That they were kept by law (but not in reality) from combatant status made these women particularly helpless and vulnerable. Since they were not considered combatants, they could be treated like Partisans and thus be shot according to martial law. Soldiers, in contrast, enjoy the protection of international agreements.

54. Franz W. Seidler, *Frauen zu den Waffen? Marketenderinnen, Helferinnen, Soldatinnen* (Koblenz, 1978), pp.163 ff.

55. *AMI* 23, 1 (January 1992): 22.

56. Sabalic, *Nirgends erwähnt*.

57. Ibid., p.9.

58. Significant in this context is that the economic and social committee of the United Nations warned in 1972 that war cruelty, especially toward women, has been occurring at virtually the same level despite the Geneva Conventions.

Turning Rape into Pornography: Postmodern Genocide

Catharine A. MacKinnon

Everything was dark, but the bed on which they were raping was lit up, like when they interrogate you and point the light only on you. Only that bed was lit up with a spotlight. . . . I had a feeling that they were sometimes recording or filming." In what is called peacetime, pornography is made from rape in film studios, on sets, in private bedrooms, in basements, in alleys, in prison cells, and in brothels. It should be no surprise to find it being made in a "rape theater" in a Serbian-run concentration camp for Muslims and Croatians in Bosnia-Herzegovina— as reported above by one survivor, a twenty-eight-year-old Croatian and Muslim woman. Still, it comes as a shock, a clarifying jolt. When Linda "Lovelace" reported her coercion into the pornographic film *Deep Throat,* Gloria Steinem reworded the essence of the disbelief and blame Linda encountered as amounting to asking her, "What in your background led you to a concentration camp?" If this was ever only an analogy, it isn't anymore.

Exploding the strategy pioneered a year earlier in Croatia, Serbian military forces in Bosnia-Herzegovina have been, as the world now knows, carrying out a campaign called "ethnic cleansing." This is a euphemism for genocide. It means removal or liquidation of all non-Serbs from the territory that was called Yugoslavia. This campaign of expansion through ethnic extermination has included rape, forcible impregnation, torture, and murder of Muslim and Croatian women, "for Serbia." A Bosnian

73

Muslim soldier – call him "Haris" to protect his identity – who spied on Serbian forces, described what he saw them do, from Vaganac in Serbian-occupied Croatia to Grabez in Serbian-occupied Bosnia: "Everything that's Muslim or Croatian, they slaughter, kill, set on fire. Nothing's supposed to remain alive, not even a chicken, cat, or bird, if they know it's Muslim or Croatian. . . . One said, 'There's a dog; it's Muslim, kill it.'" The raped women, the filmed women, the pregnant women, and probably the murdered women as well as the men suffer not only from these atrocities but also from knowing that they are intended to be the last of their people there.

This genocidal war has repeatedly been mischaracterized as a "civil war," aggressor equated with victim, "all sides" blandly blamed for their "hatred." Yet Serbian aggression against non-Serbs is as incontestable as male aggression against women in everyday life. Wars always produce atrocities, especially against women civilians. But there is no Muslim or Croatian *policy* of territorial expansion, of exterminating Serbs, of raping Serbian women. This is not reciprocal genocide. The reluctance to say who is doing what to whom is reminiscent of the mentality that blames women for getting ourselves raped by men we know and then chides us for having a bad attitude toward them. Asja Armanda, of the Kareta Feminist Group in Zagreb, theorizes that the closer to home atrocities come, the more they are domesticated, made into love gone wrong. The more "feminized" the victims thus become, the more hesitant other men are to intervene in a family quarrel, and the more human rights can be violated and atrocities condoned.

The rapes in the Serbian war of aggression against Bosnia-Herzegovina and Croatia are to everyday rape what the Holocaust was to everyday anti-Semitism: both like it and not like it at all, both continuous with it and a whole new departure, a unique atrocity yet also a pinnacle moment in something that goes on all the time. As it does in this war, ethnic rape happens every day. As it is in this war, prostitution is forced on women every day: What is a brothel but a captive setting for organized serial rape? Forced pregnancy is familiar too, beginning in rape and proceeding through the denial of abortions; this occurred during slavery and still happens to women who cannot afford abortions – who in the United States are disproportionately African American or Latina. Also familiar is the use of media technology, including pornography, to make hatred sexy. Women are abused by men in these ways every day in every country in the world. Sex has also been used before to create, mobilize, and manipulate ethnic hatred, from the Third Reich to *Penthouse*. Yet the world has never seen sex used this consciously, this cynically, this elaborately, this openly, this systematically, with this degree of technological and psychological sophistication, as a means of destroying a whole people.

With this war, pornography emerges as a tool of genocide. Natalie Nenadic, an American of Croatian and Bosnian heritage, writes from Zagreb that she learned from Muslim sources that "some massacres in villages as well as rapes and/or executions in camps are being videotaped as they're happening." One woman who survived the Bucje rape/death camp in Serbian-occupied Croatia reports the making of pornography of her rapes this way: "In front of the camera, one beats you and the other – excuse me – fucks you, he puts his truncheon in you, and he films all that. . . . We even had to sing Serbian songs . . . in front of the camera." Account after account documents that Serbian forces film as they rape. As they do it, they watch, laugh, encourage each other, and spew ethnic curses and epithets. "Ustasha whore" is particularly commonplace. "Ustasha" is a derogatory political term that refers to the fascist regime in Croatia (then including Bosnia-Herzegovina) that collaborated with Hitler. Serbian soldiers use it for Muslim and Croatian women – most of whom were not even born until after World War II.

In a war crimes trial in Sarajevo in March 1993, Borislav Herak, a Serbian soldier, testified that the rapes he committed had been ordered for "Serbian morale." As an instrument for their morale building, the Croatian-Muslim survivor quoted earlier – one of whose twin sons was decapitated in her arms – reports that, as they raped her, "Serbian soldiers were telling me 'Croatia needs to be crushed again. *Balijas* need to be crushed completely. You are half this and half that. You need to be crushed to the end. Because you're Croatian, you should be raped by five different men – and because you're a *Bula*, you should be raped by five more.'" *Balija* and *Bula* are derogatory names for Muslims. Xenophobia and misogyny merge here; ethnic hatred is sexualized; bigotry becomes orgasm. Whatever this rape does for the rapist, the pornography of the rape mass-produces. The materials become a potent advertisement for a war, a perfect motivator for torturers, who then do what they are ordered to do and enjoy it. Yes, it improves their morale.

Some of the rapes that are made into pornography are clearly intended for mass consumption as war propaganda. One elderly Croatian woman who was filmed being raped was also tortured by electric shocks and gang raped in the Bucje concentration camp by Serbian men dressed in generic camouflage uniforms. She was forced to "confess" on film that Croatians raped her. This disinformation – switching the ethnic labels – is especially easy where there are no racial markers for ethnic distinctions, and it is a standard technique. Another such incident of switched victims and murderers was dismissed as "a shameless lie" by relief officials, according to a UN spokesperson in Sarajevo, quoted in the *New York Times* on April 14, 1993. One woman captured by the Serbs described how she was forced to participate in such lies by reading a scripted false "confession" about her activities as a "terrorist" for a Television Novi Sad camera. She knew the fabrication aired because she was recognized by a Serbian guard who said he had seen her on Belgrade TV.

Serbian propaganda moves cultural markers with postmodern alacrity, making ethnicity unreal and all too real at the same time. Signs and symbols, words, images, and identities are manipulated to mean anything and its opposite – all in the service of genocide, a single reality that means only one thing. When human beings are "represented" out of existence, playing reality as a game emerges as a strategy of fascism.

Actual rapes of Muslim and Croatian women by Serbian soldiers, filmed as they happen, have been shown on the evening news in Banja Luka, a Serbian-occupied city in western Bosnia-Herzegovina. The women were presented as Serbian and as being raped by Muslim or Croatian men. In September 1992 one woman about age fifty, entirely naked and with visible bruises, was shown being raped on television. A Serbian cross hung around her neck; the rapist – using a term for Serbian fascist collaborator that has become a badge of pride among Serb forces – cursed her Chetnik mother; someone was yelling "harder." The verbal abuse was dubbed – and unmistakably Serbian in intonation and usage. The man's face was not visible, but the woman's was. In another televised rape a few days later, a woman near age thirty-five, with short, dark hair, was shown on the ground; her hands were spread and tied to a tree, her legs tied to her hands. Many men watched her raped in person; thousands more watched her raped on television. This time, in an apparent technical lapse, about four or five seconds of the actual sound track was aired: "Do you want sex, Ustasha? Do you like Serbian stud horses?" Earlier in the war, according to Asja Armanda of the Kareta Feminist Group, a news report showed Serbian tanks rolling in to "cleanse" a village. The tanks were plastered with pornography.

How does genocide become so explicitly sexually obsessed? How do real rapes become ordinary evening news? Before the war, pornography saturated Yugoslavia, especially after the fall of communism. Its market, according to Yugoslav critic Bogdan Tirnanic, was "the freest in the world." A major news magazine, *Start,* with a *Newsweek*-like format and the politics of *The Nation,* had *Playboy*-type covers and a centerfold section showing naked women in postures of sexual display and access. Select women who were privileged under the Communist regime, and who presented themselves as speaking for women, regularly published there and even occasionally served as editors. (The presentation of pornography as a model of feminism repelled many women.) When pornography is this normal, a whole population of men is primed to dehumanize women and to enjoy inflicting assault sexually. The *New York Times* reported finding "piles of pornographic magazines" in the bedroom of Borislav Herak, the captured Serbian soldier who calmly admitted to scores of rapes and murders. At his war crimes trial in Sarajevo, when asked where he learned to kill, he described being trained by killing pigs. No one asked him where he learned to rape, although he testified that his first rape in this war was his first sexual experience. Pornography is the perfect preparation – motivator and instructional manual in one – for the sexual atrocities in this genocide.

Pornography, known to dehumanize women for its consumers, pervades some rape/death camps, according to survivors. In one military prison, the pornography was customized to suit the guards' sexual tastes, in echoes and parallels to the acts they performed. One woman in her mid-thirties, a mother of two, recalls how some men drew little penises next to women in the pornography with whom they wanted to have sex and wrote their names on the penises. Next to the *men* in the materials, they wrote, "I have a longer one than you" and signed their names. One Serbian guard "draws a picture of his own dick and an arrow showing where he'd go with it." In other words, these men do to women in the materials what they do to women in the camp: "The women were cut out, but the man remains whole." And speaking of personalized weaponry, survivors in the Bosnia-Herzegovina Refugee Women's Group, Zene BiH, in exile in Zagreb, report finding the name of Jovan Tintor, a Chetnik commander, inscribed on the remains of projectiles that were aimed at, and hit, a Sarajevo maternity ward.

When pornography is this common and this accepted, the lines dividing it from news, entertainment, and the rest of life are so blurred that women may know no word for it. The woman who survived the Serbian military prison described a thick sex book that made the rounds. It showed, she said, "men with animals and women with animals, how you get AIDS." The book was "so read that it was completely falling apart." Another woman spoke of seeing "those magazines with the nude women, the sex." The women in the military prison grasped for words to describe them: "Either they remain standing and are nude or . . . you have a woman lying on a woman or a woman lying on a man, all those poses that are done. I don't know what those magazines are called." Asked what was on the walls of the room where the guards slept – pictures of political leaders, perhaps? – another woman answered, "I can't say I saw Milosevic or Tito. These pictures were mainly naked women . . . those usual pictures from *Start* and those things. Male things."

The conditions in the camps throughout the occupied areas of Croatia and Bosnia-Herzegovina are subhuman. Some peacetime brothels have become rape/death camps – a kind of surreal camouflage through blatancy. Some are outdoor pens ringed with barbed wire. Some are animal stalls. Some were arenas, factories, schools. Women are typically allotted one thin slice of bread a day. Humanity is jammed into closet-sized concrete cells, begging even for boards to sleep on, waiting for the few to be selected out for systematic torture, to be taken to the rooms with the beds with the bloody sheets. "When night came," as one survivor put it, "death in life came." Those who were allowed to live often had to sexually service their captors. One woman was forced to keep her Serbian captor's penis hard in her mouth from midnight to 5:00 A.M. for fourteen nights in a Serb-run concentration camp in Vojvodina. "My job was to please him, to excite him that whole time, so that he would be able to ejaculate. . . . Sometimes I began to suffocate, and when [he] began to spurt out on the cement, he would beat me up. I had to remain kneeling."

Often the atrocities are arranged to be watched by other soldiers. In televised rapes, the viewer can see other boots standing around, walking around. The Croatian-Muslim woman quoted earlier says of her experience: "These soldiers would invite their friends to come watch the rapes. That was like in the movie theater. All sit around while others do their job. . . . Sometimes those who were watching put out cigarette butts on the bodies of the women being raped." The Serbian soldier Borislav

Herak described how other soldiers watched him rape one young girl after another – all of whose names he remembered.

This is live pornography.

We will never know what happened to most of the women who were killed – until we uncover the mass graves, or the pornography. A gang rape observed by Haris, the Bosnian soldier, gives a rare glimpse into the sexual spectacles staged for private viewing, proceeding on orders from a superior at Licko Petrovo Selo, a village in Serbian-occupied Croatia: The woman was tied to four stakes in the ground, "in a lying position, but suspended." While they were raping her, the soldiers said "that Yugoslavia is theirs . . . that they fought for it in World War II, partisans for Yugoslavia. That they gave everything for Yugoslavia." The national politics are fused with sex. Haris reports that the men laugh and chide each other for "not satisfying her," for not being able to "force a smile out of her," because she is not showing "signs of love." They beat her and ask if it is good for her. The superior who is ordering them says, "She has to know that we are Chetniks. She has to know this is our land. She has to know that we're commanding, that this is our Greater Serbia, that it'll be like this for everyone who doesn't listen." Does it ever occur to them that the woman is a human being? "I don't know if they ever even think this is a *person*," Haris says.

Is there a relationship between the pornography consumed, the sexualization of the environment of torture and predation, and the sexual acts that are performed? This is not an academic question. One woman reported that she saw done to a woman in a pornography magazine what was also done to her. Describing materials in the camps, she says, "Those pictures with those things you hit them with . . . like you have a chain like this, and like this they hang you to a bed. He hangs her from the ceiling." Without missing a beat, she moves from describing the materials to describing what was done to her: "I know there was some kind of wooden board on the side, a woman tied to it by chains, she had a mask over her eyes and he was hitting her with some kind of thick whip-crop. I mean that whip-crop reminded me of the Begejci concentration camp, because there in Begejci, they had a thick whip, a crop made like that one – from leather – and they beat the captives in that way. I mean, I was whipped like that once in Begejci with that whip-crop, so I know that it hurts."

Many tortures in the camps are organized as sexual spectacles, ritualized acts of sadism in which inflicting extreme pain and death are sexual acts, performed and watched for sexual enjoyment. Haris, hiding in a tree, observed a small concentration camp in Serbian-occupied Croatia in April 1992. It was wholly outdoors, with "hungry, tortured people, beaten, bloody." He watched a man and a woman – who appeared to be seven or eight months pregnant – being taken to a clearing in the woods. The woman was tied vertically to a cross, legs pressed together and arms extended. They ripped her pregnant belly open with a knife. "It was alive . . . it moved." The woman took fifteen minutes to die. The man, apparently her husband and father of the baby, was bound to a nearby tree and forced to watch. The attackers attempted to force him to eat the baby's arm. Then "they hacked him up, cut the flesh on him so that he would bleed to death." While they were doing this, "they were laughing. . . . 'We're going to slaughter all of you. This is our Serbia.'" Haris is certain it was filmed.

Change the politics or religion, and victims of ritual torture in this country report the same staged sexual atrocities ending in sacrifice. Some say these "snuff" scenes too are videotaped.

The Nazis were precocious with the media technology of their time. They used it to create images of events that never took place. They also took pictures of some of their horrific medical experiments and executions. They imprisoned women in brothels, forced women in camps to run naked before cameras, and paraded naked women for pictures just before their executions. They published sexually explicit anti-Semitic hate propaganda. Since then, visual technology that uses human beings as live targets has become cheap, mobile, and available. Nearly half a century of deployment of pornography worldwide has escalated explicitness, intrusiveness, and violence. With this at hand, the Serbs make the Nazis efforts look comparatively primitive.

Rape was not charged in the post–World War II indictments of the Nazis at Nuremburg, although sexual forms of torture, including rape, were documented at the trials. Perhaps this omission was a casualty of the tribunal's emphasis "not on individual barbarities and perversions" but on the Nazi "Common Plan." Rape in war has so often been treated as extracurricular, as just something men do, as a product rather than a policy of war. Yet the propagandist Julius Streicher – editor of the anti-Semitic newspaper *Der Stürmer,* which contained pornographic anti-Semitic hate propaganda – was indicted for "crimes against humanity" for incitement to hatred of the Jews. Streicher, described by prosecution documents at the Nuremburg trials as a brutal sadist who carried a leather whip attached to his wrist, was found guilty and condemned to death by hanging. In the war crimes trials for the genocidal war against Bosnia-Herzegovina and Croatia, will those who incited to genocide through rape, sexual torture, and murder – the Serbian pornographers as well as the high policymakers and the underlings – get what they deserve?

Women hesitate to report that pornography is made of their rapes even more than they hesitate to report the rapes themselves. Disbelief from outside combines with humiliation, shame, and a sense of powerlessness inside. It is unbearable to know that even after you are dead – maybe soon, on tape – thousands will see you this way. The depth of despair at stopping the rape becomes an infinity of hopelessness at stopping the pornography of it.

Even though women in rape/death camps know that the same things are being done to other women, and sometimes are even forced to watch them, still the sense of isolation is total. Always they fear reprisals, especially for speaking out against the pornography, even when they are what is called free – meaning they and their families are not literal captives of armed men.

What do we owe them, women for whom "you were lucky if they only raped you"? What will make it possible for them to speak of what was done to them? As one survivor put it, "I have no use for telling you the rest. I have no security. I have nothing." When the films of her rape are sold as pornography – emblem of democracy and liberation in post-Communist Eastern Europe and increasingly protected as speech worldwide – she will have even less than that.

Acknowledgments

Catharine MacKinnon wishes to acknowledge the contributions of Asja Armanda and Natalie Nenadic in every aspect of this article, its analysis and theory as well as research and translations. Without them – and Kareta Feminist Group, Zorica Spoljar, and the survivors with whom they work – it would have been impossible.

The Rapes in Bosnia-Herzegovina

Alexandra Stiglmayer

We were rounded up on the playing field. The men were locked up in the school. They burned a few men in trash bins in front of the windows, so that the smoke and stink of the burned flesh would drift into the school. We saw them rape the hadji's* daughter – one after the other, they raped her. The hadji had to watch too. When they were done, they rammed a knife into his throat.[1]

The refugees and displaced people from Bosnia-Herzegovina have brought with them stories of the terror they have left behind. In all these tales, rapes play a role, yet at first they seemed to me only one more detail in the horrible scenario that the fleeing people had lived through, one more outrage of the Bosnian-Herzegovinian war. It was months before I took special interest in the suffering of the women. What I then learned in my investigations saddened and amazed me. Women and girls who were systematically raped, rape camps and forced brothels, intentional impregnation of women – the atrocities knew no bounds.

    My first contacts were doctors, women's groups, Bosnian government agencies, and a few of the women involved. What they reported seemed plausible and conclusive, for I knew that the war in Bosnia-Herzegovina was a war against the civilian population and that when territory was conquered, the non-Serbian population was expelled: Why

*hadji = local Muslim cleric

shouldn't the conquerors set upon women with the most powerful weapon men possess?

And yet it seemed monstrous, almost unbelievable. In order to get to the bottom of the matter, my friend and colleague the American journalist George Rodrigue and I set out for Bosnia-Herzegovina to find other women with similar stories. Psychiatrists had told us that raped women in Bosnia-Herzegovina, where the danger is more immediate, would be more likely to speak about what they had suffered than women who had escaped to the "safe haven" of Croatia.

In central Bosnia, the region around Zenica, Travnik, Visoko, and Tarcin, which was controlled by Muslim and Croatian troops and had become a receiving ground for refugees and displaced people from the parts of Bosnia-Herzogovina occupied by Serbs, we found rape victims: intimidated women who now lived uncertain lives as refugees, broken women, but also furious women who were planning revenge.

It was not easy to find these women. In the refugee camps we visited, how frequently we were told: "Of course we have cases of rape; I can show you the women, but they don't talk about it. They withdraw, they don't say much, they sit in a corner and cry. If you ask them what happened to them, if they want to return to their homes, they say, 'Oh no, absolutely not.' But they don't say why. They won't talk with us, let alone with you."[2] At first it was one woman who was prepared to talk with us, and then in the next refugee camp another one, one who understood the rape for what it is: a humiliating act of violence, but no mark of dishonor to be kept secret. And so, little by little, we spoke with many women and young girls.

The conversations were difficult. Even for these women, who wanted to tell the foreign journalists what had happened to them, rape is that terrible, humiliating, almost unutterable "it." They had to be approached carefully, with questions about their current situation as refugees, about events when the Serbian troops invaded. Only then could we speak about what had been inflicted on these women personally.

When they faltered and began to cry, I myself often had a lump in my throat, the feeling that I was hurting them by forcing them to live through the rape one more time. And throughout everything the sober questions, repeated at various points during the interview, to test the truth of their stories: "Who raped you, when exactly did it happen, how many women were there, what were their names and where are they now, do you know the names of the rapists, what did the men say, how did they look, how do you know that your neighbor was raped too?" These and many subsequent conversations confirmed the first results of my investigation: in Bosnia-Herzegovina a war is being waged against women. Not because they are women, but because they are Muslim, Croatian, or Serbian women. Yet because they are women, men are using against them their most effective weapon: rape.

Women have always been raped in wartime, of course. There were mass rapes even in wars that were not wars of expulsion. Rapes seem to be part and parcel of a soldier's life, a "normal" accompaniment to war. Some people, especially men, say that soldiers simply need women because they have had to be "chaste" for such a long time; they say that male sexuality includes the predisposition to "take" a woman. Yet those are only the usual excuses for wartime rapes.

A rape is an aggressive and humiliating act, as even a soldier knows, or at least suspects. He rapes because he wants to engage in violence. He rapes because he wants to demonstrate his power. He rapes because he is the victor. He rapes because the woman is the enemy's woman, and he wants to humiliate and annihilate the enemy. He rapes because the woman is herself the enemy whom he wishes to humiliate and annihilate. He rapes because he despises women. He rapes to prove his virility. He rapes because the acquisition of the female body means a piece of territory conquered. He rapes to take out on someone else the humiliation he has suffered in the war. He rapes to work off his fears. He rapes because it's really only some "fun" with the guys. He rapes because war, a man's business, has awakened his aggressiveness, and he directs it at those who play a subordinate role in the world of war.[3]

In war, men rape for various motives, and we can identify nearly all of them in every war. Yet not all wars are the same, and each war provides its own specific motivations for rape. For the Russians who raped German women by turns during the invasion of Berlin in 1945, the key motives might have been revenge, a desire to break the pride of the German master race, and the feeling of having earned "thanks."[4] For the Americans in Vietnam the motive was more likely the frustration of being in a foreign country and having to fight a war that was not "their" war.[5] In neither case was the goal to drive away the women and their community; both the German and the Vietnamese women were to remain where they were.

But dispersion is precisely the goal of the Serbian forces in Bosnia-Herzegovina. Their purpose is to drive Muslims and Croats away from the conquered territories. Besides brutal terror, deliberate murders, mass executions, internment camps, deportations, and torture, one of the means they are employing is rape. Rapes spread fear and induce the flight of refugees; rapes humiliate, demoralize, and destroy not only the victim but also her family and community; and rapes stifle any wish to return. A rape is a "surefire weapon that doesn't need any fuel or ammunition," as the Zagreb feminist Asija Armanda once said. The military leaders and politicians in positions of responsibility have obviously accepted this. Until now there has been no known case of a local authority's saving a woman of "enemy nationality" from rape or even helping her afterward.

"In Bosnia-Herzegovina and Croatia, rape has been an instrument for 'ethnic cleansing.'" The UN commission of experts that investigated the rapes in the former Yugoslavia has concluded.[6] "Rape cannot be seen as incidental to the main purpose of the aggression but as serving a strategic purpose in itself," reports the European Community mission concerned especially with the situation of Muslim women.[7] The report of the humanitarian organization Amnesty International states: "Instances that have included sexual infringements against women are apparently part of an inclusive pattern of war conduct characterized by massive intimidation and infringements against Muslims and Croats."[8]

The American human rights organization Helsinki Watch believes that rape is being used as a "weapon of war" in Bosnia-Herzegovina: "Whether a woman is raped by soldiers in her home or is held in a house with other women and raped over and over again, she is raped with a political purpose – to intimidate, humiliate, and degrade her and others affected by her suffering. The effect of rape is often to ensure that women and their families will flee and never return."[9]

Against this background, it is obvious that rapes in Bosnia-Herzegovina are taking place "on a large scale" (UN and EC), that they are acquiring a systematic character, and that "in by far the most instances Muslim women are the victims of the Serbian forces" (Amnesty International). Estimates of the number of rape victims – including Croatian and Serbian women – range from 20,000 (EC) to 50,000 (Bosnian Ministry of the Interior).

But we must not forget that Bosnia-Herzegovina is not an exceptional case. Soldiers do not rape only when they want to drive out the population of the "wrong nationality." "Ethnic cleansing" in Bosnia is only an additional factor, explaining why the rapes there are so extensive and so particularly humiliating.

The names of the women mentioned in this chapter have been changed for the women's own protection. Other name changes have been noted in the text.

The "Ethnic Cleansing" of Prijedor

An example of a successful "ethnic cleansing" using rape as a weapon is the district of Prijedor in northwestern Bosnia. Prijedor is a rural area with gentle hills, green meadows, fertile fields, and the thickly wooded Kozara mountain range. Most of its inhabitants lived in seventy villages, some large, some small, and pursued agricultural occupations. Muslims, Serbs, and lesser minorities lived here, and they all got along, say the Muslims from Prijedor.

Today they no longer live there. Prijedor has become "Serbian territory." Fifty thousand Muslims and 15,000 other non-Serbs were driven off or murdered, twenty-five mosques and eleven Muslim sanctuaries were blown up, more than 10,000 houses and apartments were searched, looted, and destroyed. Only burned ruins are left to indicate that Prijedor once had more inhabitants than it does today. The "ethnic cleansing" of Prijedor was carried out quickly, brutally, and efficiently.

According to the census of 1991, there were 112,500 people living in the district of Prijedor, of whom 44 percent were Muslims, 42 percent Serbs, 6 percent Croats, and 8 percent of other ethnicities. Thus there were approximately 65,000 non-Serbs. Of these 65,000 people (according to reliable calculations of the Prijedor Homeland Club in Zagreb) 20,000 were murdered, 30,000 were driven away, and approximately 3,000 are still living in Prijedor.

The reports of refugees allow us to reconstruct what happened in Prijedor after the Serbian leadership had decided to make it a pure Serbian community.[10] In April 1992 important posts and functions were newly filled; Muslims and Croats lost their jobs, and "reliable" Serbs took over their positions. There was no resistance, because the Muslims and Croats owned virtually no weapons. In May all telephone connections were disrupted, and the Bosnian Serbs set up roadblocks.

On May 24 the Serbian army, which had been reconstituted in Bosnia-Herzegovina from parts of the former Yugoslavian Federal Army, attacked the almost exclusively Muslim village of Kozarac (27,000 inhabitants, including environs). Along with irregular units, they entered Kozarac after three days of artillery fire. Then the "ethnic cleansing" of Kozarac began; more than 20,000 Muslims had to clear out.

"Cleansing squads," special units of the Serbian army and Serbian irregular units, broke into Muslim houses. "Suspicious" Muslims were usually killed on the spot. Suspicious meant anyone who had an influential position, who was educated, rich, or politically active. Local Serbs handed over lists with the appropriate names or promptly took part themselves in the cleansing. All men whom the Serbs considered potential opponents, as well as a portion of the women, children, and old people, were brought to internment camps. When people are being expelled, such camps fulfill three important functions: first, they serve as collection points for the population before their final deportation; it is more practical to have everyone in one place. Second, the population there is combed through one more time, and all those who could later be dangerous threats – able-bodied men who might plan revenge or potential leaders who could organize and incite the people – are killed. And third, they instill fear in everyone – women, men, children, old people, young people. The purpose is to scare them to death so that they never get the idea of wanting to return to their homeland again. That is why there are murder, torture, and rape in the camps.

The internment camps in Prijedor were opened on May 27, directly after the fall of Kozarac. They consisted of Trnopolje, a settlement near Kozarac, which was transformed into a strictly guarded ghetto; Omarska, a former iron-ore mine sixteen kilometers south of Kozarac; Keraterm, a former ceramics factory near the town of Prijedor; and some smaller camps as well. In the three large camps thousands of people were held prisoner; at times there were as many as 11,000 men in Omarska, according to a UN report.

Refugees report that Trnopolje was a "decent" camp, for here there were a few arbitrary murders, but no systematic ones. But Trnopolje was a mixed camp for men and women, and almost all of the non-Serbian women of the district of Prijedor passed through it. They were subject to rapes.

Omarska and Keraterm, both of them almost exclusively male camps,[11] are considered death camps. In Omarska hundreds of prisoners were at first penned up together in a tower that had earlier been used for ore dressing; untold numbers suffocated. At night men were killed in a slaughterhouse belonging to the complex, and ten to twenty prisoners died there every night. From one to two thousand Muslims are said to have been murdered in Omarska; some are said to be buried in the mine shafts. In addition, the prisoners were subject to cruel abuse. Thus on June 17, 1992, Serbian guards forced the twenty-one-year-old Muslim Emin J. to drink a liter of motor oil and then bite off and swallow the testicles of three fellow prisoners who had already been beaten half to death. Emin also reports that the Serbian guards once played soccer with the heads of decapitated Muslims. The reports of many other former prisoners from Omarska confirm Emin's statements.

Similar things happened in Keraterm. On July 27 a few hundred men who had been kept for days in an overcrowded, stuffy storeroom without water were at the point of suffocation. When they pressed forward in the direction of the exit and called out increasingly loudly for water and air, their guards shot them with large-caliber machine guns, literally tearing them to shreds. Approximately 190 men are said to have been killed. And there are many witnesses to this as well.

The first prisoners in the camps were from Kozarac, but shortly after it was captured the "cleansing" of the other Muslim villages in the district of Prijedor began as well, so that new prisoners followed. In order to make room for them, the people the Serbs considered less dangerous – women, children, the old, and the sick – were deported. They were taken in cattle cars to the front line near Doboj in northern Bosnia or in buses and trucks to the front near Travnik in central Bosnia, where they were forced over to the Muslim-controlled side under sniper and artillery fire.

These camps were finally discovered by journalists, and on August 7, 1992, pictures from Trnopolje and Omarska were sent around the world by the British television agency ITN, pictures of emaciated figures behind barbed wire. Under pressure of the world community Serbian leaders opened some of the camps to journalists and the International Red Cross. Before doing so, however, they had either killed those prisoners who looked most wretched or else transported them to other camps. During the regroupings there were frequent mass executions, which some witnesses survived in perilous close calls.

In August Omarska and Keraterm were closed, and after the middle of

August Trnopolje was run by the International Red Cross. Finally, in October Trnopolje was closed. Today the area of Prijedor is almost entirely "Muslim- and Croat-free." Except for a few neighborhoods in the town of Prijedor and one or two villages, all the Muslim villages and neighborhoods have been burned and destroyed, and some now go by Serbian names.

RAPES IN THE TRNOPOLJE INTERNMENT CAMP

As the district of Prijedor was being "cleansed," rapes took place during the invasion of the Muslim villages, and occupation, in the Trnopolje camp, and in brothels. At first, however, nothing happened after Kozarac was captured and the internment camps were opened. "In the beginning everybody was surprised and shocked, you see," explains the twenty-eight-year-old Muslim physician Jusuf Pasalic (pseudonym),[12] who had worked in the clinic at Kozarac before his capture and whose job it was to treat his fellow prisoners in Trnopolje.

> As a doctor I was considered an authority, even by the Serbs, and in the first days many Serbian soldiers came to see me in the camp. They wept, they came to cry their hearts out, and they asked for apaurin [a sedative]. "What's going on here?" they kept asking. They used to think the Muslims were their friends and neighbors, but then the propaganda clouded their minds. They told me that the Muslims had lists with the names of Serbian children who were going to be butchered. That was the propaganda lies of Serbian TV from Banja Luka.

After this lull, which lasted about two weeks, there was a new wave of violence. Serbs who wanted to bring food to their Muslim friends in the camps were brutally driven off, the doctor reports, and Serbian fighters began to rape.

> It began when Mile, an ordinary Serbian soldier, kidnapped and raped a seventeen-year-old retarded girl. It happened in Balcic, a settlement two kilometers from Trnopolje. She was doing the wash, and he drove up in his blue Lada, knocked her mother unconscious with his rifle, and carried the girl off to the woods. Some people saw it. She never came back, and Mile kept on driving through the neighborhood in his car, but no one punished him. And that was the beginning. Then the soldiers started to rape. . . . The people in authority all knew what was

happening. I had the feeling that the more it happened, the more there was rape and murder, the better they liked it. They liked it because of "ethnic cleansing." What mattered to them was that the people from our region should clear out, should never come back; and rapes are a splendid way to get that result.

Everyone who was in Trnopolje experienced the rapes at first hand. Forty-two-year-old Enisa Vehabovic from Prijedor reports: "They'd always come at night. They'd shine their flashlights and choose a few women and girls. Most of them never came back again."[13]

In the five days that Enisa spent in Trnopolje in July, about fifteen women were led off from her room in the school building, she says. Only two of them came back: one of them approximately thirty years old, Mesic, who was four months pregnant and had a miscarriage after the rape, and a fourteen-year-old girl, the sister of Enisa's brother's girl friend. "She was bleeding something awful and kept yelling: 'Mama, take me to a doctor.'"

"There was a big movie theater in Trnopolje, where they used to show films. One night, it was Bayram, the Muslim holiday [June 11], they came seven times to get women," the twenty-eight-year-old Muslim Suad Halilovic (pseudonym) from Kozarac relates: "A woman with children was raped. They also raped a fourteen-year-old girl, and she turned mute and hasn't been able to speak since. On that night they came seven times."[14]

As soon as the rapes began, great fear erupted among the women and girls in Trnopolje. "We tried to look ugly," seventeen-year-old Zernia Grozanic from Kozarac relates: "I stopped washing my hair; it was long, oily, and awful. I didn't wash my face either; it was dirty and sticky, and I had on some baggy, ripped-up clothes."[15]

According to the physician Jusuf's observations, the first women to be raped defended themselves fiercely:

At first the raped women and girls were beaten black and blue, especially in the lower body region. Later on we didn't find that kind of injury on them any more. The first ones probably told the others the best way to survive. A nineteen-year-old girl told me that she closed up tight inside. She lay down, tried to think of something else, and wasn't there; she blocked it out mentally. She said that all she felt was a foreign object penetrating her, something cold and hard, that caused a ripping feeling. Then she said, "When I could hear that he was drinking and cursing, I came to again. I stood up, and he said furiously, 'You're pathetic.'" The women probably figured out that that was the best way to survive and it was the least fun for the rapists. 'Cause if they resist, the men can take it as a challenge.

The women and girls were usually raped in abandoned houses around Trnopolje or brought to soldiers on guard duty. No one knows what happened to all the girls who disappeared. Jusuf says:

> My reason tells me they're dead, but I hope they're still alive. Maybe they brought them to the Mrakovica Hotel; that's twelve kilometers from Trnopolje and used to be army headquarters. Some of them have certainly been killed, but maybe some others are in all those other army barracks or in brothels. I've heard that some were also taken to brothels in Knin Krajina [Serbian-occupied territory in Croatia].

But Jusuf also mentions that it was supposed to be usual to kill the girls after raping them.

> One girl told me that an older soldier saved her life. She'd been taken to a control point in the woods and was raped there by several drunken soldiers. They were supposed to kill her afterward, but this older soldier brought her back to the camp.

No one knows how many women and girls were raped in Trnopolje. Even though he was in Trnopolje from May 27 until August 25 and well informed because of his contacts with many prisoners and Serbian soldiers, Jusuf does not know the number of victims. He estimates that five to ten women and girls were raped every night. In the whole period, however, only fifteen girls and women came to the doctors in Trnopolje and told them that they had been raped; fifty others came without saying explicitly what had happened. "There's a psychological problem here," says Jusuf. "Muslim society is patriarchal. A woman's honor is important, and the men are jealous. If a man has even the slightest suspicion that his wife may have cooperated voluntarily, the marriage is over."

Hatiza
One of the rape victims from the Trnopolje camp is twenty-four-year-old Hatiza, mother of a six-year-old daughter.[16] When I spoke with her, she was working in Travnik with the medical corps of the Bosnian-Her-

zegovinian army, wearing heavy black boots, a uniform, and a thick sweater over it. It was the beginning of November 1992, just when the neighboring Muslim-Croatian town of Jajce had fallen and the advancing Serbian army began shelling Travnik. Everyone was afraid; 50,000 refugees, many of whom had arrived from Jajce with serious injuries, were swelling the town, as were the agitated soldiers who had retreated from Jajce.

As chaos reigned outside, Hatiza told me her story, the reason she was now in the army. "At the end of July they took me to the camp, to Trnopolje. They said, 'We're bringing you to a concentration camp. The next time we meet, you'll have one of our kids in your belly.' I swore that I'd die rather than let myself to be raped." After a pause, somewhat softer: "But when it happened, I thought only about my little daughter, and I let it happen. I had to help her survive."

"It was a former Serbian acquaintance," she says. He took her to a little room in the cellar of the school building in Trnopolje and raped her there. "He told me if I resisted, he'd go get all the others. He also said I was the hundredth one to be raped anyway, and I certainly wouldn't be the last."

> That's something you never forget. I still carry it around with me in my heart, in my soul. I think of it when I go to bed and I think of it when I get up. It doesn't let you go. . . . Before I got my first period afterward, I was about to have a nervous breakdown. I couldn't sleep, and I kept smoking one cigarette after the other. . . . They did it to humiliate us. They were showing us their power. They stuck their guns in our mouths. They tore our clothes. They showed the "Turkish women" they were superior.

Along with a group of other refugees, Hatiza and her daughter were deported in mid-August to Travnik, where they were able to cross over to Muslim-controlled territory. Hatiza first went to relatives in Slovenia, but she remained there only one month. "I couldn't stand it, even though I could have gotten citizenship and a job. But I had to go back and prove to them that we can't be driven off so easily." Hatiza left her daughter with relatives and volunteered for the Bosnian-Herzegovinian army. She goes on:

> All the dead people are continually before my eyes. Once I saw three dead children. They were playing, and they just killed them. My thir-

teen-year-old cousin, a kid, was in Keraterm and later in Manjaca [a military prison near Banja Luka]. In Hambarine at the end of June, I found the body of my twenty-seven-year-old cousin; his stomach was covered with knife wounds, and his brain was spilling out of his crushed skull. His hands were tied behind his back.

"And those are our brothers, our true brothers," she says sarcastically. "I was in the camp, I was raped, and I still can't understand that our friends are doing it, people who until yesterday were our friends. I'm thinking legal conviction would be too good for such a bloodthirsty people."

RAPES DURING INVASIONS

Sadeta

Two days after the Serbian army's invasion, on July 24, 1992, twenty-year-old Sadeta was raped in her village of Rizvanovici.[17] I spoke with her in the large refugee camp of Gasinci in northern Croatia, a former barracks of the Yugoslavian Federal Army, where approximately 5,000 refugees and displaced persons from Bosnia-Herzegovina and Croatia are housed. The young Muslim woman recounted very calmly and slowly, almost haltingly, what happened in her village and what was done to her:

> They kept telling us they would be searching our village to make sure we weren't keeping any weapons in our houses that we hadn't turned over to them yet. 'Cause they ordered us to turn over all our weapons. We didn't know exactly which day they were going to search the village. They came all of a sudden on July 22. About 2,000 of them came up the main street. They came on foot, a group of about twenty to fifty, then a tank, then another group, and so on. It was a long column. My house was the first one they went into. I was home alone with my mother, my two sisters, and my little brother. Three of them came up to our front door and told us to go outside. While we were standing out in the courtyard three more of them went inside. They made a mess in our house, threw everything all over, broke everything. Then they all went back out to the street, joined the column, and moved on.

Sadeta and her family fled to her aunt's house. She witnessed how all the men of the village were herded together and taken in buses to the Keraterm camp. Ten busloads was all the camp could hold, she reports.

> In the eleventh bus, the last bus, there were about twenty or twenty-five men. During the trip the Serbian soldiers heard there wasn't any

more room in Keraterm and they could do whatever they wanted with the men. They brought them back, near my house; they had them get out in groups of five or six at four different places, and they shot them there. I know all this 'cause a boy who survived the shooting came to us asking for help. He was wounded in the shoulder. On that one day, July 22, all the men were already either in the camps or dead, killed in front of their own houses or somewhere else. Only women and kids were left in the village. There was no one to offer resistance.

The women were told that they had to get out by noon on July 24. With five other women and ten children, Sadeta spent the two days in her aunt's house. On July 24 a column of several hundred women and children was formed and marched off in the direction of Prijedor. On the way they were stopped by Serbian sentries and instructed to wait in the courtyard of a house.

We all sat together in the courtyard. First one man came over, took out his cigarettes, lit one up. An older women asked him for one. He offered her and everybody else his cigarettes. When he came over to me he demanded I take one. I told him I didn't smoke, but he insisted. Finally he started yelling at me. He did the same thing with my friend Esma, and then he went away. Ten or fifteen minutes later he came back and ordered both of us to go with him and bring along our identity cards so they could check them. He brought another guy with him too. One of them was about twenty-five years old, the other guy maybe thirty. They had camouflage uniforms on, lots of chains around their necks, with the [Serbian Orthodox] cross, and they were also wearing these earrings with crosses. One of them wore a red headband. I didn't know them from before, but they came from western Bosnia, 'cause they were speaking the same dialect we do.

We stood up and followed them. They took us into an empty house. There was only one room with a bit of furniture. And that's where they did what they wanted to with us. . . . They gave us orders about what we had to do, how we had to act, get them excited one way or another, and then satisfy them. They made us fondle them and kiss them. . . . They just behaved like they could do anything they wanted. They made jokes, they said we didn't know what real pleasure was, and they thought the other ones – they probably meant other girls they raped – were much better than we were. . . . They swore, they cursed our *balija* mothers,[18] and they made fun of us [both girls were virgins]. They said we were pretty girls, and we'd been saving ourselves just for them. Then they asked us to marry them, laughing hysterically. . . . Since the first guy wasn't satisfied with me, he suggested they switch partners. He took my friend, and I had to go to his friend. Then we had to lie down and, the way they said it, relax and enjoy it. . . . It hurt for a minute. After that all your feelings vanish, you become a stone and don't feel anything.

When they were done with us – one wasn't satisfied, the other one said he was more or less satisfied – they told us to clean up and get dressed. They got dressed too, took their weapons off the table, and brought us back to where they'd gotten us, back to the women. On the way back they threatened to kill us if we let on anything about what happened.

Maybe ten or fifteen minutes later they came back again and told my friend she had to get into a car that was out in the street, she and her mother. They took them away, I don't know where. Then the guy who offered us his cigarettes and then took us away said that I had to go to his commander, he wanted to talk to me. He took me to another house. He told me to go inside. When I went up the steps, about five or six of them were standing in front of the door. They asked me if I was the girl the commander had asked about. They called him.

He came out of one room, opened the door to another room, and told me to go inside. It was a bedroom. He ordered me to take off my clothes and lie down on the bed. He did the same thing. He began to kiss me and fondle me. When he saw that I wasn't feeling anything – I was just lying there staring at a point in space – I looked into his eyes and asked him if he had a wife. He said no. I asked him if he had a sister. He said yes. Then I asked, "How do you think your sister would feel if someone did with her what you're doing with me?" He jumped up and ordered me to get dressed and leave. As I was leaving I said, "If you're thinking of sending someone else to take me someplace again, I'd rather you just kill me here and now." He said I didn't need to be afraid, that no one would come get me anymore, and after that no one else did come.

On that same day Sadeta and the other women and children who were waiting in the courtyard were taken to the Trnopolje camp. After spending five days there, Sadeta was deported to Travnik. Her biggest fear, she says, was that she might have gotten pregnant.

> First I talked with my mother. . . . If I was feeling bad, she'd change the subject and talk about something nice from before. She calmed me down and said she was sure it wouldn't end badly. 'Cause you should believe in God and he would help. Later on, when we left Trnopolje and got to Travnik, I met a teacher who took me to a gynecologist. She examined me and found out that I wasn't pregnant. Somehow I felt better after that. That was a month and a half after the rape.

She cried a lot, says Sadeta, with her mother and a friend whom she had met in Trnopolje.

> She was much worse off than me. She said that she and her mother and two other sisters had been at home when the Chetniks came. One of them asked who was still a virgin. She told them she was, 'cause you could see she was anyway. He told her to go with him so she could pick out a man. They tortured her and beat her. Luckily, she survived. And she didn't get pregnant either.
>
> Maybe that's their way of hurting Muslim women and Croatian women, and the whole female race. Killing them isn't interesting enough for them anymore. It's a lot more fun to torture us, especially if they get a woman pregnant. They want to humiliate us . . . and they've done it, too. Not just in my case, either, all the women and girls will feel humiliated, defiled, dirty in some way for the rest of their lives. . . . I feel dirty myself somehow. And I feel as though everybody can see it when they pass me in the street. Even though it isn't true, no one could know about it. But the humiliation is there.

Sadeta has lost faith in her Serbian friends:

> They're all the same for me. For me, the word "Serbs" means "all of them." They're all of them ready to do the most horrible things, the local guys as much as the guys from other places. Maybe the local guys are a little bit better, maybe they're afraid we'll come back someday, that they'll be there and we'll get even with them. The mercenaries and the other guys from outside feel much freer. They know they won't be staying; they'll be going back where they came from.
>
> I know I can't join the army. I was thinking about it, but I'm the

only one who can help my mother and look out for her later on. 'Cause I don't know where my father is or if he'll ever return. If it weren't for her I wouldn't have to think very long about taking up a gun. I'm not a brave girl really, but in this case I would be. Maybe I'd be brave because revenge is spurring me on. . . . But since I know I can't take up a gun, I'll at least tell about what they did. These things are really happening. Then maybe someone will help us, and maybe it will finally be clear what's happening. That it's not just stories, but that these things are really happening. When people know about this maybe someone will help us, help our fighting men so we can prevent it ever happening again, 'cause the women and girls'll be in even more danger if no one helps us.

Emina
Twenty-year-old Emina tells how Biscevo, her village near Prijedor, was captured:[19]

On June 22 the Chetniks entered our village with their tanks and armored cars. They came from Prijedor and Volar [a Serbian-inhabited neighboring village]. About thirty Chetniks went into each house. They killed men between the ages of fourteen and sixty right off. They questioned kids about their fathers and brothers, and then they beat them. I saw how they took Sead Kadic away; he's twenty-six years old. They made him walk like a sheep and bleat, and they hit him. They made him call all the young men of the village together. Finally they killed him in front of Rifet Duratovic's house. They killed Hamzo Karagic and his son Samir Karagic, Rasid Duratovic, and Aldo Kadiric there, too. First they beat them up, and then they shot them. Then they came to my uncle Vahid Kadic's house. They made him lie down in a ditch in front of his house and drop his head, and then they shot him with machine guns.

Then the Chetniks came to Emina's house and interrogated her, her fourteen-year-old brother, and her seventeen-year-old sister. They wanted to know where their twenty-seven-year-old brother was staying.

They went to the house next door and came back half an hour later. They brought our neighbor's daughter Sanela, fourteen years old, and a girl from the neighboring village. They dragged us to the cellar and raped us there. Two of them held me tight, and the third one raped me. I tried to defend myself, but they used a knife on me [she shows a scar on her leg].

In the evening, when the Chetniks were gone, my brother Semsudin and his friend Asim Muic came back from the woods where they were hiding. My brother sewed up the wound on my leg. Then we went outside to see what had happened in the village. There were mutilated bodies of dead people lying everywhere, in front of all the houses, in the gardens, on the street, and in the fields. I knew all of them. These people were my relatives, friends, neighbors. I felt a great pain, but I wasn't able to cry. It was hot, it was summer, and the smell of blood was in the air. The Chetniks didn't let us bury the dead for five days. Then, two days before they took us to Trnopolje, me and my sister and a few others who survived, we buried the corpses. After those five days they all stank, and worms were crawling around on them.

"THEN THESE TWO OTHER GUYS CAME" — RAPES AT HOME

Not everyone was taken or forced into camps immediately after the villages were captured and occupied. Frequently women, children, and old people were left behind for a while. They were terrorized by itinerant groups of soldiers until they finally moved away of their own accord. For the women, that often meant rape.

Razija

"Almost every women who was still there after the 'ethnic cleansing' began was raped," claims twenty-seven-year-old Razija from the village of Tukovo,[20] "even seventy-year-old women. They came into our houses as if they owned them, forced us to make them coffee and wash them, and satisfied their needs on us."

Razija had been a bookkeeper with the Bosnian railroad, but she had lost her job. Before the "ethnic cleansing" began, she had sent her husband and her eight-year-old daughter to Germany and had remained in Tukovo herself to watch over the family house. As a woman, she thought, not much could happen to her.

It was a Monday, July 13, I think. I was home alone, when my former co-worker Brano K., a real primitive peasant, came by. I'd been working with him for six years. Now he was with the Serbian military police. . . . Six other guys were with him. All of them raped me, one after the other.

Razija too joined the army after deportation, and she works together with Hatiza in the medical corps of the Bosnian-Herzegovinian army in Travnik.

I think the main reason I put on a uniform is to get revenge. When I was still there I just wanted to get away, at any price. But now . . . we have to get even somehow, not in the same way, no, 'cause then we'd be no better than they are, but somehow.

Razija and Hatiza, soldiers now, are exceptions. Most of the rape victims are broken, not thinking about revenge, for the horror of their rape and expulsion has also taken away whatever power of resistance they might have had.

Furthermore, the refugee women rarely have anyone to whom they can entrust their children, a second reason they rarely join the army. Family communities are torn apart in the internment camps and during the deportations, and after that the individual members of a family live dispersed in refugee camps, often without knowing anything about one another.

Munevra

Forty-eight-year-old Munevra from Hambarine, another victim of the "ethnic cleansing" of Prijedor, is one of the women who have lost all hope.[21] A traditional Muslim peasant woman, she looks much older than her forty-eight years and weeps quietly to herself almost constantly.

Three years ago she lost her husband in an auto accident and was left alone with her three sons, who are now twenty-seven, twenty, and seventeen years old. She wanted to make it possible for them to live respectable lives. When the "ethnic cleansing" began, she decided to stay in Hambarine and watch over the two houses belonging to her family. For a bare four months she stuck it out, hiding and taking care of her sons, constantly harassed by itinerant soldiers and finally raped. She relates:

I kept my sons hidden in the cellar. Most of the time I was down there with them. But I came out to do the cooking. I couldn't wash for three months, 'cause I was afraid they'd come just when I was in the bathtub. Every day they came through the village, and almost every time they came into my house. I kept saying that I was alone. I'd also hidden our valuables in the cellar. I always said, "There's no one here but me, and other soldiers have already taken our things away." Later on we didn't have any food left. I went into the houses of our neighbors who weren't there anymore and found cornmeal. I made *mekinje* bread, and that was all we had to eat.

One time three soldiers came. One of them, Milan S., was a schoolmate of my twenty-year-old son, and so I wasn't afraid. I showed him our hiding place. They said they just wanted to question my son, the twenty-year-old. But this Milan turned out to be the worst one of all. He went into the garden with my son and beat him. I sat in the house; I wasn't allowed to move. I asked the other soldier if I could bring my son his shoes, he was barefoot. He said, "He won't need any shoes where he's going to end up. He'll end up in a cesspool." I heard a shot. Then this Milan came back without my son and said, "He's lying in the cesspool." Then he took my oldest boy away, to the house next door.

I thought, no, I'll never get over the death of my one son, and now they're also taking a second one away. I'll lose both of them. I'll be left alone with the little one. And they didn't come back, they didn't come back, I was dying of fear. They made my son walk over broken glass for fifteen meters. Milan slammed his head and his nose against an iron door. He said, "Show me where your kidneys are." And he beat him with an iron bar from an old boiler. My son told me about that later. The other two had finished searching the house and then went away. I was with my youngest son in the house. He said, "My god, mother, now it's my turn." Suddenly I heard my oldest son calling, "Mama, are you alive?" I opened the door. Then all of a sudden the twenty-year-old turned up too, in the garden. I said, "You're still alive. Oh God, I heard the shot, and he said you were lying in the cesspool." I was so glad I had them back again, you can't imagine. Only Allah knows how glad I was.

Another time three other soldiers came through. They found everything. They even found the *mekinje* bread; it fell on the floor and they stepped on it. We picked it up again later, 'cause we didn't have anything else to eat. I don't have the strength left to cry anymore; I don't have any words. They took the color TV and the VCR and the cassette player; they even wanted to take the detergent with them, too. I asked them to leave it 'cause I hadn't washed in three months. They left it behind.

Then these two other guys came. One of them was blond and the other one dark haired, both about as old as I am, about fifty. I didn't know them, but they spoke our dialect. Maybe they were from Ljeskare [a neighboring village]. They said, "Mother, you have a nice house, a modern house." I cried and said, "Yes, it's my husband's. We built it together when he was still alive." They wanted German marks. And gold. I said, "I don't have any gold." That was true. One of them came up to me and said, "Sit down." I said I didn't want to sit down. But he ordered me to sit down and moved up closer. He said, "You don't have to be afraid." I said, "I don't want you to come any closer. I'm not hiding anything, and I don't have anything. I'm a diabetic, I don't even have sugar." He said, "Don't worry, you'll get everything you need as long as we're around here. You'll get everything. But first we want something from you." I said, "I don't need anything. I don't want anything at all, leave me alone. Please, leave me alone, don't do this to me."

I was afraid my sons would hear me. I was dying of fear 'cause of my sons. They're decent people. You'll meet them and then you'll see. I was afraid something would happen and I'd lose my kids. Then this man touched my breasts. He pulled up my blouse and took out my breasts. My breasts look just the way the breasts of older women do. I asked him to leave me alone, but he didn't pay attention. He said, "For a woman your age your breasts aren't bad." Then they brought me to the other room. I squeezed my legs tight together. One of them was with me, the other one was waiting in the living room. I begged him and cried, and I crossed my legs. Then he took out his thing, you know, and he did it and it sprayed on me. When he was done the other one came and did the same thing, but I kept my legs crossed the whole time.

When they left, my sons came out and found me in a complete mess. They asked me what happened: "What'd they do to you?" I said, "Nothing." I couldn't tell them about it, I really couldn't tell them about it. I'd rather die than have them find out about it. You mustn't tell them what I just told you, no matter what. The next day one of them came back again. I told him there wasn't anything for him here and he should leave me alone. He went away and never came back. After that I couldn't sleep any more, not at night and not in the daytime either.

On September 13, Munevra, her three sons, and the wife of her eldest son left Hambarine. They reported to the local police, where her sons were interrogated once again. In July and August they had already spent two weeks in the Keraterm internment camp and had been let go as "harmless." After that they were allowed to leave Hambarine.

Today Munevra, her three sons, and her daughter-in-law live in a refugee camp in Zenica (central Bosnia), where they have no heat and only one hot meal a day, consisting of rice or noodles with a watery sauce. When I spoke to them her oldest son, whose kidneys had been damaged by the blows he received, was taking regular doses of pain killers; the operation he needs cannot be performed in Zenica. His wife was seven months pregnant, in severe pain and bleeding. Munevra, who used to weigh 198 pounds, was now down to 132. She says:

> They've taken everything from me, I don't own anything anymore. Our second house, which was supposed to be for my oldest son, has been looted. I used to have enough so that I could furnish three households for my three sons. I was collecting household goods for them, for their future families. I thought they'd have everything they needed when I die. Now I don't have anything anymore; they didn't leave me anything. I don't even have a handkerchief to dry my tears.

The Women of Foca

Wherever the Serbian troops invaded in Bosnia-Herzegovina, whether in the Muslim communities in western Bosnia, or in the Croatian-Muslim villages and cities in northern Bosnia, or in the historically Muslim cities along the Drina, the border river in eastern Bosnia, they always carried out an "ethnic cleansing" of the terrain, combined with rapes.

After the first wave of violence, it was usually women with children who were left behind; their husbands had been taken prisoner or killed, or else they were hiding in the woods. The town of Miljevina near Foca in eastern Bosnia seems to have been transformed into a true bedlam for women. While I was traveling through central Bosnia, I happened to meet four women from Miljevina, who told me about the events in their village and subsequently in Foca. I also had access to the statement of another woman from Miljevina, and I spoke with Velvida, a little girl who was raped in Foca. All these testimonies gives us a rather precise picture of what the Muslim women in this area had to suffer.

MAYHEM IN MILJEVINA

Miljevina is a small working-class town whose inhabitants, Muslims and Serbs, worked primarily in a nearby coal mine. It is part of the district of Foca, in which 40,513 people lived before the war – 52 percent Muslims and 45 percent Serbs.

In April 1992, at the very outset of the war, Serbian troops captured the town of Foca, and in May they began to "cleanse" it of Muslims. The surrounding localities were also affected by the "cleansing" of Foca. A forty-five-year-old Muslim woman describes the first "cleansing" of Miljevina at the beginning of May:

> They told us if our men turned over their weapons nothing would happen to us. We did turn them over, but they didn't keep their promise. They tricked us. They took our men to the jail in Foca and killed many people. On one day alone they killed seventy-six people and threw them in the river. The Chetniks set fire to my parents' house. They took my brother and my father prisoner. My husband was in the Miljevina prison two times, his uncle was shot in front of his house. They called to him so that he'd come out, and then they shot him. When our men saw what the Chetniks were doing, what they were going to do, they had to escape. They fled to the woods. The Chetniks told us women and children that nothing would happen to us. We believed them, but the next day at twelve o'clock at night they came to take their revenge on the women and kids of the men who escaped.
>
> Two cars with four Chetniks stopped in front of my house. At twelve o'clock at night they knocked on my door: "Open up!" My mother-in-law and three children were with me. She got up and opened the door; we had to open it up, 'cause they were threatening to shoot. They forced their way in with their weapons, and the kids screamed and cried. One of them grabbed hold of me; his last name is Todorevic, I don't know his first name. They claimed they were from Montenegro. I recognized them, but I couldn't let on that I knew they came from Miljevina, that they were our neighbors.

They pushed me out of my house and took me into the house of my husband's uncle who had been shot. Four young women were there already; one of them was my daughter-in-law. They dragged us one after the other into the room, and what all didn't they do with us there! They beat us, tortured us, raped us – they did whatever came into their heads. They said if we told anyone about it they'd come again and butcher us and our kids. I decided to run away to the woods, so the Chetniks wouldn't catch me at home.[22]

The four women from Miljevina whom I interviewed personally stayed in hiding during the first wave of cleansing. The following June passed relatively calmly, apparently, but by July the hunt for the remaining Muslim women, children, and old people had begun. No longer could they go shopping or let themselves be seen on the street. Sometimes Serbian neighbors helped them, or else they lived on previously stockpiled supplies. But they had to be careful: passing hordes of riotous soldiers would shoot at random, burst into Muslim homes and apartments, loot them and rape any woman they could get their hands on. According to the statements of the four women I interviewed, there were approximately one hundred Muslim women still in Miljevina, and every one of them was the victim of at least one rape and sometimes several.

Fatima

"They probably planned it," says thirty-three-year-old Fatima. She used to work as a cleaning woman and now lives in a refugee camp in Zenica in central Bosnia.[23] "They used to get together and sing 'O beautiful *bula*,[24] a Chetnik's beard will scratch you,' or about how Muslim women would give birth to Serbian children." Fatima's husband was taken prisoner on May 2, 1992, and has since disappeared without a trace. Fatima remained behind in Miljevina with her two little daughters, nine and eleven years old, because she wanted to wait for her husband. In mid-August three soldiers in camouflage uniforms with Serbian insignias came into her house.

They pretended to be policemen. One of them stayed with my daughters in one room while two of them went with me into another room. My little girl began to cry and called out for me. But he put a rifle to her head and said, "If you cry for your mama again, I'll kill you." They ordered me to get undressed, and they cursed my mother. I screamed and wept. They yelled at me not to cry, they threatened me with their guns: "We'll knock out all your teeth, we'll butcher your kids, hack them to pieces, and make you watch."

I recognized one of them, it was Sasa G.; he used to be a neighbor of mine in Foca; he's about twenty-five years old. I said, "You're Sasa." He was in disguise, wearing a scarf and a headband so that I wouldn't be able to recognize him. When I told him I recognized him he started whispering with the other guy. Then they really did begin to threaten me, and all three of them raped me. I couldn't do anything to stop it; they threatened me. One after the other they came in from the room where my girls were. I pleaded with this Sasa; I said, "Think of your mother, think of your sister, what would you say if something like this happened to them? Aren't you ashamed?" But he just said, "I've gotta do it, or else they'll kill me." But that was just an excuse.

After the rape Fatima fled to her Serbian neighbor and friend Persa F., where she spent the next few days.

Her son was on my side, too. It's true he was in the Serbian army, but he was a good guy. He cried when I told him what happened. He felt for me. He was a married man with one kid. He couldn't do anything about being in the army. Every Serb had to join; all of them were mobilized, they all got weapons, uniforms, they had to fight with the other guys. If someone refused he got sent to KP-Dom [the local men's camp, a former jail] in Foca.

Afterward Fatima went back to her house. Whenever anyone came she escaped through the back window with her daughters and hid. "We didn't have any way out. The Serbian authorities had already told us we couldn't leave Miljevina, and no one would help us."

Azra

Twenty-year-old Azra from Miljevina, now living as a refugee in Tarcin, thirty kilometers southwest of Sarajevo, had similar experiences.[25] Her husband was taken prisoner on May 3, 1992, and put in jail near Foca. "He told me it was awful there," says Azra. "They didn't have any food at all, and in seven days he lost thirty-eight pounds."

After the seven days Azra's husband was released, but he had to work at forced labor in a flooded coal mine. On June 9 he was arrested again and has since disappeared. Azra was left alone with her one-year-old son and decided to stay where she was in case her husband returned.

On August 5 her Serbian neighbor, a policeman named Dragan J., about twenty-five years old, knocked on Azra's door and asked her if she wanted to go with him for a cup of coffee at his apartment. Azra refused. "The next morning at 8:30 he came again and arrested all of us." All of them – that was Azra and her baby, her mother-in-law, and her mother-in-law's two little children. But whereas the others were quickly released, Dragan J. detained Azra in prison.

> After four hours he came and led me to another cell and raped me there. He threatened me with his rifle. He told me I was very attractive and all the soldiers wanted to have me. But he only told me that to make me scared. He also said, "It's war now, you don't have to bother defending yourself. There's no law or order anymore."

After the rape Azra was permitted to go home.

Esma and Mirsada

Two other women from Miljevina, acquaintances of Azra's who are now also living in Tarcin, confirm Fatima's and Azra's accounts.[26] Esma, twenty-eight years old, was raped in her home in Miljevina by three Montenegrin soldiers whom she did not know.

> Each one of them weighed at least 220 pounds. They were horses, beasts. . . . They played with their knives and said they were going to butcher my kids.

Twenty-nine-year-old Mirsada was also raped by several men in her house in Miljevina.

> And I was lucky I was only raped once. I hid. All the Serbs, the soldiers, the Chetniks, they were all raping, all of them, and they didn't rape only grown women. They raped twelve-year-old girls, too.

The four women report that "local Chetniks" led by Pero E., a forty-year-old Serb who had been a truck driver and smuggler before the war, were "better" than the Chetniks who came from neighboring villages or even from Serbia and Montenegro. As Fatima relates:

> When Pero E. was in Miljevina, nothing happened. But as soon as he went somewhere else we were persecuted, and all these terrible things

happened. Our own Chetniks didn't bother us too much; they went to other villages and raped and killed and looted there.

But Pero E. is no saint. He brought twelve-year-old girls from Kalinovik [a village about twenty kilometers away] to a brothel in Miljevina. They're still there; he keeps them there as his playmates. And our Chetniks must have given information to the other guys: when they came, they knew exactly who lived where, and where we were hiding. These Montenegrins couldn't have known that all by themselves.

The brothel in Miljevina, the women report, was set up in the abandoned house of a Muslim named Nusret Karema, who was working in Germany. Mirsada's apartment was only fifty meters from the brothel, just on the other side of a river. "I saw how they came with their cars and dragged young girls into the brothel. At night I heard them screaming and crying." She tells of speaking about the brothel with some Serbian neighbor women. "They said I was hearing ghosts," Mirsada says bitterly. "Ghosts! And all the time they knew exactly what was going on."

All four women talk repeatedly of the fear they lived in. "Every night there were rapes, I heard the women screaming," says Fatima. "Every night there were more rapes than you could count." Even her eleven-year-old daughter was almost raped:

That happened sort of near the beginning, about a month after they took my husband prisoner. This was when we could still go out of the house, and I was just visiting a friend of mine next door. I was having coffee with her, and my daughter was playing outside. He caught her by the stairs, and first he put his hand over her mouth and then he began to kiss her. It was Zdravko I., a Chetnik. Then someone else came through the stairwell, and he let her go and threatened her, "If you tell anybody about this, I'll butcher your mother and your sister." My girl came running to me, she sat down on the sofa and didn't say a word. She was stiff as a board. I asked her, "What happened, baby?" She cried and said, "Nothing, mama, it's nothing, I just can't breathe, I need some air." She ran out onto the balcony and began to scream. Tara [Fatima's friend] and I kept asking her what happened. At first she kept answering, "Mama, I can't tell you, or else we'll all be killed." "Who do you think would kill us, dear?" "This guy in the stairwell." And then she told us what happened, and Tara knew it was this Zdravko I.

In early September the Serbian authorities rounded up the last Muslims in Miljevina, approximately 150 women, children, and old people. They were taken to the Partisans' Hall in Foca, which was now being used as an internment camp. All four of the women, Fatima, Azra, Mirsada, and Esma, were in this convoy.

Fatima and Esma spent only six hours in the camp and were then driven to the front near Gorazde, along with the other prisoners. From there they were able to cross over to Muslim-controlled territory. Shortly before they were released, Fatima relates, a girl was carried off.

> Her name is Alma B. She was twelve years old and gorgeous. While we were between Ustikolina and Osanica they stopped the bus and took her out. Later in Gorazde I met Edi, a man I knew from Miljevina. The Serbs had taken him prisoner and made him work removing land mines for them; later on our soldiers set him free. I asked him if he knew anything about Alma, and he told me she had been in the brothel in Miljevina and slit her wrists there.

Mirsada and Azra were taken from the Partisans' Hall, together with their children and two other Muslim women. Azra relates:

> It was a group of Chetniks, they called themselves Zaga's People. They had long hair and beards and Rambo headbands, and they were wearing the Serbian cross on long chains. Three of them I knew from before; I went to school with them. Even then they were crazy, they took drugs and didn't know which way was up. They told us they were going to rape all the young women. They were going to beat us up, rape us, and then kill us. Then we had to go off with them. They said they'd kill my baby if I didn't go along.

The four women and their five children were brought to an apartment on the sixth floor of a building near the police station in Foca, where they were raped. Azra continues:

> Two of them raped me. Then more Chetniks came, and they wanted to rape me too. I didn't want to do it. They said they were going to throw my baby out the window, I screamed and cried, and then they left me alone. . . . It was no normal rape. When it was over the blood kept

flowing out of me. The other women in the apartment were raped some more by other men.

Mirsada tells how the men put a pistol to her head and made her take off all her clothes.

> They put their fingers into me all over, to see if I was hiding money anywhere. Then four of them raped me, one after the other. They told us we were going to give birth to Serbian children and they would do everything they could so we wouldn't even dare think of coming back again. After the fourth guy I fainted. If I hadn't fainted, they'd have kept on going.

Her four-year-old daughter had been with the other children in the adjacent room, and the children were able to watch what was happening to their mothers.

Two of the men stayed with the women the whole time, while the others came and went. Mirsada states:

> I think everyone knew what was going on in the apartment. They knew they just had to drop in for it. They came and went, they drank and smoked marijuana. They laughed, they had fun. . . . They said they were going to show us what real Serbian men were like. But they weren't men at all, they were animals, monsters.

Azra:

> They ordered me to do the dishes. When I stood up they roared at me, "How dare you stand up without permission!" They said we were at war now, there wasn't any law and order anymore; they shouted curses: "Fuck your Turkish mother" or "Death to all Turkish sperm."

After Mirsada fainted, she was allowed to return with the children and one of the other two women to the Partisans' Hall. In their despair the women went to the police station that stood directly next to the building where they had been raped. There they spoke with a Serbian policeman, Gojko Jovic (pseudonym), who was about thirty years old and had been a traffic policeman before the war.

> He told us it wouldn't be the first time he'd had to rescue Muslim women, and he promised to watch out for us. But he warned us that

we weren't safe at the police station, and he brought us to his apartment, in the same building where they raped us.

The policeman's mother gave the exhausted women and children something to eat and drink.

Then we heard Azra scream when they were about to throw her baby out the window. Gojko ran up there, but they chased him away. They yelled, "Piss off; tomorrow you'll find a bomb in your apartment," and Jure [one of the rapists] told him Azra was his woman and she had to stay where she was.

After that the policeman stayed up the whole night with the women.

He told us that for all intents and purposes the Chetniks are like mobsters; they're always raping and looting. They did get called to account a few times, but it didn't do any good. There wasn't any kind of power or law that could control them. But that's idiotic. Responsible people knew exactly what was going on and didn't do anything about it.

Azra agrees with this judgment:

All they had to do was give two or three of them a stiff punishment and it would've stopped. But they never did that; practically speaking it was legal to rape Muslim women and all the rest of it.

While Mirsada was with the policeman, Azra was still in the hands of the rapists.

The next morning they locked us in the apartment and left. We were supposed to clean it up. It looked awful; there were bottles everywhere, blood, filth . . . I wanted to jump out the window and kill myself. Why should I go on living? To be raped every day and then have to work for them on top of that? But when I was standing by the window I saw Pero E., this Chetnik leader from Miljevina. I called him and he forced open the apartment and set us free.

Mirsada had asked the Serbian policeman to get Pero E. "He didn't apologize when he got there," says Azra. "He said we ought to clear out, cause he couldn't keep going from apartment to apartment to protect us." The Chetnik leader ordered a few policemen to drive the four women and their children to the front near Osanica, and from there they walked over to Gorazde.

Today Azra, Esma, and Mirsada are living as refugees in Tarcin, a little town about thirty kilometers southwest of Sarajevo. The constant rumbling of Serbian artillery can be heard in the distance. "Maybe they'll come here too, and we'll go through the same thing all over again," the women say fearfully. Azra relates:

> In the beginning I was paralyzed with fear. I kept having nightmares that it was happening to me again. They're very realistic dreams, I can't get rid of them. And I'm afraid I'm pregnant, it's been three months since I had my period. But the doctor says I'm not pregnant. He says it's the whole situation that's to blame, the tension and the fear.[27]

The women now have reservations about Serbs. "I can't see anything good in them anymore," says Esma. "I'll never be able to forget this; I'll always have this picture in front of my eyes." Fatima said she thought she wouldn't go back, not even if the war were over and all the war criminals punished.

> I really don't trust anybody anymore; I've gone through too much. I'm really doing fine now compared with the way I was before. I don't know. . . . Of course there were a few decent people who helped us or at least tried to help us, but there were so many of the other kind.

These "others" have achieved what they wanted: Miljevina has been "cleansed," and the danger that the displaced people might return has been removed. The weapon called rape has done its job.

Little Velvida

The story of twelve-year-old Velvida shows the extent of the violence against the women of Foca. In August 1992, a few weeks before the Miljevina women arrived there, she spent ten days in the Partisans' Hall in Foca.[28] Velvida is still a child. I met her in Tarcin, where I had spoken with three of the four women from Miljevina. As always, I inquired in the refugee camps about victims of rape, and this little girl was introduced to me. During the whole interview Velvida looked at me quietly and kindly, with wide eyes. Like a good schoolgirl she answered every question, but she never uttered more than three words. Once in a while she wept softly; I didn't notice it until I saw a tear running down her cheek.

Her mother is a plain, calm peasant women who has had eight children in her thirty years. She was present at the interview, and Velvida seemed to be glad about that. The interview itself was one of the most unpleasant I ever conducted. I felt like a criminal while I pressed the little girl, who did not speak very much, with questions about her rape, and I was glad when the interview was over. To give a sense of our conversation, I reproduce it here verbatim.

Their early family history is no different from that of all Muslim displacees: Velvida's family comes from the village of Jelec near Foca. Here too "ethnic cleansing" began in May, Velvida's mother reported, and people were taken prisoner, murdered, robbed, raped. At first the family only had their farmhouse searched a few times. But then in August the father was taken to the men's camp KP-Dom in Foca, while the rest of the family was brought to the Partisans' Hall.

At that point, according to Velvida and her mother, there were about seventy prisoners there, exclusively women and children. Velvida's mother and another thirty-year-old were the only young women, and Velvida was the oldest of the children.

QUESTION: What were conditions like in the camp?

MOTHER: In the ten days we were there they gave us only two meals, only two. They beat us; they beat all the women who had money. They took our jewelry away if we had any, and our money too, German marks. They forced the kids in the hall to tell them who still had money, who still had gold. I had just the one ring; they took it away from me. At night they came to get women. The first evening when they took Velvida away, I waited and waited, but she didn't come back. And I begged them [the guards] to bring her back.

QUESTION TO VELVIDA: Where did they take you?

VELVIDA: To an apartment.

Q: Was the apartment far away from the camp?

V: We walked to it.

Q: Did they take other people out of the hall too?

V: I was by myself.

Q: How many people came to get you?

V: Two.

Q: What did the two look like?

V: They were soldiers, Chetniks.

Q: What did they do in the apartment?

v: They raped me.

Q: Both of them?

v: Both of them.

Q: Did they say why they were doing it?

M: They did it because of the money. They raped us and stabbed us with knives, all over our bodies, they wanted to know who had money. Here, look. [The mother shows a scar on Velvida's neck.]

Q: You were raped too?

M: Yes, one time they raped me, my daughter, and this other young woman, all three of us. And that was just one guy. First we had to wash with cold water. Later they didn't want to bring us back to the Partisans' Hall. They said, "If you have permission, go by yourselves." But we didn't have permission to be on the street at night. So we slept there naked, without blankets.

v: They didn't let us get dressed again.

Q: Did the men spend the night there too?

M: Yes, they slept with us.

Q: How many times were you raped?

M: They took me away twice and her [Velvida] nine times.

Q: You said that you were in the Partisans' Hall for ten days all together. Does that mean that Velvida was taken away on nine nights?

M: Yes, almost every night.

Q: Did the men tell you anything about why they were doing it?

v: They said they were looking for gold.

Q: Did anyone still have any gold by that time?

v: Yes.

Q: And did you tell them that?

v: No.

Q: What did you tell them, then?

v: That I didn't know anything about it.

Q: Did they take you away every evening?

v: Every evening.

M: Once when they came to take her away the other kids shouted: "Go, go with them." They didn't know where she had to go. She didn't want to go, she didn't want to, didn't want to, just didn't want to, and she began to cry. Then he kicked her with his boot and pulled her away.

Q: Did you try to help your daughter?

M: No, they didn't let me. They didn't let me do anything or say anything. At first I screamed, "Don't do it; what do want with a kid?" Then one of them said, "Shut your trap or I'll butcher you all." I did say it once, but I wasn't supposed to say anything.

Q: Did these soldiers have weapons?

M: Yes, knives and machine guns.

Q: Was anyone else raped besides you and your daughter?

M: This other young woman that I already told you about.

QUESTION TO VELVIDA: Was it always the same men who came to get you?

V: Different ones.

Q: Did you know any of them?

V: No.

Q: Did you try to resist?

M: She would always scream, but they didn't let us resist.

V: I cried.

Q: Did they always take you to the same apartment?

V: To different ones.

Q: Were the apartments empty?

V: Yes. But once my mother and this other woman were with me.

Q: Why did they rape you? To punish you because you didn't tell them who was hiding money?

V: Yes.

Q: Didn't they tell you that you were pretty or anything like that?

V: No.

Q: Or that they wanted to marry you?

V: No.

Q: How many men came to get you?

V: Sometimes five or six.

Q: And did all of them rape you?

V: Sometimes one, sometimes two. Always different.

Q: Are you afraid even now?

V: At first I was afraid, even of our own soldiers. But not anymore.

M: She survived it. Only if something happens now, if a grenade falls, then we're afraid. [Tarcin is shelled from time to time.]

Q: Did you go to a doctor?

V: Yes.

M: She's okay, he just gave her some pills to take.

Q: Do you want to go back when the war is over?

M: Where should we go? Everything's burned up; there's nothing left.

Q: And you're better now? Can you sleep?

V: Yes.

Q: Did you used to have a boyfriend, or was this the first time you had contact with boys or men?

M: She didn't have anything; she was a virgin.

Q: Do you know any of the men who raped you, their names?

BOTH OF THEM: No.

Rape Camps

"Rape camps" – this outgrowth of the war against women in Bosnia-Herzegovina has called forth worldwide dismay and outrage, repugnance and disgust.

We became familiar with this concept when women reported prisons in which hundreds of them had been held like animals, facing daily humiliation and deliberate impregnation. It is those images that are now invariably suggested by the word. Again and again women have related their experiences in such camps; women's groups and commissions have published lists of locations. They say there were such camps throughout Bosnia-Herzegovina. Women's camps are also said to have existed on the Muslim-Croatian side, though on a smaller scale.

All the lists, whether Bosnian, Croatian, or Serbian, have one thing in common: they are usually undocumented and very vague. Furthermore, the camps cannot be checked out on the spot. All the places in which women are held prisoner, whether large camps or simply cellars, houses, former cafés, are kept secret by the people in charge and are dissolved immediately when they are discovered. They are normally found in areas that are inaccessible, even to the International Red Cross, the only organization in the former Yugoslavia authorized to inspect camps and prisons.

It is easy to keep undesirable visitors at arm's length: the military just refers to the "cunning sharpshooters" who are making the region unsafe or to the land mines in the vicinity; or perhaps the authorities in charge even grant permission, but the Red Cross delegation is then held up at a checkpoint.

"All of a sudden you're not allowed to go through," reports the Red Cross security coordinator Didier Pradervand.[29] "And then they have to contact the head office by radio, and they in turn have to contact the higher authorities in charge to find out what's going on, and all that can take days." Sometimes after long negotiations the Red Cross does get permission to visit one or another of the suspicious locations – but it's empty. "You know that can't be right, that the prisoners are still there the same as before and that they've just been moved somewhere else for the length of the visit, but there's nothing you can do," says Pradervand.

In order not to jeopardize its workers, the Red Cross never goes anywhere without the consent of the local authorities, and for the same reason it never enters war zones. All in all, it operates only in a very limited area. The above-mentioned district of Foca, for example, is a "taboo zone," and not until early August 1992, two and a half months after the beginning of the "ethnic cleansing," was the Red Cross allowed to go to Prijedor.

At the moment it is only the women concerned who can give information about "rape camps," and the picture remains incomplete. But there is no doubt that they existed and perhaps still exist. In what follows I will present two women's camps, each of which was described to me by at least two women.

THE RAPE CAMP IN DOBOJ

According to the statements of three women, there was a women's camp in the northern Bosnian town of Doboj in which approximately 2,000 Muslim and Croatian women as well as a few children were detained in May and June 1992. This number is very high, and I have discussed it at length with the women. They insist it is correct and say that the gymnasium of the Djure Pucar Stari school in which they were housed was very big, that international handball tournaments were held in it previously, that it even had tiers of seats, and that it was "completely overcrowded." "We couldn't move without stepping on somebody," says forty-year-old Kadira.[30] "There might even have been 2,500 women." She goes on:

Up on the ceiling there were glass blocks, like little windows. They really should've turned the lights on in the gym, but we were in the dark. There wasn't any light; it was dark. We hardly knew when it was daytime or nighttime. And then they'd come and pick out women, take them away to classrooms so they could rape them. They looked for the women with little lights, flashlights.

The guards, too, went through with flashlights, trampling recklessly on the women and hitting them with clubs if they moved even a little bit.

You never even knew who was sitting next to you; you couldn't see your neighbor, and you weren't allowed to look at her, let alone talk to her.

Every few days the women were thrown a few slices of bread, and water stood around in dirty buckets, according to twenty-six-year-old Ifeta.[31] Empty buckets were used as toilets, "but most of them had holes in them, and everything ran out."

All three of the women who were in this camp – forty-year-old Kadira, twenty-six-year-old Ifeta, and forty-five-year-old Ziba[32] – come from a Muslim village near Doboj captured by Serbian troops in early May 1992.[33] After their village was occupied one group of women and children was deported immediately, while all the Muslim men and another group of women and children were arrested. Kadira relates:

They went according to a list. Usually they arrested the clever, educated people that everybody looked up to, also co-workers that they might have had a fight with at work sometime, but also women they found attractive.

Ifeta

Ifeta, who used to be a salesclerk, was arrested by a group of Serbian soldiers, most of whom she knew. Among them was her former schoolmate Slaven T., twenty-six-years old, as she was. "Those were my friends, people I'd gone to school with, and I thought they'd help me." Instead, Ifeta says, Slaven rammed his rifle into her back and said, "How come you're moving so slow, you bitch!"

She had to get into a bus that was already filled with women, and after an intermediary stop she was brought to the women's camp in Doboj. There three drunken soldiers from the Red Berets, a special unit of the Serbian army, dragged her into a classroom on the fourth floor of the school building. The chairs and tables had been shoved aside, and in the middle of the room were a few mattresses. Here she was raped by all three men, "at the same time," says Ifeta, pointing to her mouth and backside. "And while they were doing it they said I was going to have a baby by them and that it'd be an honor for a Muslim woman to give birth to a Serbian kid."

After that, rapes were a part of Ifeta's daily life. During the next five weeks that she had to spend at the camp, she reports, she was raped every second day on the average by two or three men. It was always a gang rape, they always cursed and humiliated her during it, and the rapists very frequently forced her to have oral sex with them. "For them the camp was like a fruit stand . . . or to put it better, a livestock stand. Anyone could pass by and just take whatever he wanted, just do whatever he wanted. The Serbs had the power."

Kadira

Kadira and Ziba were brought to the camp somewhat later, at the beginning of June. They too had been arrested during the Serbian army's invasion, but they first spent three weeks in a "decent" internment camp in the neighboring village. The horror began when they arrived at the women's camp in Doboj. Kadira relates:

> It was a camp of abuses, humiliations, rapes . . . I don't know how to put it into words. Everything, everything, the very worst thing there is, that's what they did there. Sometimes they'd be coming back from the front, where they suffered some losses. Then they'd be completely out of control. They'd just run through the hall, pull us out by our hair, and beat us.

It is hard for her to speak about what she experienced: "You know, you can only talk about it with someone who's gone through the same thing. You can't describe it with words."

After a while:

> They pushed bottle necks into our sex, they even stuck shattered, broken bottles into some women. . . . Guns too. And then you don't know if he's going to fire, you're scared to death, everything else, the rape, becomes less important, even the rape doesn't seem so terrible to you anymore.

Haltingly Kadira tells what was done to her. Once she was forced to urinate on the Koran. Another time she and a group of women had to dance naked for the Serbian guards and sing Serbian songs. Sometimes the rapists put their cigarettes out in her hair. She has forgotten how many times she was raped. "They said that each woman had to serve at least ten men a day." She herself was raped about every other day, always by several men.

> God, what horrible things they did. They just came in and humiliated us, raped us, and later they told you, "Come on now, if you could have Ustasha babies, then you can have a Chetnik baby, too."

Kadira reports further:

> Women who got pregnant, they had to stay there for seven or eight months so they could give birth to a Serbian kid. They had their gynecologists there to examine the women. The pregnant ones were separated off from us and had special privileges; they got meals, they were better off, they were protected. Only when a woman's in her seventh month, when she can't do anything about it anymore, then she's released. Then they usually take these women to Serbia.

Kadira thinks she knows a few women who got pregnant in the camp, but none of them has been seen again since.

> They beat the women who didn't get pregnant, especially the younger women; they were supposed to confess what contraceptives they were using.

She herself had an IUD, which she of course had not revealed. And she was tortured, says Kadira and shows a red scar over her breast.

> That's where they wounded me with a knife. I refused to get undressed, and then they ripped up my clothes with a knife, and this is where he wounded me.

Ziba

Forty-five-year-old Ziba, a simple woman, has difficulty speaking about what she has gone through. She usually leaves the talking to Kadira, who became her friend after their shared camp experience and simultaneous release. Ziba just nods in agreement, and when asked what was done to her she replies: "My daughter was raped along with me. First he raped me, and then I had to watch while he raped my little girl." For months her daughter, fourteen years old, suffered from bleeding and infections. "Now she wants to join the army," says Ziba, "but I'm not going to let her. She's still too young."

The rapists didn't even shrink back from children, Kadira believes:

> I saw about seven or eight little girls who died after they were raped. I saw how they took them away to be raped and then brought them back unconscious. They threw them down in front of us, and we weren't allowed to look at them; you had to keep looking at the floor the whole time. And then they'd announce: "Look, that's what'll happen to you too if you resist and disobey Serbian law." . . . If it was in the morning they'd leave them lying there the whole day; if they threw them in in the evening they'd stay till the next morning. Then they'd come and collect the bodies. We don't know where they took them.

Older women were killed too: "One time they killed a woman who wouldn't cooperate," Ifeta reports. "They beat her till she was unconscious, and then they took her away."

What pains the women more than anything else is that former friends also took part in the violence. Kadira says:

> I knew a lot of them; they were our friends and neighbors. . . . some of them enjoyed doing it, and others were forced to do it. I know a few guys who used to work with me; they were forced to do it. You can tell, and one of them in particular, a close friend of my husband's, that's what he told me, too. . . . The local Serbs, they went easier, they weren't so extreme. But as soon as the foreigners came, whether they were Arkan people or Seselj people, then they had pressure on them, and you knew they just had to do it too. There were three men I knew, they're dead now, they refused; they didn't want to go along with it, and so they killed them.

Kadira is convinced that the rapes were happening on orders:

> How could it be anything else? 'Cause I'm sure our Serbs wouldn't have done that to us on their own, not our neighbors. There was only one Muslim village, that was our village, we were all mixed up together there. The other villages were Serbian, but we never had any problems with one another, we were good friends; we watched out for each other and helped each other out. . . . The orders came from Serbia, those were Serbian directives.

Ifeta isn't so sure about that:

The ones who were completely drunk told me they had orders from above to do it. Not from the Serbs in Doboj, but from the commanders in Serbia. But they could have done it just as well without orders.

After Kadira and Ziba were in the camp for three weeks, and Ifeta for five, they were exchanged for Serbs who had been taken prisoner by Muslim troops.

The amazement remains. "They wanted to kill us slowly, torture us to death, they wanted us to suffer, they wanted to show us in every way they could that they were stronger," says Kadira. Ifeta observes matter-of-factly: "They didn't want sex. They were gloating because they were humiliating Muslim women." Both women look for explanations for the violence but cannot find any. "I have no idea why they did it," says Kadira; "maybe because we're not Serbs, and for no other reason. The way I see it at least there's no other reason except that we're not Serbs." Ifeta thinks that the idea of "ethnic cleansing" was the reason for the extreme violence. "They said they wanted to drive us out, that there shouldn't be any more Muslims in Europe."

They did drive them out, not from Europe, but from their homeland Bosnia-Herzegovina. Ifeta is now a refugee in Sweden, while Kadira and Ziba are still waiting in Zagreb. Both women know that their husbands are still alive: they were recently released from a Serbian internment camp and have gone on to European countries under protection of the UN Commission on Refugees. Kadira and Ziba will follow them as soon as they have taken care of the necessary formalities. Because of their husbands, both of them asked me not to publish anything more precise about them. "I'd like to spare my husband the details," says Kadira. "He's been through too much himself. Maybe later sometime."

The rape camp in Doboj is probably no longer in existence. According to information from the Doboj Displaced Persons Club in Zagreb, there are only about 1,500 Muslims left in Doboj, and they are no longer held in camps and are gradually being exchanged; the last Muslims to come out of the area said that in recent months Serbian refugees were being housed in the Djure Pucar Stari gymnasium.

THE "VILINA VLAS" HOTEL IN VISEGRAD
The Vilina Vlas (Fairies' hair) Hotel in Visegrad in eastern Bosnia was once a large spa with thermal baths and a vast park. "It was gorgeous," say the displaced Muslims from Visegrad, with a certain stubborn pride.

According to information from Bosnian authorities, the hotel was transformed into a women's camp in May 1992, and two or three hundred young Muslim women were detained in it. These girls are still missing today. Some of the refugees from Visegrad, like thirty-year-old Zehra Turijacanin, the only survivor of a Muslim burning[34] and herself covered with burns, claim that the girls were murdered after they had done "their duty." Even the October 1992 report of the Bosnian "Government Commission on the Investigation of War Crimes" states that the prisoners of Vilina Vlas were killed and thrown into the river Drina in the nearby village of Sase. But circulating among the refugees in central Bosnia is the rumor that the captured girls were removed to Serbia to give birth to Serbian children. But this rumor may also spring from the relatives' desperate hope that their daughters, cousins, and nieces have survived.

Two women, seventeen-year-old Muniba and twenty-year-old Hasiba, each spent one night in the hotel.

Muniba

Muniba, a Muslim girl from a good family,[35] relates that she did not leave her parents' apartment after Visegrad was occupied by the Yugoslavian Federal Army in April. In May the Federal Army withdrew because Serbian president Slobodan Milosevic wanted to create the impression that the rump Yugoslavia, consisting of Serbia and Montenegro, had nothing to do with the war in Bosnia-Herzegovina. But the Yugoslavian Federal Army left all its weapons behind for local Serb leaders and paramilitary groups. And thus "ethnic cleansing" began in the district of Visegrad, in which approximately 13,000 Muslims and 7,000 Serbs were living before the war.[36] According to refugee reports, between 4,000 and 6,000 Muslims were killed in the process.

Accompanying the "ethnic cleansing" were the rape and deportation of Muslim girls. Muniba's mother forbade her two daughters, seventeen-year-old Muniba and her fifteen-year-old sister, to leave the apartment. Living with them at the time were also an eighteen-year-old friend of Muniba's and that girl's mother. Muniba's father had fled. For several weeks their little society of women was not discovered, but on June 9 two Serbian soldiers entered their apartment. As Muniba describes it, one of them, about twenty-eight years old, tall, slender, dark haired, introduced himself as Milan L.; the other one, about forty years old, an "awful looking man" with a scar-covered face, did not give his name.

Muniba relates:

The first time, they came in the morning. They said we were supposed to write the apartment owner's name on our door. They talked with us in an ordinary way. We didn't look at them, we turned our backs to them, but they asked us in a normal way how old we were, what school we went to, whether we had any brothers or sisters. We told him about our oldest sister, she's a student in Zenica. Everything was perfectly normal. The second time, they came about eight o'clock at night, more or less for no reason at all. We didn't know them, but they came to have a cup of coffee. This Milan told us what he liked about Muslim women, that they're faithful to their husbands and they don't go out much. He had this image of Muslim women as if they're still wearing veils like they did before; that's the kind of image he had. At 11:30 at night they came to get us. He was completely different. He yanked open the door like he was going to ask, "What're you hiding in there?" He ordered us to get dressed 'cause we had to go identify a few of our schoolmates. He claimed they didn't want to give their names, and we were supposed to go along to the police station to identify them.

All three girls, Muniba, her little sister, and her friend, had to go with the two men. But instead of going to the police station, they drove the three girls to the Vilina Vlas Hotel.

When we got to the hotel, the whole place was dark. This Milan asked for keys at the reception desk. He led us up the stairs to a room. First he called my sister and a soldier over; I don't know what his name was. And he said, "Here are the keys. Go interrogate her, but don't overdo it." And they laughed, 'cause . . . it wasn't any interrogation at all. Then he called my friend and another soldier over and said the same thing again: "Here, go interrogate her thoroughly, but don't overdo it." And they laughed again. And so I was left alone in the room. He said, "Wait five minutes, I'll be right back." Then he left. When he came back he locked the door and put a table in front of it. He sat down and asked me who in Visegrad still had weapons and where they were hidden. I said I didn't know, 'cause everybody had to give over their weapons when the army came. He said I was lying and he knew who still had weapons. Then he asked me who my father was and things like that. And he began to get undressed. When he got undressed he ordered me to do the same thing . . . and then. . . . I didn't want to get undressed.

Muniba gulps and starts to cry; only after a while does she go on:

When he ordered me to get undressed I got undressed. But I didn't want to give myself to him; I resisted, and he hit me. He said: "It's an honor to belong to me. We could've thrown you in the Drina or into a quarry. It's an honor for you to belong to me." I began to scream. Then he stood up and said, "Okay, I'll go get ten other guys for you, and they'll tear you apart." I didn't have any strength left. I gave up.

About three o'clock I heard someone screaming. A woman screamed, stopped, screamed again, stopped. I think she was being raped while she was screaming like that. It lasted about five minutes. Scream, stop, scream, stop. Then I heard a door unlocking and a soldier cursing. And then I heard my sister crying in the corridor. I think she said, "Where is my Muniba?" I'm not quite sure, but I think that's the way it was. Then the crying got softer; she went down the stairs. I think they were taking her away.

It was the last time Muniba heard anything of her sister.

Milan L. brought her back home the next morning, but her little sister and her friend have not yet returned. While they were still in Visegrad, Muniba's mother tried to make some inquiries about her youngest daughter. She went to the police station every day; the police chief Risto P. was her daughters' former teacher. But no one was ready to help her, she says: "When I said that Milan L. had abducted my daughter, they said there was nothing they could do about it."[37] But she thinks that was just an excuse, because the police themselves made sure that the hotel was shielded from any unwanted visitors.

One time Milan L. showed up at the police station too. "He was just furious," the mother says, "and he pointed his rifle at me. He said to me, 'It's not your business who I take away.' And he said he did give one daughter back to me after all." She says the soldiers at the station told her, "Nothing will happen to your daughter, they're just having a little fun with her. They won't hurt a hair on her head." Even the commandant of the local Serbian forces, Veselin V., who had been one of her husband's best friends, did not want to help her. "He told me I shouldn't go back there anymore, I'd be upsetting the soldiers with my crying. He treated me as if he'd never seen me before." After Muniba's rape, mother and daughter hid in the Bikavac quarter in Visegrad, where large numbers of Muslims had sought refuge. There they heard about many other girls who had been taken away. Muniba says that just among her own friends and acquaintances ten have disappeared. Until now none has returned. They also learned that Milan L. was one of the most feared "cleansers" of Visegrad. "Everyone knew him. 'We know him, he took my husband away, he took my daughter, he killed my brother.' He'd taken someone away from every family." Muniba and her mother finally had to leave Visegrad in late July because it was the day when the last deportation convoy was departing.

Today Muniba's mother is living as a refugee in Donje Mostre near Visoko in central Bosnia. She cries continually for her youngest daughter and hopes she may still be alive; sometimes, however, she says that she'd be more peaceful knowing that her daughter was dead rather than having to think that she was being abused and raped every day.

Muniba is living with her older sister in Zenica. Her sister had come to get her because their grieving mother was in no condition to help her raped daughter. Muniba, who had been a virgin before this happened, reacted to the rape with panic anxiety and withdrawal. "In the beginning I was afraid of everyone and everything. When we got to Visoko I didn't talk to anybody. I was afraid of everybody. Now I'm slowly getting better." The stories about the fury of the Serbian men in Visegrad are terrible. Muniba's older sister says that the girls were seized systematically.[38]

> The Serbs who came from Visegrad knew the [Muslim] girls from before. They knew who was especially pretty. They went after one of my friends, Jasmina, in particular; they knew her name and knew where she lived. They abused her family until they found her. Finally, they burned down the house where she was hiding and killed her cousin.

Mina Kasapovic, a refugee in Donje Mostre near Visoko, tells how her sixteen-year-old cousin Dzenana Gocka "disappeared":[39]

> For quite a while her parents kept calling us up and saying a certain Milan L. was going to come and rape Dzenana right before their eyes. They were awfully afraid, but none of them was allowed to leave the

house. Later on, one of us sneaked over there. Dzenana's parents and her brother were dead, their throats were slit, and Dzenana had disappeared.

Hasiba

Twenty-year-old Hasiba, the mother of a three-year-old son and a five-year-old daughter, became the victim of several gang rapes in Visegrad; one of them took place in the Vilina Vlas Hotel.[40] Hasiba comes from Zepa, a region in the eastern Bosnian mountains that had continued to be held by Muslim units. The Serbian soldiers were interested in getting more detailed information about Zepa from her. Rape was one of the methods they used. But Hasiba remained silent at all her "interrogations." "What would you have done?" she asks.

> Would you betray your own people if you were born and raised there? Would you tell them how many people are still there and what kind of weapons they have? Nothing in the world could have made me do it. Better I lose my own life than that three or four hundred people lose theirs.

Hasiba comes across as self-confident and in charge. Of the sixteen rape victims I spoke with, she is the only one who tried to inject some "humor" into the story of her ordeal. When she told me how she had to try for hours to help a completely soused Chetnik "get it up" with no success, we both burst out laughing. Her position is clear:

> You have to be cold-blooded, not let anything show, and just do whatever they ask you to. You're in their hands, and you just want to survive; you'd go along with anything, if only you can stay alive.

Hasiba was arrested in late May near Visegrad and taken to the Visegrad fire station, an internment camp for approximately 130 Muslims, among them 20 men who were later murdered. All the new arrivals were first searched for money and jewelry; 15 children had to stand in a row, and the others were threatened that the children would be shot if anyone tried to hide anything. On that night two girls and a woman were led away to be raped. The next morning two Serbian soldiers came to pick Hasiba up. "I thought they were going to rape me right away, but they took me to the police station." There they wanted her to identify a young man from Zepa who'd been beaten half to death. Although they threatened her and beat her so roughly that she lost consciousness, she pretended not to know him. "Of course I knew him, but I wouldn't have told them that for anything in the world," she says dryly.

After that she was taken back to the fire station. About two o'clock Zoran L. showed up, the twenty-three-year-old brother of the feared Milan L., who had raped Muniba.

> He came about two o'clock and asked, "Where's the girl from Zepa?" I didn't say anything, I was just coming around again a little bit and had lit up a cigarette. "Where's the girl from Zepa?" he asked again. I stood up and said, "Here I am." He announced that he wanted to marry me, but I didn't say anything to that. Then he pointed his gun at me and led me away. We left the building, and he took me to a house in the Bikavac quarter. When we got there, you couldn't see anybody, but inside the house there were suddenly twenty of them, and they called out, "Leave something for us, Zoran, don't forget about us." As soon as one of them was done, the next one came. Twenty of them took turns with me. I never told this to anyone before. And they didn't use any protection at all, not one of them. Afterward Zoran said, "Now I don't want to marry you anymore, now that all of them have" – you know the word – "fucked you down the line."

On the same evening Hasiba was once again taken away, along with two other women. They were taken to a room on the second floor of the fire station.

> Four of them were standing there. First it was the other two women's turn. "Take off your clothes!" and they pointed their rifles at them. They followed orders. One woman was about thirty-seven years old, the other one thirty. "Tell us, who here is still hiding money and jewelry?" "No one's got anything left anymore. How could we have anything left after you searched us I don't know how many times?" And then one of them went up to the woman and grabbed hold of one of her breasts and said, "There isn't much left here, someone sucked you dry a long time ago." And he said to the other one – I don't know, maybe because she smelled of sweat – "They can smell you for miles around; you're not good enough for us."
>
> I just stood there; I didn't have to get undressed, nothing. Then he shouted, "So what're you waiting for, get going!" I shouted back, "I

won't get undressed, you can forget about it!" "If you don't, I'll do it for you!" "Just try it," I shouted back. I had on a white blouse, and he grabbed it and tore it. Then he yelled at me again to get undressed. I had to do it; he was pointing his rifle at me, and I got undressed. The other two women were allowed to go; they threw their clothes at them and ordered them to get dressed again. Then one of the men began to get undressed. "Sit down," he said to me. I had to sit down Turkish style with my legs crossed. So I was sitting in front of him naked, and thinking now he was going to rape me. But he sat there, naked too, took his big Serbian cross in his hand and said, "Kiss this cross!" I thought, well that's the end of me. I took the cross and kissed it. "Kiss it three times!" I kissed it once, twice, three times. "Cross yourself!" I'd never crossed myself before and didn't know how you do it. I said, "I don't know how to cross myself." "What, you don't know how to cross yourself?" "No, I don't know how." "Cross yourself!" he ordered me again. Then one of the other guys who was standing behind him showed me how you cross yourself, you know, first you tap your forehead and then your shoulders, like that.

After I crossed myself he said, "Now you've changed religion, now you're a Serb." He got his jacket, and I wondered what was coming next. He took two pouches full of jewelry out of his jacket. He emptied them out in front of me and said, "Take what you want." I said, "I've never cared much for jewelry; I don't need anything." "Take something!" "I don't want to; I don't need anything, I've never liked jewelry." He wanted to force me to take it. "Go ahead and kill me, but I don't want this jewelry. I used to have my own gold, but you took it, and I'm not interested in this gold." Then he claimed that lots of women couldn't have waited to get their hands on the jewelry. "You're the only one who didn't want it."

In the meantime the other three men had gone and I was left alone with this crazy guy. Finally he forced me to give him a blow job, he held a knife to me, and I had to do it to him and he came in me. Then the next one came back, everything happened again, and then the other two. After that they let me go.

About two o'clock in the afternoon on the following day, the third day of her stay in the fire station, three Serbian soldiers came to fetch Hasiba. They took her to the "New Bridge" over the Drina,[41] where approximately ten Muslims, men from Hasiba's village, and a group of Chetniks were waiting. There she was raped in public, Hasiba reports:

> One of them screamed: "I'll fuck your mother, all your mothers. Here, I brought you one of your women; look how the Chetniks love them." And they started to kiss me right in front of them, they did everything, there wasn't anything they didn't do. It made no difference to me, I was in their hands, and as long as I was going to survive I could take anything. After that one of them took my chin and said, "So, you pretty thing, now tell me, how many people are there in Zepa, how many weapons do they have and how do you get there?"

Hasiba denied knowing anything, although the rapists had learned from tortured Muslims that she had frequently been in Zepa. Even when the Chetniks put a gun to her head, she remained silent. "Then one of them said, 'Let's knock off these Ustashas [the ten Muslims on the bridge] first, and then we'll see about her.'"

Hamet Kesmer, approximately fifty years old, a peasant and a distant relative of Hasiba's, who had been a member of the Muslim SDA Party, was the first to be killed.

> One of the Chetniks took a knife and cut his throat, but not too deep, so Hamet just bled and didn't die for quite a while, maybe ten minutes. I had already seen so much, been through so much, I didn't care. Then the Chetnik cut off Hamet's head; he took his head like a ball, kicked it, and said, "One Ustasha less," and the head flew into the Drina. He saw how the blood was squirting and laughed hysterically, he almost fell over laughing, and he watched the blood dripping from his knife.
>
> The next victim was Husein Vujic, a forty-year-old man. The Chetniks said, "Let's play with him for a while; he's always playing the fool and hiding machine guns to kill our people with." They tortured him for a long time. They cut up his body and head with their knives. They carved Serbian crosses in his skin, they forced him to drink his own blood. When he was finally more dead than alive, they shot him in the head and threw him in the Drina. Then they mowed down the rest of the men with their machine guns and said, "And now the girl from Zepa will tell us what she knows about her town. See what we did to these guys – we'll do even worse things to you."

But just then one of the Chetnik commanders who had been watching the whole time called Hasiba over. Hasiba thinks he said his name was Niko from Foca. He drove her to the Vilina Vlas Hotel.

> The whole hotel was filled with our girls and women, each one prettier than the next. We went in downstairs by the reception desk and he took a key.

On her way to the third floor Hasiba was able to look into the other rooms, since the doors were usually open.

> The Chetniks were there with the girls. There was nothing they didn't do with them, you only had to stop and look. In every room there were women, men, screams, noise, songs, everything. They said they were bringing the women there to bear Chetnik kids. This was the only hotel they were taking them to, they said, nowhere else. That was the story this guy from Foca told me. He said, "Look, the only people in this hotel are girls and women who'll carry our babies, babies for the Chetniks."

When they got to their room Niko threatened Hasiba with his rifle and forced her to get undressed and douche with cold water. After that he got a bottle of whiskey. Hasiba refused to drink any of it.

> He emptied the whole bottle all by himself in three or four gulps, a whole liter. Then he got undressed and I had to . . . do everything to him. I did it and did it and did it, but it didn't work, he couldn't get a hard-on. He swore, "I'll fuck your mother; you get it up for me." I did everything I could. He was with me for an hour or two, I think, I was almost dying when he finally came. After he came, he left the room and brought in the other guys. They'd all been waiting for him, and I had to do it with all eight of them. I was utterly exhausted. I finally got back to the fire station at midnight.

Her last "interrogation" took place on the same evening; three men led Hasiba to a nearby doorway.

> They said, "Back there on the bridge you didn't want to tell us how many people live in Zepa and what weapons they have. Tell us now." I told them I didn't know anything, I couldn't go on anymore; I began

to cry and said, "Go ahead if you want to, kill me and get it over with; I don't know anything."

All three soldiers raped her.

On the next day all the prisoners from the fire station were supposed to be deported – but not Hasiba: some Chetniks were waiting for her a short distance away, but she was able to slip undetected onto one of the trucks and hide under the skirt of a fat peasant woman. And so she was able to escape.

Today Hasiba and her two children are living as refugees in a little village near Visoko in central Bosnia. Her greatest wish is to go to Zepa and fight against the Serbs at the side of "her" people. But she has no one she could entrust her children to. When asked how she is coping with the rapes she answers only, "Okay, but sometimes I do have nightmares."

"The Thing in Your Belly"

Senada

On December 25, 1992, in Sarajevo, thirty-year-old Senada gave birth to a girl, a child she does not consider "her" child and with whom she would have nothing to do.[42] "It was a hard birth. It hurt a lot. But after what the Chetniks did to me for four months it wasn't anything. . . . I looked up at the ceiling. They took it away, washed it, and I never saw it." One night in early May, Senada relates, local Chetniks entered her little village near Sokolac (fifty kilometers east of Sarajevo) to deport the few Muslims who were still there. She was the only young woman among them. Four Serbian neighbors, Milomir B., Radomir T., and Drago and Rade J. hustled her into a car and took her to the Sokolac elementary school, a white building with a red roof. There she was shoved into a classroom where about thirty women and some children were lying on mattresses. All the women were between twenty and thirty years of age. Senada asked them, "What're they doing with you here?" "They're raping us," was the answer.

About six o'clock in the evening on the next day she received a slice of dry bread and some tea and then, near midnight, they came to fetch her. The rapists brought along a captured Muslim who was forced to rape her. After that six Serbs raped her: the four neighbors who had taken her away, as well as Brana L., whom Senada had gone to school with, and Drago K., the police chief of Sokolac and director of the camp, a bearded dark-haired man about forty years of age. "He was usually the last one and stayed longer than the others," Senada says. After that she was raped almost daily. "If they didn't come to get me between twelve and one, then they came between three and four." It is her impression that the rapists wanted to humiliate her.

> They said, "You see, that's what happens when you fight against Serbia." They sang songs about how they were cutting Alija's [Bosnian president Izetbegovic's] throat. Sometimes they brought prayer beads, and I had to say Islamic prayers and they beat me. I still have the imprints of their boots on my back. Sometimes they also beat me up with their guns.

The rapists kept changing.

> Drago [the commandant] brought different gangs who were supposed to rape me. . . . Some men didn't want to go along with it. He hit them and asked, "You mean you really don't want her?" and then they did rape me after all.

When the women weren't being raped they were usually locked up in the classroom. There they had one bucket with water and one that served as a toilet. They could wash themselves very rarely. "We were dirty and stank, but they stank too."

From the beginning the rapists announced that she was going to have to bear a Serbian child.

> They told us how much they'd like to see us raise their kids, they sang rhymes with words like, "A mother raises a baby, he's half a Muslim, half a Serb."

Senada asked them why they were doing that. They answered:

> Look what your Muslims are doing, they're fighting against us and killing our people. We have to get revenge, and we can't let any Muslim get away.

By the end of May she should have gotten her period, but it didn't come. In August it was obvious that she was pregnant. Drago's reaction was: "Very good; now Alija will have to provide for a Chetnik." Drago never got her a doctor.

On September 20 the women's camp was dissolved. "They let us go because we were pregnant," Senada believes. "They thought it was too late for us to do anything about it." The rapists drove the women to a suburb of Sarajevo and let them walk over to the Muslim-controlled side. Eleven of the women who were taken to Sarajevo with Senada were pregnant; Senada does not know where they are now.

Senada's father, brother, and sister live in Sarajevo. She went to them, but she hid the fact that she was pregnant. "I was too ashamed to tell my father or my brother." Her sister had just lost her husband and so Senada didn't want to bother her with her problem. Not until early November did she go to a hospital, "and then it was too late for an abortion."

Senada decided to kill the child as soon as it was born.

> I knew it wasn't my kid. I knew what I went through. It wasn't a child born of love or from a respectable marriage. If anyone had tried to show it to me after it was born, I'd have strangled them and the baby too. . . . If I'd ever had any chance to kill the kid inside me, I'd have done it.

Her doctors considered her suicidal and put her under strong sedation. By the end of December it was over. The baby is now in England: a British journalist smuggled it out of Sarajevo. "This kid has nothing to do with me. He can do whatever he wants to with it, it makes no difference to me," says Senada.

Today Senada is living in Sarajevo and has found a job as a cook. She's feeling better, she says. While she was pregnant she was on the brink of madness.

> I used to be afraid and cry nearly all the time. These days I don't feel anything. Or I feel a little better. Especially when I think of everything I've been through. I still have to have my blood checked to see whether the Chetniks infected me with something or other. . . . I'll stay here for the time being and try to forget. I hope no other woman has to go through anything like this . . . and I hope I'll survive this war.

Snezana

One month earlier, the twenty-year-old Serbian woman Snezana from Sarajevo had given birth to an unwanted child in Belgrade. The Belgrade journalist Seska Stanojlovic spoke with her in December 1992, shortly after the birth. Snezana's mental condition at the time, according to her psychiatrist, was still greatly altered; she swung "between euphoria and depression." Seska reports:

> At first glance Snezana is no different from the other young women who gave birth to children in the Belgrade hospital. She wears light makeup, is noticeably merry and loud. But her hands keep trembling uncontrollably. Snezana has never seen her child, a girl. When the newborn baby let out its first cry, Snezana covered her face with a pillow. Later the child was taken to the Belgrade orphanage.

Seska thinks that Snezana was almost eager to talk about what she had suffered.

> No matter what topic we start out with, every conversation invariably ends with the tragedy she lived through, and to judge by external appearances at least, she tolerates talking about it quite well.

Before the war Snezana worked in Sarajevo at a hairdresser's salon. On the evening of April 4, 1992, she was on her way home with a friend, who made a short stop in a supermarket to buy something. While Snezana was waiting on the sidewalk a car stopped next to her. Some men pulled her into the car and blindfolded her. They did not take the blindfold off again until she was in a cellar. Snezana and a fifteen-year-old girl shared this cellar, which contained only some blankets and a little chair, for twenty-five days.

On the very first evening of her captivity Snezana was raped by the owner of this "private prison," Ismet B., a well-known criminal from Sarajevo. After him, eleven other men took their turns. This became Snezana's daily lot. Her young coprisoner suffered similar brutality.

Fortunately, Snezana's friend had seen her being abducted. This friend was married to a Muslim who searched for Snezana, found her, and brought about her release. On April 29 she was deposited on a backstreet in Sarajevo. Snezana went to her friend's house and remained there over five months. In October the first rescue convoy set out for Belgrade, and with the help of her friend's husband she got a place on it. She could never live in Sarajevo again, Snezana informed Seska. When asked whether she would testify in court should her torturers have to answer for their crimes, she replied that she would.

The UN commission that investigated the rapes in the former Yugoslavia in January 1993 in the larger women's clinics of Zagreb (Croatia),

Unwanted Pregnancies

Place	Cases	Abortions	Unwanted Births	Current Pregnancies
Zagreb	35	27	4[a]	4
Tuzla	45	41	4	
Sarajevo	15	14	1	
Zenica	19	19		
Belgrade	5	3	2	

a Whereas for all the other births medical documentation makes it clear that they were unwanted – it was too late for an abortion – for two births of these four there is no indication whether they were wanted or unwanted.

Sarajevo, Zenica, Tuzla (Bosnia-Herzegovina), and Belgrade (Serbia) found 119 cases of pregnancy resulting from rape.[43]

Women who become pregnant following a rape normally reject both the pregnancy and the children. In 104 of the 119 cases the women decided to abort the pregnancy. In 9 cases women were forced to carry the child to term because it was too late for an abortion. (In the remaining 6 cases – 4 current pregnancies and 2 births – there is no information about whether the woman decided to have the child voluntarily or had to carry it to term for medical reasons.) These statistics show that women generally do not want to accept children who are the result of a rape.

In Bosnia-Herzegovina as well as in Croatia and Serbia, the old Yugoslavian abortion law is still valid. Women are permitted to abort within the first trimester without having to give a reason. That makes things easier for raped women. Furthermore, in war-torn Bosnia-Herzegovina the three-month deadline is not observed very rigidly, as a doctor in the Zenica hospital told me: "As long as we can still terminate a pregnancy according to the customary methods we don't ask questions, we just do it. How can you expect any woman who's had to flee, who's lost everything, to bring a baby into the world?"[44]

According to law, however, a hospital commission on ethics meets to consider requests for abortions after the first trimester. A woman presents her reasons to this group, which then makes a decision about the abortion after weighing the medical risks. According to Croatian women's groups, some raped women in Catholic Croatia have been denied abortions even though the pregnancies could have been terminated. Croatian doctors dispute this and claim that they make a point of performing abortions in rape cases unless there are serious medical reasons against it.

In the hospitals of Bosnia-Herzegovina, on the other hand, doctors are frequently not in a position to perform abortions after the first trimester. They lack the necessary drugs for inducing premature births, and hospital beds are occupied by the wounded. In addition, hospitals in a dissolving Bosnia-Herzegovina are not always easy to reach. The story of thirty-year-old Melisa from the eastern Bosnian city of Gorazde serves as an example.[45]

Melisa

Melisa was raped at the end of April when Serbian troops entered the Gorazde neighborhood where she was hiding along with ten other women and a few children.

> The Chetniks came into our house; there were about ten of them. We didn't have any electricity, no lights, only a candle. All of them were wearing masks over their faces; all you could see was their eyes, and they had on camouflage uniforms and caps with the Serbian cockade [Chetnik insignia]. As soon as they came in they began to yell and scream; they cursed our "Muslim mothers" and said, "You sent your husbands off to the front, but now we'll show you what's what, and then you'll go to a concentration camp." First they dragged me and Semsa U. (who's thirty years old) into the bedroom. I recognized two of the Chetniks in there; they were my neighbors, Dragan K. and Bora J. I recognized them from their voices. They tore all my clothes off of me until I was naked, and then two of them held me down and two of them raped me. They forced me to do it with my mouth. I was awfully scared, and they kicked me around and beat me. They raped Semsa at the same time, in the same room. I don't remember exactly how many there were, 'cause I fainted.

As soon as Melisa regained consciousness she sneaked out of the house where the Chetniks were still going wild and fled as fast as she could. She intended to go to her sister in Zagreb. But the journey through war-torn Bosnia-Herzegovina lasted months. Melisa accomplished most of it on foot and had to submit to long detours in order to circumvent the war zones; every so often she had to report to the military authorities in order to get travel permits.

Before long she noticed that she was pregnant. At first she tried to abort herself with injections of hot water. She thought she had succeeded, because she was bleeding heavily. Some weeks later she determined that she was still pregnant. She asked for an abortion at the first opportunity, in the Kiseljak hospital, but doctors denied her request. She did not arrive in Zagreb until December 1992, and then it was too late for an abortion.

Melisa also had trouble coping with pregnancy; she referred to her child only as "the thing." According to her psychiatrist, Dr. Jarmila Skrinjaric, she was in a "hypomanic state." She was uncommonly merry and jolly, and then again desperate. "She's compensating for her depression, trying to pretend that everything's okay. But in reality she's completely torn up," Skrinjaric said at the time. Melisa too was under sedation.

In addition to her psychological rejection of the child, she was afraid of a possible rejection by her family. She said, "Where I come from, everybody, my husband, my daughter, the whole town, everybody would think of the kid as filth." Her husband, who had stayed in Gorazde, knew nothing about her rape. "He'd never take me back again if he knew what happened," Melisa asserted. In spring 1993 she gave birth to a dead child in Zagreb. She left the hospital without telling anyone where she was going.

Rapes of Serbian Women

Because of the suffering of Muslim and Croatian rape victims, we frequently forget that Serbian women in Bosnia-Herzegovina are also being raped. Of course they are not affected by rape as frequently as the Muslims. For one thing, the Serbian army is the victorious army and can better protect its civilians; for another, Muslims and Croats only rarely carried out "ethnic cleansing actions" in the territories under their control (where Serbs are still living) — although hostility toward Serbs is constantly growing and there are recurrent instances of misconduct toward Serbs.

To be sure, it is also difficult to find Serbian rape victims, for refugees in Serbia are normally housed with friends and relatives, where they are hard to locate. But the real reason that Serbian women seldom appear in the reports of rapes in Bosnia might be a different one: they are the wives, sisters, and daughters of the aggressors. There is hardly a journalist who feels motivated to seek them out, to check up on what has happened to them and thus offer propaganda material to the Serbian side – that is, the "bad" side, the side "responsible for the war."

But on this side too there are victims of the war, and among them are women who were raped. The UN commission investigating the rapes in Bosnia-Herzegovina emphasizes that it found "victims among all ethnic groups involved in the conflict,"[46] and Amnesty International also avers "that all the sides participating in the conflict have been guilty of [sexual] misconduct."[47] Perhaps Serbian women have not been systematically raped, perhaps the aim behind these rapes is not to expel civilians but rather to get revenge, show contempt for women, annoy the enemy, celebrate male supremacy. But it is a fact Serbian women have been raped.

Jelena

One of the victims is the twenty-eight-year-old nurse Jelena from Brcko in northern Bosnia. The Belgrade journalist Seska Stanojlovic spoke to her in early December 1992 when Jelena was visiting friends in the Central Belgrade Hospital. At that time, Seska wrote,

> The scars on Jelena's hands (from the knives she was "caressed" with during the rapes) and on her back (from the cigarettes that were put out on her back) are slowly fading. Her friends in the hospital say that something similar is going on in her mind. She isn't as depressed as she used to be, especially since this former nurse has gotten a new job in a clinic in Belgrade.

In late January 1992 Jelena was traveling home to Brcko after a visit in Germany when her tour bus was stopped near the Croatian town of Sisak by Croatian militiamen. Six Serbs, four young women and two men, were pulled off the bus, and Jelena was taken to a Croatian internment camp in the warehouse of the Slavonski Brod oil refinery. There, like the other female prisoners, she was raped. "They came to 'relax' with us after their successful military actions." Jelena did not tell Seska how many coprisoners she had or who their torturers were. She said that "many women" were being held prisoner in the camp and that the rapists were Croats.

In April the women were transferred to Odzak in northern Bosnia on the other side of the border river Sava. The new detention camp was a former school, and Jelena, who was already pregnant by this time, continued to be raped. She was not released until July, when she bought her freedom with foreign currency that she had kept hidden. Jelena went first to Brcko and then to Belgrade. In the Central Belgrade Hospital she learned on September 8 that she was in her thirtieth week of pregnancy. She wanted to abort, but one of the clinic's leading gynecologists, Dr. Miomir Krstic, was against it: although Jelena had been severely traumatized mentally, she and her unwanted child were in good physical health. In early October Jelena gave birth to a girl whom she immediately put up for adoption.

Katica

The twenty-four-year-old salesclerk Katica, another rape victim, comes from the village of Nisici, thirty-five kilometers north of Sarajevo. On December 5, 1992, she gave the following deposition that was recorded by a clerk of the (rump) Yugoslavian federal government.

> I was taken prisoner on May 26, 1992, in the woods near our house. There were two other women with me, refugees from Visoko: Jadranka and Nevenka R. Ten men in nonregulation uniforms took us prisoner. On their caps they had the insignia of the lily [the Bosnian insignia]. They carried us off in a truck and took us to the Breza camp [twenty-nine kilometers northwest of Sarajevo]. There they locked us up in a dirty, damp cellar. They raped us right off; they raped us in gangs and beat us too. I spent two days there. Then I was transferred to a room in another building. There were five other young women there: two Nadas, Rosa, Mira, and Olja. I stayed there until the end, that is, until August 15, 1992, when we were released. . . .
>
> Later when I came back home I heard that the director of this prison was named Kula and that he comes from Semizovac [thirteen kilometers northwest of Sarajevo]. I never saw this man. When they let me go, they also released the five young women who were held prisoner along with me. Two of them committed suicide as soon as they arrived back in their village; the other ones moved away with their parents. They released us because we were pregnant and they wanted us to stay pregnant.

Katica went directly to Belgrade and had her pregnancy terminated in September. After that she returned to Bosnia.

Slavenka

Forty-year-old Slavenka from the vicinity of Zenica in central Bosnia was also forced to learn that Serbian women, despite all contradicting claims by Muslim politicians and despite the sometimes serious efforts of authorities in Muslim-controlled territory, are not safe. In December 1992 she told the German journalist Heidi Hecht what had happened to her.

According to her statement, three Muslim soldiers broke into her house in Zenica early one morning in summer of that year. One of the men had a knife in one hand and in the other a piece of glass that he held up to Slavenka's throat. While doing so he threatened her: "I'll cut your throat; your husband's a Chetnik." Besides Slavenka, her children and her parents-in-law were staying in the house. The men beat up her in-laws and cursed her mother-in-law as a "Chetnik mother." One of them told Slavenka, "I fancy you," and pulled her into the bathroom. There he ordered her to get undressed and threatened her with his pistol. He forced her to have oral intercourse with him and announced that he would kill her children if she refused. Afterward Slavenka had to lie down on the floor and he raped her, saying, "I'm going to give you a little Muslim." When he was finished, the next man came into the bathroom, pulled her hair, and screamed, "You whore, I'm going to fuck you in the ass and then do it to your husband in the slammer, too." Before he left the house he went into her children's room and urinated on one of the children, says Slavenka in conclusion.

After the rape Slavenka fled with her children to relatives in Zvornik, a city in eastern Bosnia that is controlled by Serbs. She never wants to return to Zenica.

THE "FIERY STEEDS" OF NORTHERN BOSNIA

According to statements of the women involved, a group of men calling themselves "Vatreni Konji" (Fiery Steeds) wrought havoc during June and the first half of July 1992 in northern Bosnia, which was at the time controlled by Croatian and Muslim units. Three Serbian women from the northern Bosnian town of Novi Grad reported to the British journalist Yigal Chazan and a BBC reporter that they had been not only raped, but raped by their Croatian neighbors, who were now members of the Fiery Steeds.[48]

One night, so the thirty-seven-year-old Ljubica L. relates, these neighbors came into her house, searched it, and accused her of hiding Chetniks. On the following night she and three other Serbian women were taken into a house where approximately fifteen men in camouflage uniforms were waiting.

> They began to abuse us. Then they ordered us to get undressed. They told us the Chetniks had raped 150 women and now they were about to do the same thing to us. Seven men raped us. They kept us there for five hours. They were all of them my neighbors — I'd known them for over fifteen years. They didn't beat me as much as they could have, I think, 'cause I kept hollering at them by their first names while they were raping me. After that they herded us onto the street naked and scared us away with gunshots.

Ljubica went back home. The next night Croatian fighters broke into her house again. This time they abducted her thirty-seven-year-old friend Smilja. According to her own testimony, Smilja was stowed on the floor of a truck where there was also another Serbian woman, forty-five years old. On the trip, the truck had to stop at a checkpoint of the regular Croatian military police. The two women called out for help, but when the military police were about to check the truck, the abductors fired and stepped on the gas. They finally stopped near a forest and raped Smilja; the other woman was taken away. Smilja reports:

> There were eight of them. While they were raping me they sang anti-Chetnik songs. I thought they killed the other woman, but they brought her back later in terrible shape. After that they drove away and left us behind with only a few rags to wear. I still can't believe it. They used to be my co-workers once.

In Novi Grad on June 24, 1992, thirty-six-year-old Gordana was likewise the victim of a gang rape by the Fiery Steeds.

> One night a group of drunken men in camouflage uniforms broke into the house where I was living with some older women. One of them pulled me up by the hair and stuck a rifle in my back. They ordered the other women to be quiet and dragged me over to a nearby house. Three of them raped me there. I had to swear I thought it was fun.

When I screamed, one of them beat my head against the floor. That all lasted three hours. After it was over they said I was going to have a Ustasha baby.

RAPES IN THE HOS INTERNMENT CAMP AT DRETELJ

In summer 1992, units belonging to HOS, the Croatian right-wing extremist paramilitary group, ran a prison camp for Serbs in Dretelj (five kilometers north of the Herzegovinian city of Capljina). Its existence has been documented by the visits of various foreign journalists. In the camp women were also held prisoner, but they were not shown to the journalists.

One HOS soldier admitted to a Croatian journalist that there were two women there, a doctor and a teacher, both of them members of the Serbian SDS Party and "fomenters of the Serbian uprising in Bosnia-Herzegovina." The two women were in no condition to be shown publicly, however. The Croatian journalist said that "there is no doubt what this soldier meant by saying this."

In a report of the Belgrade women's political action group Women Helping Women,[49] one case from Dretelj is cited – very briefly, to be sure, and without verification – and yet it does concern a doctor.

Dr. O. D., a Serbian born in Capljina in 1958, was arrested in her apartment on April 25, 1992, and raped daily by HOS members. They forced her to go about naked and branded her with a hot iron. She tried to commit suicide. Then she was transferred to Dretelj. There, in August 1992, she was exchanged.

In the pamphlet "Bordeli jauka" (Brothel of sorrow), published in February 1992 by the editors of the Belgrade refugee newspaper *Odgovor* (The answer), we find the testimony of another rape victim from Dretelj, whose story is also mentioned in the Amnesty International report on rapes.[50]

I was born in 1937 in the district of Capljina, where I still reside. I am a worker by profession, and a Serb by nationality. On June 10, 1992, three HOS policemen came into my apartment, Mirsad R. and Mile V., and the third one stood guard outside the door. They said, "This apartment is for a Muslim family." They ordered me to lie down on the floor, and they let off a couple of warning shots over my head. While I was lying there like that they looted my apartment. Anything they liked they took away. They also took my papers and said I wouldn't be needing them anymore.

After they searched through my apartment I had to go with them; they didn't even let me change clothes. Along with my neighbor Branko B., they took me to the Dretelj camp. When I got to Dretelj the HOS soldier Zvonko B., called Little Red Riding Hood, confiscated all the gold jewelry I was wearing. Later he participated when I was interrogated and abused. In Dretelj I was led into a room with barred windows. The room was about three meters by two, and there were already other women there, the doctor D. O., the teacher M. J., the housewife V. A. Every other day they brought in new prisoners, men and women. They housed us women separately from the men, and we only saw them when the HOS soldiers were leading them off to work.

We were interrogated and abused. They beat us with clubs on our hands and over our whole bodies, they boxed our ears, shoved needles under our nails, lit our hair with candles, put cigarettes out on us. They cut up my underwear with a knife so that, as they threatened, they could rearrange my breasts. I was tortured by Mirsad R., Zvonko B., and Ivan M. from Ljubuski; I don't know the names of the others. They raped me right away at the first interrogation.

The interrogations kept on for seven or maybe ten days. They interrogated, abused, and raped the other women too. Under my breasts I have the scars from where they put out their cigarettes. You can't see the bruises from the club blows on my hands anymore, but my hands still hurt me.

A month after I arrived in the camp we were transferred to assembly halls. The women were put in one of them, the men in another. Every day they brought in new prisoners, so that the rooms were getting too crowded. The floor in the hall was made of concrete and the ceiling from rods and corrugated tin. We slept on the concrete. There wasn't any water or electricity; the hygienic conditions were terrible. In my hall there were about seventy women between the ages of thirty and eighty. They told me that they were torturing me because in my apartment they found a book about the persecution and annihilation of Serbs from 1941 to 1945 [in the Croatian Ustasha state]. Ten days later they also found a pamphlet in my apartment, and they raped me some more until I was transferred. Other women were abused there, too.

On August 17, 1992, the Dretelj camp was taken over by the regular Croatian army in Bosnia-Herzegovina (HVO), and the fifty-five-year-old Serbian woman was transferred to a prison in Mostar and later to Ljubuski. In October she was released in a prisoner exchange organized by the International Red Cross.

Rapes in Croatia

The first rapes of the war in the former Yugoslavia took place in Croatia, in the autumn of 1991.[51] At the time they were thought to be isolated incidents. Not until the mass rapes in Bosnia became known did a few Croatian organizations begin to concern themselves with war rapes in their own country. Although these rapes have not reached the extent of those in Bosnia-Herzegovina, the same political objective behind the Bosnian rapes is recognizable here too: the intimidation and expulsion of the population.

Representing the Croatian women who became rape victims in this war, let me tell the story of fifty-year-old Marija from the village of Berak near Vukovar in eastern Slavonia. Her testimony was recorded by Dr. Mladen Loncar on October 15, 1992.[52] In the first part of her testimony Marija goes into the details of events in her village after it was occupied. This section appears here in shortened form; the rest of Marija's testimony is cited verbatim.

The Yugoslavian Federal Army (JNA) entered Berak on September 2, 1991. Before the war, 926 people were living in Berak, among them 515 Croats and 348 Serbs. Most of the inhabitants had already fled a short time before the JNA entered. On the first day of the occupation, some of Berak's inhabitants were killed, all the houses were searched, able-bodied Croatian men were arrested, and all Croatian inhabitants were interrogated. One of Marija's sons was able to flee, the other one was arrested. She herself was interrogated.

A month later, on October 2, Berak's remaining Croatian inhabitants, about 100 people, were rounded up and locked in the house of the Croat Peter Penavic on Orolicka Street. This camp was managed by local Serbian paramilitary men who at first wore JNA uniforms and later the uniforms of the "Autonomous Serbian Province of Krajina." There were also regular JNA soldiers in the village.

At first the prisoners were allowed to go home every day under military escort to get food and to feed their livestock. Later they were only rarely allowed to leave the camp. On November 14, when Marija was permitted to go home, she discovered that her house had been looted and that all her farm equipment and livestock had been stolen.

The imprisoned men and women were interrogated several times; some of them were tortured and deported to unknown destinations – they never returned. During the harvest season the prisoners were forced to work in the fields.

On December 16 the camp was closed. Shortly before it closed a local Serb, in the company of a high JNA officer, announced to the prisoners that they could no longer remain in Berak. The Croats were supposed to declare in writing where they wanted to go. Marija wanted to stay. She went home. The next day she was speaking on the street with her Serbian neighbor. Both women were threatened by some members of the White Eagles, an irregular Serbian group. One of them said to Marija's neighbor: "Go tell all your Croatian neighbors that there's no more room for them here. We're going to destroy all their seed. There's not even any room here for their bones."

On the same evening nine Serbian soldiers entered Marija's house to spend the night. Marija assumes they were members of the White Eagles, but they had no insignias on their uniforms. She was expressly forbidden to sleep anywhere else. During the night there was a coming and going in Marija's house, and in the middle of the night she had to go with a soldier to army headquarters. There he blindfolded her and led her on farther to the headquarters of the White Eagles.

He knocked on the window, "Open up, I'm bringing you guys a real lioness." When he led me into the house he said, "Here she is, I've done my job." They stripped me naked right away and forced me to kiss and lick their penises. Seven of them raped me and I had to satisfy them orally. I had the blindfold on the whole time. They raped me, one after the other. They held knives to my breasts and other parts of my body. When one of them pressed a knife to me again, I heard someone call out, "Obrad, we didn't agree to that!" For me the worst part was that I had to swallow their semen and urine. The whole time someone kept swearing, "Fuck the Ustasha mother, where's the gold your son stole?" He grabbed my breasts several times and punched me in the belly. When I couldn't swallow anything anymore they threw me out onto a cement floor. Later they brought me back in again. The whole thing lasted more than two hours.

Suddenly I heard steps outside, and they pushed me behind a sofa. One of them went out and spoke to three men. These men went away again, and one of the men in the room said, "Throw this Ustasha trash out of here. We should kill her." They dressed me. One of them stuffed a pair of underpants in my mouth and said, "You won't get out of here until you swallow it." I almost choked. Then one of them said, "It's about time we got lost," and they led me out through the back door. After about four hundred meters they let me go. I was just about to take my rosary out of my trousers pocket when someone took the blindfold off me and took the rosary away from me, a little man with a mustache. He said I should run away as fast as I could. I wanted to run, but I fell down. Just then I heard machine-gun fire. A second man showed up, but both of them disappeared again. I just kept lying there for a while; my body hurt something awful. After that I ran through cornfields for three hours. I saw a tractor, but I'd lost my orientation. And then I realized that I was in the vicinity of my own house. I went to a barn, because I was sick to my stomach. There I remembered my [Serbian] neighbor, who'd offered to help me. I ran to her house, climbed over the high fence, and fainted. After that I don't remember anything else.

I woke up in my neighbor's house; she'd carried me inside. My mouth was full of pus and blood. She made me a cup of tea. When I drank it I had to throw up. I didn't stop throwing up until early in the morning. My neighbor's husband offered to take me to the military hospital. When my neighbor said good-bye she told me, "Maybe we'll never see each other again, 'cause when you leave, the same thing that happened to you could happen to me." She gave me her brother-in-law's address in Zagreb and asked me to tell him to call her kids in Belgrade and let them know that they shouldn't return to Berak. After she washed me and gave me a change of clothes, her husband took me to the military hospital. He told the army doctor everything that had happened to me and the doctor said, "My god, is this possible?" The doctor was tall and thin. The local Chetnik headquarters opened up at seven o'clock in the morning. A few people who had been mistreated the night before were standing around there. My neighbor asked for permission to take me to Negoslavci, and they allowed us to travel. When we got there we spoke with some high army officers about it; I didn't tell them the names of the men who had done this to me, because I knew that it had been planned. I got an exit visa, and half an hour later three cars escorted us out of the village to the train station in Sid.

The Perpetrators

> Men who rape in war are ordinary Joes, made unordinary by entry into the most exclusive male-only club in the world. Victory in arms brings group power undreamed of in civilian life. Power for men alone.[53]

This observation by Susan Brownmiller also applies to the rapists in the war in Bosnia-Herzegovina. Everyone participates in the rapes: regular soldiers as well as members of paramilitary groups; simple foot soldiers as well as high officers and commandants; policemen as well as friends, coworkers, and acquaintances of the raped women – "ordinary Joes." Yet how are they brought to the point of doing what they do?

George Rodrigue of the *Dallas Morning News* spoke with three rapists who are now the prisoners of Muslims or Croats. Their testimony has probably been doctored, yet it is revealing.

Borislav Herak

In October 1992, twenty-two-year-old Borislav Herak from Sarajevo made the mistake of running into a Muslim patrol and is now being held in the military prison of Sarajevo.[54] In March 1993 he was condemned to death by a military court in Sarajevo, but he has filed an appeal.

Borislav completed elementary school and then worked at odd jobs. During the war he joined Serbian fighters in Vogosca (ten kilometers north of Sarajevo). He admits that in the brothel called Sonja's, a former restaurant in Vogosca, he raped Muslim girls and later killed some of them, in addition to killing dozens of other Muslim civilians.

GEORGE: In general they say that you have killed many men, women, and children with guns and with knives, and that you raped many women. Is that true?

BORISLAV: It is true, but I did not kill any children.

G: I would like to talk about the women you raped. I believe you have listed their names before. Could you do that again for me please?

B: Amara, Sabina, Sumbula.

G: Okay. Any more? Who was the first woman you raped?

B: Amara.

G: Tell me what happened.

B: We had an order to go to Restaurant Sonja in Vogosca. We were told that we were going to rape girls there.

G: Who told you this?

B: My captain. The commander of our unit. So as to increase the morale of our fighters.

G: What was the name of your captain?

B: I do not know his last name. His first name was Borov, and he came from Breza [thirty kilometers northwest of Sarajevo]. He was working as a captain there too, and he came to Sarajevo as a refugee and became a captain here.

G: Was this good for your morale?

B: Not at all. And before that and after that I had to go to the front lines, so it was the same for me.

G: How do you mean?

B: It was just a stupid thing to do. We hadn't any fights, and that is why it was worthless.

G: So what did you think of this order?

B: I had to obey it.

G: What would have happened to you if you had not?

B: They would have sent me to the worst front line in Trebinje in Herzegovina, or sent me to jail.

G: They would not have killed you?

B: I cannot say that. But I knew they would have taken away the house that they had given me.

G: They had given you a Muslim's house.

B: Yes.

G: Was it nice?

B: Yes. It had two floors, and it was white. There was a place to keep cows. A building for them, behind the house.

G: So you got to the restaurant, and what did you see?

B: It had a guard in front of it, and the girls were in the room.

G: What room?

B: The girls were in a room just inside the door.

G: How many girls?

B: Sixty.

G: How did they look? Clean, dirty, beaten, not beaten, young, old?

B: They were young, twenty to twenty-five years. They were looking normal, with normal clothes on them. They hadn't any bruises on them.

G: Did they look well fed or hungry?

B: I didn't notice.

G: What happened next?

B: I know that they were killed afterward.

G: I want to ask who did the very next thing. Who said the next thing?

B: They found Mordrag Vukovic and Dragan Damjanovic, they were in Seselj's army [a paramilitary group]. And they worked there. It was their work to guard the women.

G: What happened then?

B: We told them that we were sent by Borov, and they knew what to do. They brought the girls to us from the room. . . . They picked girls for us.

G: And which one was picked for you?

B: That Amara girl . . . she was tall, black hair, about twenty.

G: Did you say anything to each other?

B: No.

G: What happened then?

B: We went up to the room. On the second floor. That guy Miro showed us the way. And there we raped her, the four of us.

G: They picked out one girl for the four of you?

B: Yes.

G: You were all in the room when she was raped?

B: Yes.

G: Didn't this seem strange to you?

B: Just a little bit.

G: Why did you do it?

B: Because I had those guys with me. I had to listen to the order, or I would have to face consequences if I did not.

G: Did you say anything to each other this whole time?

B: We told her to take off her clothes. . . . She didn't want to. And that guy Misa Damjanovic started to beat her.

G: Did he beat her with his rifle butt or his hands?

B: With his hands. And then she took her clothes off and we raped her. And she put her clothes back on, and we took her away.

G: Did you feel good about this, or guilty?

B: I felt guilty. But I didn't want to say anything or to show it to the others.

G: You did not kill this one?

B: Damjanovic did.

G: How do you know?

B: I went with him. We went together to Zuc [a mountain in Sarajevo].

G: You and Damjanovic?

B: Three of us. They took her out of the car, the two of them, and I sat in the car. I saw that they had guns. One of them shot her in the head. They took her into some bushes; they sort of hid her there and then they killed her. . . . Then they came back.

G: Did they say why they did this?

B: When they finished and we were still in the restaurant, Miro Vukovic told us to kill her. Because they did not have enough food or space, and they wanted to bring new girls into the restaurant. So we should kill her.

G: What did you think of this?

B: I just kept my mouth shut. I was standing by the side.

G: I did not ask what you did. I asked what you thought.

B: I thought that what they were going to do was bad.

G: That is all you thought?

B: Yes.

G: Were you surprised?

B: I had already heard the stories about that. About killing girls. It was known to me already.

G: When they came back from shooting her the first time, were they laughing or sad or just very quiet?

B: They had music turned on in the car as we went back, and there was no conversation.

G: What was the music?

B: Serbian folk music. The usual folk music.

After that Borislav tells how during a subsequent visit to Sonja's along with two other soldiers he raped a girl named Sabina who was also killed later on Mount Zuc. A third victim was Sumbula, who suffered the same fate as Sabina and Amara, but this time Borislav killed her himself.

G: When you killed this young girl you had just finished raping, what were you thinking?

B: I can't remember. It was a long time ago.

G: I'm sorry, but I cannot believe that you don't remember. How many unarmed women have you shot in the back?

B: Three.

G: Do you remember what you were thinking while you shot any of them?

B: I knew that those were my orders. I knew I had to obey the orders.

G: If someone had told you before the war that if you did not rape and kill a Moslem girl they would have taken away your money and sent you someplace dangerous, would you have raped and killed the girl?

B: I would not have believed it. And I would not have done it.

G: Why would you do it now?

B: I had to do it.

G: Isn't that rather a bad excuse? You did not argue with these orders. You didn't even say that you didn't feel like it. You never said, Why don't we just let them go? Isn't this a bad excuse, "orders"?

B: We all had to obey the orders.

G: Let me ask you this. You have heard a lot of propaganda about how the Serbs are in danger and the Muslims want to slaughter them. Did you believe this?

B: Yes, I believed it. I had been told that in Sarajevo terrible things are going on. That they have prisons and whorehouses. That they rape little girls from five to seven years. That they throw babies and women to the lions in the Sarajevo zoo.

G: Now you grew up here, right? You had Muslim friends.

B: Yes. My brother-in-law is a Muslim.

G: Now before the war started would you have ever believed that Muslims could do such things?

B: No.

G: Had a Muslim ever hurt you in any way?

B: No. No. They only helped me. They were helping me all the time. I once had an accident, fell down and hurt my head. And a Serb neighbor was afraid. He ran away. A Muslim neighbor picked me up and took me to the hospital.

G: So how did you come to believe this propaganda about the Muslims?

B: I don't know.

G: Are you incapable of thinking for yourself? Do you believe everything that people tell you?

B: No. I don't believe everything that I hear. I can think for myself. But when I came to Vogosca, to the Chetniks, they told me that they had phoned to Sarajevo and were quite sure that my father had been killed at his house, on the street, in Sarajevo, and that my house had been burned. So that is why I believed them, and I started to think in a different way.

G: Your father is ashamed of what you have done.

B: He told me, I am your father and you are my child. And I can forgive you, but the others cannot.

G: Do you feel ashamed?

B: It is hard for me to look in his eyes.

G: How could somebody who grew up with Muslim friends, who had Muslims in his family, how could he grow up to treat Muslims this way?

B: I don't know. But while I was in Sarajevo my cousin came to my house and told me that the Muslims had put me on a list of people to be killed. And because we are close relatives, I believed him. When I escaped they told me a lot of stories about what the Muslims had done. Raping, slitting throats. And my thinking began to change.

G: What do you think now about the Serbs' claims to be great warriors and victims of the Muslims?

B: I think that they do not know what they are doing. As a matter of fact, because they act like this and fight like this they are going to ruin themselves. They are going to destroy themselves. It is easy for them while they are up in the hills. And it is easy for them while they have artillery and the Bosnians have just guns. But they will never be able to come down from the hills and visit the town. And that will be hard for them.

G: You know that by talking to so many people you have perhaps condemned yourself to death. Why have you done this?

B: They should know what they are doing on the other side.

G: What will happen to you now?

B: They will kill me.

G: Is that fair?

B: I guess so. Depends on the court.

G: Do you want to live?

B: I do not know. Muslims tell me that I am a criminal, and so does Serbian TV. They say that I have betrayed them. They are mad at me for talking against Serbs now, for speaking honestly. They say I am a lunatic.

G: Are you a lunatic?

B: I never was in a hospital.

G: Your dad said you had trouble with drinking, too. Is that right?

B: Yes. Lots of troubles.

G: And you know the Serbs all say you are crazy. Do you sometimes feel a little bit confused?

B: Yes.

G: Was there anything good about fighting with the Serbs? A feeling of togetherness or being part of a team? A feeling of being important?

B: The only good time was when we found schnapps and we could drink together. Or when we had barbecues. And then we could be together and drink and eat.

G: But I think that in the same way your bosses gave you the drink and food, they gave you the women. As a way to show you were important. Is that right?

B: Yes. For me and for all the soldiers. They wanted to keep us together.

G: Because the way the women are here, you would never be able to have so many women as a normal person, would you? In fact, you had not had any women before, had you?

B: Yes, that is right.

G: Now was it important, not to you personally but to your friends, that they had this chance? Did they enjoy it?

B: Yes, they did.

G: How would you know that? What did they say or do that let you know they were enjoying themselves?

B: Those guys, they tried to make themselves important. When we had meals together they would talk about what they had done there.

G: Specifically what would they say?

B: That they were there [in the restaurant Sonja's] and had a good time.

G: I don't think that anyone is completely different from anyone else. I think everyone has inside them a little bit of love, a little bit of hate, a little bit of goodness, and a little bit of violence. What do you think?

B: I think so too.

G: Okay. So was there a part of you that felt like your friends did? A part that really enjoyed this chance to rape and kill these women?

B: As for me, it was just a little part.

G: How did you know that that part was inside you? What did you do or feel or say that proved to you that you were feeling this way?

B: (silence)

G: What did you feel? There must have been something, or you would not have known that this part was inside you.

B: I know that it was good because when I got back I would drink and celebrate.

There is no doubt that Borislav is a very confused rapist. When interviewed he sometimes gives contradictory information about the number and names of the Muslim women he raped.[55] And yet the basic pattern of his narrative is always the same. He says that he raped all the girls in the company of other soldiers, that it had been an order whose objective was to raise the soldiers' morale. He told the American journalist Joel Brand that it really did raise his morale, "but only a little bit." He said that his commandant had also told him that the Muslims were doing the same thing to Serbian girls, and he thought that the rapes had made him hate the Muslims more than ever.

Probably Borislav himself does not know how many girls he raped, how many of them were killed afterward, and what their names were. He seems to have raped automatically, without wasting much time thinking about his victims. It is noteworthy that he always describes his victims as "tall, dark haired, and between twenty and twenty-five years of age" — there is no way he could have said more eloquently how little they mattered to him. Incidentally, it is typical of gang rapes that the perpetrators hardly perceive their victims as concrete people and that they are unable to describe them afterward unless they knew them beforehand.[56]

Cvijetin Maksimovic

Twenty-three-year-old Cvijetin Maksimovic from Lukavac near Brcko in northern Bosnia was captured by Croatian troops on May 18, 1992, and is now being held in the military prison of Orasje in northern Bosnia.[57] He too has only an elementary education and worked before the war in the Brcko brickyard.

In early May, as Cvijetin tells it, Serbian troops entered Brcko. On May 10 he, like all other Serbs between eighteen and sixty years of age, was forcibly mobilized. His assignment was to guard the notorious Luka internment camp at the Brcko harbor, right on the Sava River. According to American State Department information, at least 3,000 Muslims were killed in this camp in May and June 1992.

Cvijetin admits that, under orders, he killed eighty people with a machine gun and three additional people with a knife, and that he also raped one girl "properly" and eleven others "partway." He recounts that five or six hundred Croatian and Muslim men and women were held prisoner in the Luka camp while he was guard there. The camp was run by Seselj's and Arkan's people (paramilitary groups from Serbia), and in the beginning his only assignment was to sit in the sentry box at the entrance. He says that he saw corpses being carted off on trucks every day; their number depended on how many people had been killed that day; sometimes there were only three, sometimes eighty. His colleagues told him that the corpses were either thrown into the Sava River or else processed in the Brcko fodder factory.

According to his report, the camp consisted of two big halls. The killing took place behind one of the two halls. Some of the victims were chosen deliberately from out of the mass of prisoners, but most were picked arbitrarily. Arkan and Seselj soldiers were the perpetrators, and sometimes local Serbs were forced to participate. On the afternoon of May 17 his turn came around.

I was outside the camp area – there was a sentry box there where we used to hang out, and two men came to get me. They were called Dino and Colo; they were either Arkan or Seselj soldiers, I'm not sure which. They had on the usual camouflage uniforms, short hair, and black knitted caps with the insignia of the White Eagles. They were responsible for guarding the camp, and they were from Serbia; you could hear that from their dialect. They came to get me to butcher three men. They led them outside and gave me a knife. I said I'd never done anything like that, and I couldn't do it. I said up until then I hadn't even butchered a calf, let alone people. Then this Dino, I think it was Dino, he took my hand and put the knife into it and said, "Then I'll show you how you butcher," and then we did it together. Three other guys held the man down. He was about forty years old and not too tall. I looked at him while I was killing him. It was very hard for me to do it, I was afraid because of all the soldiers who were watching, and I was unhappy to have to do it. The soldiers were laughing and talking together. I don't know what they said; I was completely . . . I felt terrible. Then they cursed my mother and my father: "What kind of a Serb are you anyway? We traveled four or five hundred kilometers to fight here in Bosnia, and you're not even a real Serb!"

Then I had to kill the other two. They said, "If you don't butcher them, we'll butcher you." I never thought I would ever do such a thing. I don't know what the other two men looked like, they were in a bad way, they looked like they'd been beaten, and the things they had on were torn. And then I killed them; they died quickly. The other soldiers said I wasn't a real Chetnik, not a real butcher. "Let's go get eighty of them so we can see if he can at least kill them with a gun." They gave me a machine gun, and eighty people had to go stand in a row; some of them were women. And so I shot them. With a few rounds in the chest. It took one or two minutes. Later on after they led me away I heard some more shots, probably some of them were only wounded.

They said I wasn't a real Chetnik and now I would have to prove to them if I was at least a real man. They led me into a room in the camp halls. You had to take a different entrance to get there; I think it used to be an office, but now it was empty except for a table and a chair. They said, "Here are twelve broads for you." The women were already there when I got there, and five or six soldiers came in too. I was supposed to rape the women. Some of them were young and some were older . . . from twelve to maybe twenty-four years old. I figure they were Croatians and Muslims. And then they stripped a girl naked . . . she looked completely scared and lost. She was maybe fourteen, fifteen years old. She was blond, not too tall and a little chubby. She was afraid and didn't say a word; three of them held her down. All the women were afraid. The soldiers told me I should rape her, and the others too . . . that I could go ahead and have her. I was supposed to get undressed and lie down on her, and like that. . . . But I was afraid, and I didn't have an erection. They egged me on, and I had to take down my pants and lie down on top of her. I don't know how it managed to work, I had absolutely no feeling for what I was doing . . . and then I did get an erection, but I didn't feel anything. I didn't come; I was afraid and tired. It took a very short time. The soldiers said, "You guys aren't real Serbs at all; but don't worry, we'll show you how it's done."

They cursed our mothers 'cause I hadn't turned into a real man and said what a disgrace it was that they'd come from so far off just to fight for us. Then I was also supposed to strip and rape the women who were left over, catch them. . . . They showed me how you do it, how you grab a women by her breast and take hold of her sex, and they told me that I was free to rape them. I didn't feel anything at all, I wasn't excited at all, but I had to lie down on them and take hold of them. They were naked; the others guys had stripped them. The Chetniks were doing a lot of yelling, making animal noises, whistling: "Oh looky there, that's supposed to be a man! That's no man, that's a sissy." And they were bragging about how they raped the women themselves, how much fun they had with these twelve women the day before. At the end they said they'd forgive me this time, but not next time. And then they let me go.

The next day Cvijetin fled from Brcko. He was afraid, so he says, of having to kill and rape more people, and he was also afraid for his own life. Together with his friend Slobodan Panic, whose experience was similar, he went in the direction of Lukavac, his native village. On the way there both men were captured by Croatian sentries.

To explain why he is talking about what he did in the Luka camp Cvijetin says: "I believe in God, and I had to tell about it." He thinks he knows why he was forced to kill and rape:

> It's because of territory – they have to drive out the non-Serb people in Brcko and annihilate them so that Brcko can become Serbian. Otherwise this Brcko could never belong to Serbia; too many Croats and Muslims would be living there.[58] The rape is part of it; it spreads fear and terror so that the people flee and don't come back. This expulsion and all, it's made the Serbian people in Bosnia into haters, it's sown hatred. The killing and the raping were supposed to teach us to hate.

Slobodan Panic

Cvijetin's friend, twenty-three-year-old Slobodan Panic, was working as a carpenter before the war and had completed his continuing education. Like Cvijetin, he comes from the village of Lukavac near Brcko. On May 14, he reports, he was stopped by a group of policemen and soldiers at a checkpoint in Brcko and mobilized. He got a uniform and a gun and became a reserve policeman. At first he had to spend two days guarding a former cinema that had become the quarters of the reserve police, then he was sent to the Luka camp.

> I stood guard outside the camp and had to make sure no one went into the camp without authorization. Right away on the first day, May 16, a soldier in a camouflage uniform came up to me and said, "Come here!" He was big, with black hair, and heavy – he must have weighed more than 220 for sure. He took me over to the camp halls, and they had brought two girls outside there; they held them and told me that I had to rape them. I answered that I couldn't do it, and this tall guy said, "Go on, do it, or would you rather be killed?" I looked at him and saw he was serious. And so I had to go ahead and do it. About ten other soldiers were standing around watching. I think they were from Serbia, because of the dialect they were speaking. I didn't have an erection, nothing at all, only a little. . . .
>
> These two girls were somewhere between fifteen and twenty-two years old. One of them had brown hair, the other black. They had clothes on, and they had bruises on their faces like someone had hit

them. The other guys pushed them down on the ground and held their arms down. And I pulled up their skirts, but they didn't have anything on underneath, no underwear, and I had to rape them. It was just like that, more or less for appearance sake. . . . How can I say this? I didn't feel anything while I was doing it, it was only a little, each one a little bit, I didn't come. The other guys were laughing the whole time and shouting out dumb things, "Hey, looky here, go to it," and things like that, but I wasn't really listening closely. The girls were crying the whole time.

Then I said, "I can't do it anymore." The tall guy called out: "Go on, you guys, bring him another two! Maybe he'll like them better." And then they brought over three more girls, and I was supposed to rape them too. They were young too, somewhere between fifteen and twenty, maybe seventeen, eighteen, I don't know. They looked like someone had already raped them; they looked like they'd been beaten. They had bruises on their faces and their clothes were torn and dirty. They pushed them down on the ground, and they cried. One of them resisted; the other two didn't. One of the two soldiers who was holding her down hit the one who resisted; he hit her in the face. Each one only took a very short time; I didn't come. I wasn't in any one of them for more than a minute, and it didn't excite me at all. The whole thing took maybe fifteen minutes. Then the tall guy gave orders to bring two men over.

Slobodan had to shoot the two men, and later he had to cut the throats of two other prisoners. He says that he too had never before butchered any kind of fowl or swine, so that the "tall guy" had to guide his hand. Finally a soldier who obviously had some say in the camp showed up. According to Slobodan he asked, "What're you guys doing there? Don't you see he's already white as a sheet?," and Slobodan was finally able to go. Two days later he decided to flee along with his friend Cvijetin and return to his native village. As described above, Croatian sentries captured the two of them on their way home.

Slobodan cannot explain what took place in the camp. "You'd have to be crazy to think up a thing like that." He has reported it "'cause it gives me a little relief. It's better to tell how everything was instead of keeping silent. I didn't say anything at first, but then I decided to tell everything." He feels guilty for what he did, and he thinks it would have been better if the soldiers in the camp had killed him instead of forcing him to kill and to rape.

ORDERS TO RAPE?

All three rapists speak about orders. Some things in their reports have surely been glossed over, of course. And yet they sound plausible. Cvijetin and Slobodan were trying to escape when they were caught, and what Borislav reports puts him in such a bad light that he is probably not lying about very much.

Some rape victims, like forty-year-old Kadira, who was in the rape camp at Doboj, confirm that their former friends and acquaintances were forced to rape them. "These orders, they all came from Serbia; they were Serbian directives. . . . I know some men who had to do it, who were forced to do it and weren't doing it for their own enjoyment. You can tell about something like that."

Forty raped girls from the village of Brezovo Polje near Brcko also mentioned orders to the American journalist Roy Gutman.[59] During their deportation in June 1992, they were taken out of their buses, held for several days, and raped. "We have orders to rape the girls," twenty-three-year-old Mirsada was told by the young man who took her away, writes Gutman:

> According to the young girls' reports, the men discussed the rapes with them as if it had to do with a mission that they had to carry out. The women describe how many of the men took white pills that seemed to stimulate them. The men's claim that they were acting under orders seemed all the more probable at the arrival of a new group of irregular fighting forces under the command of Vojislav Seselj, one of the cruelest commanders of this war, a militant nationalist from Sarajevo. According to the women, the leaders of the local troops tried to protect the Brezovo Polje women from Seselj's subordinates. Twenty-three-year-old Zlata relates that one of the officers told Seselj's subordinates, "Don't worry, the girls have already been raped!"

Dr. Mladen Loncar, who looked into the mass rapes in Bosnia-Herzegovina for the Croatian Ministry of Health and spoke with about twenty rape victims, is convinced that there are "orders to rape." In his opinion the paramilitary groups directed from Belgrade are using rapes to build up a kind of "Serbian solidarity." For one thing, the rapes and killings teach locals Serbs who is "good" and who is "contemptible." At the same time, by forcing them to go along they destroy the bonds of friendship that existed between them and their Muslim and Croatian neighbors. In addition, Loncar thinks, there is another quite simple reason for the orders: "The local Serbs are witnesses to crimes, and those from abroad want to silence them by making them culprits too."

The statements of the perpetrators and the women concerned lead us to assume that there really are orders to rape – even if it has not been proved that the orders come from above, directly from the responsible generals and politicians. But without a doubt, mass rape does fit into the Serbian politicians' scheme of things, and there are no known cases in which local Serbian or military authorities have tried to thwart the rapes. At the very least they have been encouraging the soldiers by consistently failing to punish those who have raped.[60] It has also been proved that propaganda about the "fundamentalist Muslims" and "fascist Croats" who must be driven out and annihilated, itself an incitement to rape, does come from the highest level. Both aspects combined come close to a direct order to rape.

Reactions

The news about the mass rapes in Bosnia-Herzegovina spread like wildfire in the German media in November 1992, and soon the wave of outrage spilled over to other European countries and the United States. More and more journalists spoke with the women and girls concerned, made known the horrible details of the rapes, and quoted large numbers of victims. Since then the subject has been taken up by investigatory commissions and human rights organizations, women's groups, and aid agencies, but also by politicians. Each one sees the problem in his or her own way, and the rapes are often turned to particular ends.

Nevertheless, we do not know much more today than we did when the discussion began. We know that women have been raped in great numbers in Bosnia-Herzegovina and that the policy of "ethnic cleansing" is playing a role in it. No one knows the actual extent of women's suffering in Bosnia-Herzegovina, and all information about the number of rape victims continues to be an arbitrary estimate not based on any statistical calculations. Amnesty International quite correctly stresses

> emphatically the extreme difficulty of estimating the actual extent of sexual assault to which the women in Bosnia-Herzegovina have been exposed. Because of their shame and fear of being socially stigmatized, many women are not able to speak about what they have suffered. Furthermore, governmental structures in Bosnia-Herzegovina have been nearly completely destroyed and, except in a few centers, systematic investigations are almost impossible. The fact that women were only temporarily held prisoner in places which served this purpose has also made it very difficult for international organizations to scrutinize them. In addition, the subject of the rape of women (and the other atrocities committed in the course of the conflict) has been employed extensively as a propaganda weapon, and all sides have minimized or disputed the assaults by their own forces while exaggerating the assaults by their opponents. For these reasons it is the view of Amnesty International that all estimates regarding the number of raped and sexually abused women must at the present time be treated with caution.[61]

WAR PROPAGANDA

At first the Bosnian government registered some surprise at the response to the rapes: for them they represent only one of the countless war crimes. But the rapes quickly became part of the long list of justifications cited by Bosnian politicians when they indict the Serbian side and ask the world for help.

When they recognized the propaganda value of rapes, Serbian politicians also woke up. Television Belgrade immediately began to broadcast stories about raped Serbian women, and all over the world Yugoslavian embassies dispatched reports of raped Serbian women and forcible Muslim-Croatian brothels.

The propaganda war is also being fought by feminist women's groups who claim not to be nationalistic. Bosnian and Croatian feminists contend that the mass rapes of their countrywomen are an attempt at genocide, unique in the history of rapes, and many of them demand military intervention to rescue the women. Serbian feminists, on the other hand, claim that women have been raped in every war up to the present, that it has nothing to do with nationality, and that every military action is masculine and sexist per se – for after all it is the Serbian side that is victorious, and any intervention might jeopardize their victory.

The war has affected each side of the three warring parties so much that it cannot see or understand the other. In fact, politicians challenge the report that their own soldiers are raping. The Croatian president Franjo Tudjman, his Bosnian colleague Alija Izetbegovic, and the leader of the Bosnian Croats Mate Boban – who represent the Muslim and Croatian side – have until now gallantly passed over this topic.

For a long time, their opponent Radovan Karadzic claimed that Serbian soldiers did not commit rape as a matter of principle (!). Nevertheless, in October 1992 he admitted in an interview for the British BBC that he could not control every Serbian soldier, but that there was sexual abuse on all sides. When the mass rapes of Muslim women by Serbian forces were then reported around the world, he purported not to know anything about it. At a press conference in Belgrade on December 23 he said:

> The lies about the organized rapes of Muslim women in prisons and other locations are shameful, lacking all basis in fact and going beyond all bounds of human decency. We challenge the whole world to prove the existence of a single prison for women or a single case of an organized rape or even the presence of a single female civilian in our prisons, which for that matter are all open to inspection by international organizations.[62]

AID PROJECTS

Along with much else, knowledge of the mass rapes has instigated a wave of aid efforts. In general, I believe, one should remember the following in connection with aid measures:

• The women concerned usually come from a rural milieu. They have strong feelings of shame and disgrace, and one must probably approach the women rather than waiting for them to come forward.

• For most women the rape is only part of a many-layered trauma: many of them have had to watch as members of their families were tortured and murdered, or their nearest relatives have disappeared. They are subject to an additional trauma in that they have been driven off by their former friends and neighbors; they have lost their homes and property, and most of them look back on painful stays in camps.

- The raped women are usually not aware that they need special help related to their rape. After all the murders, tortures, and horrors they have seen and experienced, they do not understand rape as a special attack on the dignity of a human being. When I asked Muslim women what kinds of help they could imagine receiving, they said that they just want to forget the rape(s), and that if something is going to be done, then all the other displaced people should be helped too. Most of them asked that the world intervene militarily or lift the weapons embargo so that the war, and with it the rapes and expulsions, would cease.

- And indeed, all the humanitarian efforts cure only the symptoms; the causes themselves are in no way changed. The international community must finally undertake concrete measures to end the war in the former Yugoslavia.

- Bosnian men and women of the Muslim faith have been forced to wait it out in a crumbling Bosnia-Herzegovina. If they do not possess a visa for a third country, they are turned away at the Croatian border. Yet it is practically impossible to arrange for a visa, since in Bosnia-Herzegovina not even the phones or the mail are working. These are the people who need help, even if travel in Bosnia-Herzegovina is fraught with certain safety risks.

- Whether Serbia, Croatia, or Bosnia-Herzegovina, in all three countries chaos and corruption are the rule. Giving money to local aid organizations does not solve the problem; instead one should help to begin putting the appropriate structures in place.

- Further, the powerful response to the rapes in Bosnia-Herzegovina should be exploited to ensure that rapes in war are finally condemned and punished as war crimes.

Notes

1. This was reported by a thirty-two-year-old Muslim refugee from Bratunac in eastern Bosnia, which was captured by Serbian units at the beginning of May 1992. I spoke with her at the Croatian-Slovenian border on July 25, 1992, shortly before her departure for Germany. She wanted to remain anonymous because her husband was in Serbian captivity.

2. This was the view of nurse Melisa Zerin, with whom I spoke in a refugee camp in Zenica on November 3, 1992.

3. For the function of rape in war, see Ruth Seifert's and Catharine A. Mac-Kinnon's analyses in this book; Susan Brownmiller, *Against Our Will: Men, Women, and Rape* (New York, 1975); and Lepa Mladjenovic, "Universal Soldier – Vergewaltigungen im Krieg," *Scheherazade Newsletter,* no.4 (January 1993): 2–6.

4. Helke Sander and Barbara Johr, eds., *BeFreier und Befreite: Krieg, Vergewaltigung, Kinder* (Munich 1992).

5. Brownmiller, *Against Our Will,* pp.96ff.

6. Report of the team of experts on their mission to investigate allegations of rape in the territory of the former Yugoslavia from January 12 to 23, 1993. Appendix 2 of the third situation report of the UN Commission to Investigate the Human Rights Situation in the Former Yugoslavia under the direction of the UN special deputy Tadeusz Mazowiecki, published in Geneva February 12, 1992, p.73.

7. EC investigative mission into the treatment of Muslim women in the former Yugoslavia, final report, published in Brussels on February 2, 1993, p.5.

8. Amnesty International, "Bosnia-Herzegovina: Rapes and Sexual Abuse by the Armed Forces," January 1993.

9. Helsinki Watch, *War Crimes in Bosnia-Herzegovina,* vol. 2 (New York, 1993), p.21.

10. This section is based on interviews with twenty refugees and former prison inmates as well as with four rape victims from the district of Prijedor; twenty additional witness statements recorded by various Bosnian organizations; studies at the Prijedor Homeland Club, the Bosnian government office in Zagreb, and the Bosnian Center for the Investigation of War Crimes; various articles that have appeared on this topic; and the exchange of experiences with other journalists.

11. According to the American human rights organization Helsinki Watch, approximately thirty-five women were held in Omarska, whereas in Keraterm there were only occasionally a few female prisoners. These women were also raped. A thirty-nine-year-old teacher from the city of Prijedor, who spoke with Helsinki Watch, was the victim of several rapes in Omarska, and a forty-five-year-old Muslim woman from Prijedor was raped in Keraterm. See Helsinki Watch, *War Crimes in Bosnia-Herzegovina,* 2:87ff., 121ff., 163ff., 165ff.

12. Interview on November 18, 1992, in the refugee camp of Karlovac, Croatia.

13. Interview on October 24, 1992, in Zagreb.

14. Interview on August 15, 1992, in Zagreb.

15. Interview on November 5, 1992, in Zenica, central Bosnia.

16. Interview on November 4, 1992, in Travnik, central Bosnia.

17. Interview on November 27, in the refugee camp of Gasinci near Djakovo in northern Croatia.

18. In Serbo-Croatian the mother of a person who is the butt of anger is frequently the object of insults. *Balija* is a very contemptuous reference to Muslims.

19. On December 27, 1992, Dr. Mladen Loncar from the Croatian Ministry of Health spoke with Emina.

20. Interview on November 4, 1992, in Travnik.

21. Interview on November 3, 1992, in Zenica.

22. Witness statement videotaped in July 1992 in Jablanica. Excerpted from Ibrahim Kajan, *Muslimanski danak u krvi: Svjedocanstva zlocina nad Muslimanima 1992* (Muslim days in blood: Evidence of the crimes against Muslims), Kulturno drustvo Muslimana Hrvatske *Preporod* (Cultural society of Muslims in Croatia *Preporod*) (Zagreb, 1992), p.64.

23. Interview on November 3, 1992, in Zenica, central Bosnia.

24. *Bula* is the term for Muslim women with religious education who according to Islamic tradition wash the female dead and prepare them for burial.

25. Interview on November 7, 1992, in Tarcin.

26. Both interviews on November 7, 1992, in Tarcin.

27. Missing a period after a rape (amenorrhea) is a common reaction.

28. Interview on November 6, 1992, in Tarcin.

29. Interview on November 30, 1992, in Zagreb.

30. Interviews on October 26 and November 9, 19, and 27, 1992, in Zagreb.

31. Interview on November 9, 1992, in Zagreb.

32. Interviews on October 26 and November 19, 1992, in Zagreb.

33. According to the 1991 census Doboj had 102,546 inhabitants: 40 percent Muslims, 39 percent Serbs, and 13 percent Croats.

34. On June 25 seventy-two Muslims in the Bikavac quarter of Visegrad were closed up in a house that was then set on fire. Zehra was able to save herself by crawling through a little garage window, in the process burning her hands thoroughly on the searing hot metal. Everyone else, including Zehra's mother, her sister with two little children, and her brother's wife and child, was burned to death. Zehra's statement was recorded on video by a lawyer in Zenica; the tape is in the possession of the "Center for the Investigation of War Crimes" in Zenica, viewed on November 1, 1992.

35. Interview on November 5, 1992, in Zenica.

36. According to the 1991 census, Visegrad had 21,202 inhabitants: 63 percent Muslims, 33 percent Serbs, and 4 percent others.

37. Interview on November 6, 1992, in Donje Mostre.

38. Interview on November 5, 1992, in Zenica.

39. Interview on November 6, 1992, in Donje Mostre.

40. Interview on November 6, 1992, in Radovlje near Donje Mostre.

41. In Visegrad there are two bridges over the Drina, the historic "Old Bridge," which was built during Turkish rule and is also called "Ivo Andric Bridge" after a novel by Ivo Andric, and the "New Bridge."

42. George Rodrigue, a correspondent with the *Dallas Morning News,* spoke with Senada in January 1993.

43. Report of the team of experts on their mission to investigate allegations of rape in the territory of the former Yugoslavia from January 12 to 23, 1993, appendix 2 of the third situation report of the UN Commission to Investigate the Human Rights Situation in the Former Yugoslavia under the direction of the UN special deputy Tadeusz Mazowiecki, published in Geneva February 12, 1993, pp.64ff.

44. Interview on November 2, 1992, in Zenica.

45. So far I have spoken with Melisa only by telephone; the American journalist Laura Pitter (UPI) conducted two interviews with her, which she placed at my disposal, and I also have at hand Melisa's written statement, recorded by Dr. Mladen Loncar from the Croatian Ministry of Health on December 30, 1992.

46. Report of the team of experts on their mission to investigate allegations of rape in the territory of the former Yugoslavia from January 12 to 23, 1993, appendix 2 of the third situation report of the UN Commission to Investigate the Human Rights Situation in the Former Yugoslavia, under the direction of the UN special deputy Tadeusz Mazowiecki, published in Geneva February 12, 1992, p.72.

47. Amnesty International, "Bosnia-Herzegovina," summary p, 1.

48. See Yigal Chazan, "Serbian Women Gang-Raped by Their Croat Neighbours," *Guardian,* August 17, 1992, and Amnesty International, "Bosnia-Herzegovina," p.6.

49. The report "Partial Documentation of Rape in the Yugoslavian Civil War" is available in Bielefeld at the Women's Peace Initiative of Serbian Women in Germany.

50. Amnesty International, "Bosnia-Herzegovina," p.7.

51. The war against Croatia began in July 1991. Within a few months the Yugoslavian Federal Army and Serbian paramilitary groups that were still in existence at the time conquered a third of Croatian national territory. A cease-fire arranged by the United Nations went into effect on January 3, 1992, and in March

14,000 United Nations peacekeeping troops were stationed in the crisis area. They are supposed to oversee the cease-fire, return a portion of the Serbian-occupied area to Croatia (the "pink zones"), and facilitate the return of all refugees and displaced persons. Until now they have only partially accomplished this task. Even with the "blue helmets" stationed there, fighting of varying intensity continues in the crisis areas, as does the expulsion of the non-Serbian population. In Serbian-occupied areas, according to information from the Croatian office of UNPROFOR (United Nations Protection Forces), 500 people of Croatian nationality have been murdered and 2,000 displaced during this period.

According to official statistics of the Croatian Ministry of Health some 6,500 people have been killed in the war thus far, and 23,000 have been wounded. The number of the dead is based on the results of autopsies and is not complete. It is assumed that of the 14,000 people listed as missing by the Croatian Red Cross, most are dead. In Croatia there are 270,000 registered refugees and displaced persons from the Croatian crisis areas and Serbian-occupied areas.

52. *Editor's note:* The Croatian Ministry of Health has a department for the investigation of war crimes (Department for Information and Investigations) and is working on documentation of rapes in Croatia and Bosnia-Herzegovina as a new type of war crime. Rape victims are systematically interviewed for this purpose. The director of the investigation is Dr. Mladen Loncar.

53. Brownmiller, *Against Our Will,* p.32.

54. Rodrigue spoke with him in Sarajevo on January 23, 1992.

55. He told *New York Times* journalist John Burns that he had raped and killed a total of eight Muslim women in the forcible brothel of Sonja in Vogosca (see also Amnesty International, "Bosnia-Herzegovina," pp.8ff.). And he reported to the American journalist Joel Brand that he raped only three girls in Sonja's, but four others in Ilijas (approximately twenty-five kilometers north of Sarajevo) in an elementary school that had been turned into an internment camp for about 150 Muslim women and men. He said that the girls from Sonja's had afterward been killed on Mount Zuc to make room for new ones; he returned the girls who were imprisoned in Ilijas to their internment camp after he raped them. Both journalists spoke with him in December 1992.

56. See Ruth Seifert's essay in this book.

57. Rodrigue conducted the interview on December 14, 1992, in the military prison of Orasje in northern Bosnia.

58. Before the war the district of Brcko had 87,332 inhabitants: 44 percent Muslims, 25 percent Croats, and 21 percent Serbs.

59. Roy Gutman, "Mass Rape – Muslims Recall Serb Attacks," *Newsday,* August 23, 1992.

60. About this, Amnesty International writes: "There is likewise no doubt that politicians and military officers at the local level must have known about the rapes and sexual assaults against women and condoned them silently as a general rule." Amnesty International, "Bosnia-Herzegovina," conclusion, p.1.

61. Amnesty International, "Bosnia-Herzegovina," pp.1ff.

62. Quoted from United Press International.

The Muslim Woman

Azra Zalihic-Kaurin

In the kingdom of Yugoslavia as it existed before World War II, Muslim society was a closed community. Because Muslim women seldom came into contact with people of other nationalities, Muslims were able to preserve the patriarchal tradition of an upbringing based on the principles of Islam.

The role of women is laid down in Islamic *shari'ah* law, which derives from Allah's instructions as preserved in the Koran. No other law in the world pays as much attention to the distinct tasks of men and women: the *shari'ah* contains more precepts about the rights and duties of women than does constitutional law. According to *shari'ah* law, women are fully equal to men in religious rights and obligations; secular rights and obligations are another matter. Woman's place is in the home, and the role of mother is privileged. For example, according to Mohammed, Allah's prophet, a woman who dies in childbirth is given the status of *shehid*, the highest rank a person can attain.

Before World War II, Islamic traditions prevailed uninterrupted among Bosnian Muslims. The Muslim woman was thought to be the model of a good spouse, mother, and housewife. She wore the veil and the traditional long, baggy trousers, or *dimije*. (In accordance with Islamic precepts, a woman has to cover her entire body except for her hands and eyes.)

Muslim men behaved courteously toward women and honored them. Muslim society as a whole showed women the same respect. Until she married, a woman stood under the protection of her father and brothers; afterward her husband took on this responsibility. One of the Koran's most impressive designations for marriage is the Arabic word *hisen,* "fortress." The husband protected the fortress, and the wife reigned over its inner realm. At its very center were her children and their education. Muslims considered children's education in the home to be the foundation for their development and later views. A Muslim proverb states: "As our women are, so also is our community." Within this fortress, the Muslim mother was everything: the first nursery school, the first elementary school, the first source of wisdom, the first judge.

After World War II the Communists gained power in Yugoslavia, and 1945 marks a radical turning point in the history of Bosnian Muslim women. They benefited from the Communists' innovations, certainly, for earlier they had lived under many limitations and disadvantages and needed to be liberated—but not in the way the Communists wanted to "liberate" them.

Under the motto "brotherhood and unity," Muslim women were supposed to take off their veils. People turned up their noses at tradition-rich clothing like the *dimije;* they became accustomed to seeing Muslim women baring their faces and wearing skirts. Young women participated in youth brigades to rebuild the homeland, and there the Muslims encountered a new way of life. Nationalities were no longer to play a role. The Communist leadership wanted to mold the Muslim woman into a new type of Communist woman and erase all traces of the Islamic religion and its customs.

Coming from traditional Muslim families in which the role of woman was precisely defined, used to respecting and being respected and protected, Muslim women found themselves in a whirlpool of new experiences. They tried to find their identity and integrate themselves into the new community. It was difficult to bring the new way of life into harmony with old traditions and beliefs. Making Muslim women's integration more difficult, Muslims did not feel acknowledged socially: they were regarded as backward outsiders.

Nor did "old-style" Muslims make it any easier for Muslim women. They condemned everything new, talked about "women's moral decline," and clung to the traditional ideal of the Muslim woman. But it proved impossible to retain women's status in Islam and do justice to the needs of the new age at the same time. I am speaking about the collision of the patriarchal Muslim value system with the developments of the new civilization. Nevertheless, long after the war was over, the Muslim community continued to argue bitterly about whether it was more important to preserve Muslim women as they had existed in the patriarchal community or to support them in adapting to new ways of life. Even today this problem has not been resolved in some of the exclusively Muslim areas of Bosnia-Herzegovina, Kosovo, Saudjak, and parts of Macedonia.

In various ways, Muslim men tried to hinder their women from taking new paths. Only a few Muslim women were able to attend university, even if they were talented and had parents with the financial resources to send them to study in the cities. There they would come into contact with other people and grow accustomed to city life. Muslim women had to watch out for "bad company." It was unthinkable to see a Muslim woman in a café or at a private party; just as before, she drank no alcohol and ate no pork. Just as before, the Muslim woman had to remain intact and go into her marriage with a pure soul. Only to her husband could she show her body—an extramarital affair was inconceivable. Muslim women who married men of a different faith were sometimes disinherited by their parents. It was also a disgrace if a Muslim woman became pregnant and the father of her child would not marry her: there was no greater shame.

Yet over the years, the influence of traditional Muslims weakened more and more. The new ways became commonplace; only in remote villages were mixed marriages thought to be despicable, and Muslims were scarcely different from members of other nationalities. Muslim women lived new lives, transmitted this new way of life to their children, and forgot what they had learned in their fathers' houses. They were convinced that they were emancipated and were enjoying all their rights. They no longer had anything to do with Islam: the only thing they still knew was that Muslims do not eat pork. Travel, city life, education, and Communist ideology had changed them. Communist Yugoslavia noted the Muslim women's transformation with satisfaction and celebrated their emancipation on March 8, the Day of the Woman.

The Bosnian Muslims, however, never fully forgot their traditions. Young Muslim women today may wear miniskirts and have boyfriends, may study and work, but they still respect the commandment of virginity. Marriage is as self-evident as is a mother's responsibility for the education of her children. In remote villages Muslim traditions are even more alive. There it is still the custom that after the wedding night a mother-in-law hangs out the sheet on which a young couple has slept so everyone can see that the bride was a virgin.

When the influence of Communism began to diminish after Tito's death, Muslims noticeably began to hark back to old values. Once again they turned more determinedly to their faith. Muslim customs were rediscovered and cultivated; men and women attended mosques regularly and sent their children to *medresas*.* The Muslim community discussed the young people, deploring the loss of family connections and the irresponsibility of parents. For Muslim women this was tied up with the moralistic admonition that they could retain their dignity and honor only by obeying Muslim precepts. Returning to the old traditions was thought to be the prerequisite for a national renaissance.

Frequently, too, people told the story of a young Muslim woman who lived in the vicinity of Sjenica during World War II. Emina took up a gun to defend her village against the loyalist Serbian Chetniks but was not able to hold them back. When she fell into their hands she begged one of the Chetniks, "Only leave me my honor; I will forgive you my death." Emina is taken as a model Muslim woman; her honor and dignity were worth more to her than her life. She forgives the Chetniks for her murder so that she will not be raped, humiliated, and defiled. Bosnian Muslims wanted to dedicate one day of the year to her and make March 8 "Emina's Day." But then a new war broke out, bringing new rapes and new sexual abuses.

Medresas are Islamic schools. Those teaching the Koran to children are normally adjacent to mosques and attended in addition to regular school, but they can also be schools or universities whose whole curriculum centers on Islamic teachings.

Psychiatric Aspects of the Rapes in the War against the Republics of Croatia and Bosnia-Herzegovina

Vera Folnegovic-Smalc

Psychiatry approaches rapes in a special way that sets it apart from the other sciences. I shall explain this by the example of psychiatry versus gynecology. The medical histories of some patients reveal that women have been imprisoned and raped over long periods in camps.[1] One young patient who was held for four and a half months in a camp in Bosnia and abused daily by three to five rapists appears as one case in a gynecologist's statistics. For the psychiatrist, that the woman was always raped in the presence of other male and female prisoners, that by her estimate there were 180 to 250 of these prisoners, and that there was heavy turnover among them is very important, for it means that the number of victims is much greater than statistics show.

Our patient is the primary victim of protracted and repeated abuse, but even those who witnessed the rapes passively are considered victims – secondary victims of rapes. As such they represent a psychiatric-psychological problem, though not a gynecological one. In my experience the psychiatric consequences in secondary victims can be very pronounced, sometimes even greater than in primary victims. For this reason psychiatrists and psychologists are confronted with far more of the corollary problems of rape.

Type of Rape

The rapes in this war are not individual rapes but gang rapes. They represent not a primarily sexual act, but rather an aggressive act that has as its purpose the destruction of the victim's human dignity, her injury and humiliation. It has nothing to do with the personal sexual satisfaction of the rapist. The main aim of gang rapes is to demonstrate power.

Such rapes destroy not only the personal identity of the victim but also the identity of the (political, national, religious) group to which the victim belongs. The group that suffers the rapes occupies an inferior position. By the rapes, the rapist intends to create a hierarchy; it is his way of expressing his own group's superiority.

When gang rapes take place in great numbers, they represent a systematic attempt to break and annihilate the political and military enemy. Unfortunately, the sexual abuses in Croatia and Bosnia-Herzegovina are of this kind. So far we have only scanty knowledge about this kind of sexual abuse.

Typical Marks of the Rapes

Abuses are commonly described as either psychological or physical, though the two types usually take place simultaneously. For the most part, the rapes discussed here are also abuses of both a psychological and a physical nature. According to our male and female patients, not only women but also children and men are being raped. Rapes of women are the most frequent, to be sure, but even girls not yet fourteen years old are being raped. The victims are very frequently raped in the presence of other people. Rapes that are carried out in front of members of the victim's immediate family – children, parents, husband – result in severe trauma.

In the prison camps where most of our patients have spent time, there were many sorts of sexual abuse. According to our patients' statements, all the sexual abuses were accompanied by physical abuse, verbal insults, and threats. In almost all cases the victims report that the perpetrators were under the influence of alcohol. The way these sexual abuses were carried out speaks for the assumption that their aim is to destroy the political enemy. In addition, rapes perform an important function when conquered territories are being "ethnically cleansed": a woman who has been raped over several months is usually set free during an exchange of prisoners; she can then move freely and speak about the rape. Her story produces fear in the remaining inhabitants, not only the females, but also the males: the men come to realize that they are not in a position to defend their women, and thus they are not only fearful, but also severely demoralized.

At the same time, involuntary witnesses to the rape report what they have seen, and the direct rape victim and her family are "stigmatized." To avoid shame and disgrace, their only choice is to flee their native surroundings.[2] In both these ways the main goal of "ethnic cleansing" – expulsion – is achieved.

The rape victims must reckon with psychological trauma, pregnancy (which may or may not result in induced abortion or childbirth), infections (ranging from ordinary infections to AIDS), and physical trauma.

Response to Offers of Psychiatric Assistance

A relatively long time has passed between the rapes committed during the war against Croatia and Bosnia-Herzegovina and their public revelation. What is the reason for this delay?

In our sociocultural community a raped woman does in fact receive a certain amount of sympathy, but rape also evokes a negative reaction. A raped woman is considered defiled; she represents a disgrace to her family and her (national, religious, political) community. Most probably, rape victims' feelings of humiliation, disgrace, and impotence are the reason they even now respond only rarely to offers of psychological or psychiatric help and seldom ask for help on their own initiative. If they do come forward they try to remain anonymous and avoid being labeled as rape victims. They will identify themselves much more frequently by telephone, and if they do come to a counseling session they usually begin by speaking about themselves in the third person (that is, they say that someone else has been raped). It takes time for them to be able to speak about themselves.

In the beginning rape victims came to us only if they needed a psychiatric certificate about their mental health to apply for a termination of pregnancy,[3] after a suicide attempt, or if they were afflicted by other psychological disorders. I have known some women who tried to hide their rapes even then.

Psychological Consequences in Rape Victims

The intensity of psychological decompensation stemming from sexual abuse is assessed in terms of the psychiatric diagnosis of PTSD (post-traumatic stress disorder). The intensity depends on various factors, including the victim's personality structure, her previous sexual experience, her sociocultural and religious character, the sort of rape, the victim's emotional relationship with her rapist, the consequences of the rape (e.g., pregnancy), the attitude of her family and those around her, and the therapy used.

If other traumatic experiences have taken place in addition to the rape itself, the PTSD symptoms are much more pronounced. In nearly all our patients, the rape is part of a many-layered trauma whose other components may include a stay in a camp, the loss of one or several beloved people, separation from family members, the loss of a home, physical abuse, insults, death threats to the victim or her family, the loss of material goods, and so forth. The most frequent symptoms occurring in our patients are anxiety, inner agitation, sleep disorders, nightmares, apathy, loss of self-confidence, and depression.

We also frequently encounter a loss of vital instincts or even a death wish. Suicidal thoughts are evident above all in women who have become pregnant as the result of rape. After an induced abortion the symptoms change, and depression is replaced by aggression and the wish for revenge.

In all patients who have been primary or secondary victims of sexual abuse, we observe an aversion to sexuality. Some patients say, "For me there's no such thing as sex anymore; that's all in my past." Only one patient was prepared to resume sexual relations again after her rape, and that was with her husband, who knew nothing about the rape. She said, weeping, that they had stopped short of sexual intercourse at her request because she was afraid she would reveal everything to her husband, "and that could have meant the end of our life together."

If women experience strong emotional support from family and friends or even from new acquaintances in the refugee camps, their psychological disorders abate more quickly than those of women who keep the rape a secret or speak of it only to a therapist. We have discovered that women can discuss the actual act of sexual abuse and their subsequent psychological problems more fully in telephone conversations than face-to-face, and they also report their suicidal wishes more frequently by phone than when they come in for counseling. We believe this is because a telephone conversation precludes the danger of being forcibly committed.

We had two cases in which the consequences of sexual torture reached the psychological intensity of a psychosis, both stemming from gang rapes. One patient was the primary victim, the other was a passive participant who was forced to witness the rape of her daughter. The daughter did not come to us for treatment because, as her mother informed us, she was not suffering severe psychological consequences. In general it is my opinion that the indirect victim's emotional tie to the direct rape victim decisively influences her psychological decompensation.

The professional literature presents similar data regarding the type and frequency of symptoms.[4] For lack of time we have still not been able to gather data about how long isolated symptoms last or in what way they depend on the whole trauma. The literature states that the length of treatment depends on the extent of the violence experienced. It is thought that when a rape is accompanied by death threats in the early stages of the traumatic experience it tends to result in several symptoms, and that a penetration of whatever kind noticeably affects the intensity of reactions in the regeneration phase. In addition, the number of attackers is thought to determine the symptoms more strongly than anything else.

Forms of Therapy

There are various forms of therapeutic treatment for rape victims with psychological disorders; ultimately they depend on the intensity and type of symptoms, the victim's personality structure, her attitude toward treatment, and the training of the therapist. If the victim is positively disposed toward therapy, she usually receives individual psychotherapy in combination with chemical therapy. Anxiolytics, antidepressants, or both are usually prescribed, and in the case of a psychosis neuroleptics are given as well. Family therapy can be undertaken only in exceptional cases, because the victims have usually been separated from their families or else want to hide the rape from them. They usually also receive gynecological treatment. When treating rape victims, we incorporate the practical experience of members of the International Rehabilitation Council for Torture Victims and the Rehabilitation Council for Torture Victims, published regularly in Copenhagen in the magazine *Torture*.

Final Note

At the moment I am not in a position to speak about the course or final outcome of our treatments. Our work with rape victims is not intended to support research about the problem but is a purely therapeutic, professional treatment whose aim is to prevent or heal victims' symptoms of psychological decompensation.

Instead of a final conclusion, I shall simply remark that rape is one of the gravest abuses, with consequences that can last a lifetime. For that reason it is necessary to offer victims every opportunity to prevent or treat psychological injuries. To do that, appropriate steps must be taken by those authorities responsible for health and welfare insurance. Further, it is important to support victims and their families emotionally, and in this respect religious and political communities can do their share. With all of this, the victim's wish for anonymity must be respected, and if no psychosis is present, the victim should have a role in deciding what type of treatment she receives.

Notes

1. The following remarks are based on my conclusions from my therapeutic work with twenty-nine rape victims in the Vrapce Psychiatric Clinic in Zagreb and in telephone counseling sessions.

2. In some cases husbands have gone so far as to kill their wives after hearing about the rape; in others, raped wives have committed suicide.

3. In accordance with the abortion law of 1978, women in Croatia may have a pregnancy terminated up until the tenth week of pregnancy (the twelfth week after insemination) without giving their reasons. After this time a woman must present her reasons for wanting to interrupt her pregnancy before a hospital ethics committee. To that end, a psychiatric certificate supporting the termination can be helpful.

4. See IRCT (International Rehabilitation Council for Torture Victims), RCT (Rehabilitation Council for Torture Victims), *Annual Report, 1991* (Copenhagen, 1993); L. Jacobsen and P. Vesti, *Torture Survivors: RCT and IRCT* (Copenhagen, 1992); and B. Sorensen and P. Vesti, "Medical Education for the Prevention of Torture," *Medical Education* 24 (1990): 467–469.

Making Female Bodies the Battlefield

Susan Brownmiller

*T*his is all about identity," the television newscaster said earnestly, attempting to shed some light on the murderous ethnic rage that has torn apart the former Yugoslavia. Perhaps the newscaster should have amended his analysis to say *male* identity. Balkan men have proved eager to fight and die for their particular subdivision of Slavic ethnicity, which they further define by religious differences. The Serbs are Eastern Orthodox, whereas their sworn enemies, the Croats, are Roman Catholic. Bosnians – or rather the 44 percent of the population in Bosnia and Herzegovina that is neither Serb nor Croat – are Muslims; they currently side with the Croats. But Balkan women, whatever their ethnic and religious background, and in whatever fighting zone they happen to find themselves, have been thrust against their will into another identity. They are victims of rape in war.

If the Serbs have emerged as the bad guys in world opinion, it is largely because they have been wildly successful in carving a Greater Serbia out of chunks of Croatia and Bosnia and Herzegovina. Serbian land advances have been accomplished in the age-old manner of territorial aggression, with looting, pillage, and gratuitous violence that gets lumped under the rubric of atrocity.

So it is heart-rending, but not surprising, to hear of mass rapes committed in Bosnian villages recently overrun by Serbian fighters. Bosnian refugees fleeing to Croatia give horrendous eyewitness accounts. Detention camps have been turned into brothels that the Bosnian foreign minister in Washington calls "rape camps." Pregnant detainees will suffer the additional shame of bearing unwanted children of war. An emotional Bosnian appeal calls the Serbian rapes "unprecedented in the history of war crimes," an organized, systematic attempt "to destroy a whole Muslim population, to destroy a society's cultural, traditional, and religious integrity."

Alas for women, there is nothing unprecedented about mass rape in war when enemy soldiers advance swiftly through populous regions, nor is it a precedent when, howling in misery, leaders of the overrun country call the endemic sexual violence a conspiracy to destroy their national pride, their manhood, their honor. When German soldiers marched through Belgium in the first months of World War I, rape was so extensive, and the Franco-Belgian propaganda machine so deft, that the Rape of the Hun became a ruling metaphor. Afterward the actual cases were dismissed by propaganda analysts as rhetoric designed to whip up British and American support; but if the rapes had not had propaganda value, they would not have surfaced.

Women are raped in war by ordinary youths as casually, or as frenetically, as a village is looted or gratuitously destroyed. Sexual trespass on the enemy's women is one of the satisfactions of the conquest, like a boot in the face; for once he is handed a rifle and told to kill, the soldier becomes an adrenaline-rushed young man with permission to kick in the door, to grab, to steal, to give vent to his submerged rage against all women *who belong to other men.*

Sexual sadism arises with astonishing rapidity in ground warfare, when the penis becomes justified as a weapon in a logistical reality of unarmed noncombatants, encircled and trapped. Rape of an object doubly dehumanized – as woman, as enemy – carries its own terrible logic. In one act of aggression, the collective spirit of women *and* of the nation is broken, leaving a reminder long after the troops depart. And if she survives the assault, what does the victim of wartime rape become to her people? Evidence of the enemy's bestiality. Symbol of her nation's defeat. A pariah. Damaged property. A pawn in the subtle wars of international propaganda.

Sexual Conscripts

During World War II, when the Germans were on the march again, atrocious rapes were committed on the bodies of Russian and Jewish women in the occupied villages and cities, while still more women were dragged to brothels or to death. When the tide reversed and the Soviet army began advancing into German territory on the road to Berlin, it was the turn of German women to experience the use of their bodies as an extracurricular battlefield. In the Pacific, the euphoric Japanese occupation of China's wartime capital in 1937 was accomplished with such free-wheeling sexual violence that it became known as the Rape of Nanking. Astounding though it seems, it was not until this year that Korean "comfort women" sufficiently overcame their shame to tell of *their* unwilling role in World War II as sexual conscripts for the Japanese army.

How short is the memory of those who see warfare strictly in terms of national and religious pride. The mass rapes committed by Pakistani soldiers in newly independent Bangladesh were also called "unprecedented" in 1971, when the government of Bangladesh appealed for international aid to help with the aftermath. As in Bosnia now, Bengali women were abducted into military brothels and subjected to gang assaults. Although the raped women of Bangladesh were termed heroines of independence and permitted to secure abortions, they were ostracized by their own men when they returned to their Muslim villages. And lest this brief overview be accused of its own ethnocentric bias, sporadic cases of gang rape appear in the records of courts-martial for American soldiers in Vietnam, and further accounts are contained in the Winter Soldier Investigation conducted by Vietnam Veterans against the War.

The plight of raped women as casualties of war is given credence only at the emotional moment when the side in danger of annihilation cries out for world attention. When the military histories are written, when the glorious battles for independence become legend, the stories are glossed over, discounted as exaggerations, deemed not serious enough for inclusion in scholarly works.

And the women are left with their shame.

Rape, Genocide, and Women's Human Rights

Catharine A. MacKinnon

Human rights have not been women's rights – not in theory or in reality, not legally or socially, not domestically or internationally. Rights that human beings have by virtue of being human have not been rights to which women have had access, nor have violations of women as such been part of the definition of the violation of the human as such on which human rights law has traditionally been predicated.

This is not because women's human rights have not been violated. The eliding of women in the human rights setting happens in two ways. When women are violated like men who are otherwise like them – when women's arms and legs are cut and bleed like the arms and legs of men; when women, with men, are shot in pits and gassed in vans; when women's bodies are hidden with men's at the bottom of abandoned mines; when women's and men's skulls are sent from Auschwitz to Strasbourg for experiments – these atrocities are not marked in the history of violations of women's human rights. The women are counted as Argentinian or Honduran or Jewish – which, of course, they are. When what happens to women also happens to men, like being beaten and disappearing and being tortured to death, the fact that those it happened to are *women* is not registered in the record of human atrocity.

The other way violations of women are obscured is this: When no war has been declared, and life goes on in a state of everyday hostilities, women are beaten by men to whom we are close. Wives disappear from supermarket parking lots. Prostitutes float up in rivers or turn up under piles of rags in abandoned buildings. These atrocities are not counted as human rights violations, their victims as the *desaparecidos* of everyday life. In the record of human rights violations they are overlooked entirely, because the victims are women and what was done to them smells of sex. When a woman is tortured in an Argentine prison cell, even as it is forgotten that she is a woman, it is seen that her human rights are violated because what is done to her is also done to men. Her suffering has the dignity, and her death the honor, of a crime against humanity. But when a woman is tortured by her husband in her home, humanity is not violated. Here she is a woman – but *only* a woman. Her violation outrages the conscience of few beyond her friends.

What is done to women is either too specific to women to be seen as human or too generic to human beings to be seen as specific to women. Atrocities committed against women are either too human to fit the notion of female or too female to fit the notion of human. "Human" and "female" are mutually exclusive by definition: you cannot be a woman and a human being at the same time.

Women are violated in many ways in which men are violated. But women are also violated in ways men are not, or that are exceptional for men. Many of these sex-specific violations are sexual and reproductive.

Women are violated sexually and reproductively every day in every country in the world. The notion that these acts violate women's human rights has been created by women, not by states or governments. Women have created the idea that women have human rights out of a refusal to believe that the reality of violation we live with is what it means for us to be human – as our governments seem largely to believe.

Women have created the idea of women's human rights by refusing to abandon ourselves and each other, out of attachment to a principle of our own humanity – one defined against nearly everything around us, against nearly everything we have lived through, certainly not by transcending the reality of our violations, but by refusing to deny their reality as violations. In this project, women have learned that one day of real experience is worth volumes of all of their theories. If we believed existing approaches to human rights, we would not believe we had any. We have learned to look at the reality of women's lives first, and to hold human rights law accountable to what we need, rather than to look at human rights law to see how much of what happens to women can be fit into it, as we are taught to do as lawyers.

In pursuit of this reality-based approach, consider one situation of the mass violation of women's human rights now occurring in the heart of Europe. In this campaign of extermination, which began with the Serbian invasion of Croatia in 1991 and exploded in the Serbian aggression against Bosnia and Herzegovina in 1992, evidence documents that women are being sexually and reproductively violated on a mass scale, as a matter of conscious policy, in pursuit of a genocide through war.

In October 1992 I received a communication from an American researcher of Croatian and Bosnian descent working with refugees and gathering information on this war. She said that Serbian forces had exterminated Croatians and Muslims in the hundreds of thousands "in an operation they've coined 'ethnic cleansing'"; that in this genocide thousands of Muslim and Croatian girls and women were raped and made forcibly pregnant in settings including Serbian-run concentration camps, of which "about twenty are solely rape/death camps for Muslim and Croatian women and children." She had received reports of the making and use of pornography as part of the genocide. "One Croatian woman described being tortured by electric shocks and gang-raped in a camp by Serbian men dressed in Croatian uniforms who filmed the rapes and forced her to 'confess' on film that Croatians had raped her." She also reported that some United Nations troops were targeting women: "In the streets of Zagreb, UN troops often ask local women how much they cost. There are reports of refugee women being forced to sexually service the UN troops to receive aid. Tomorrow I talk to two survivors of mass rape — thirty men per day for over three months. We've heard the UN passed a resolution to collect evidence as the first step for a war crime trial, but it is said here that there is no precedent for trying sexual atrocities."[1]

Here is the rape, forced motherhood, prostitution, pornography, and sexual murder, on the basis of sex and ethnicity together, that is inflicted on women every day in every country in the world, targeted, escalated, organized, and intentionally directed against these specific women. Whether or not these practices are formally illegal — and it is easy to say with complacency that rape, prostitution, pornography, and sexual murder are illegal — they are widely permitted under both domestic and international law. They are allowed, whether understood, one man to another, as an excess of passion in peace or the spoils of victory in war, or as the liberties, civil or otherwise, of their perpetrators. They are legally rationalized, officially winked at, and in some instances formally condoned.

Whether or not they are regarded as crimes, in no country in the world are they recognized as violations of the human rights of their victims.

This war exemplifies how existing approaches to violations of women's human rights can serve to confuse who is doing what to whom and thus can cover up and work to condone atrocities. These atrocities also give an urgency, if any was needed, to the project of reenvisioning human rights so that violations of humanity include what happens to women.

The war against Croatia and Bosnia-Herzegovina, and their partial occupation, is being carried out by Serbian forces in collaboration with the Serbian regime in Belgrade, governing what remains of Yugoslavia. This is an international war. All the state parties have adopted relevant laws of nations that prohibit these acts; they are covered in any case by customary international law and *jus cogens*.[2] Yet so far nothing has been invoked to stop these abuses or to hold their perpetrators accountable. The excuses offered for this lack of action are illuminating.

In this war the fact of Serbian aggression is beyond question, just as the fact of male aggression against women is beyond question, both here and in everyday life. "Ethnic cleansing" is a euphemism for genocide. It is a policy of ethnic extermination of non-Serbs with the aim of "all Serbs in one nation," a clearly announced goal of "Greater Serbia," of territorial conquest and aggrandizement. That this is a war against non-Serbian civilians, not between advancing and retreating armies, is also beyond question. Yet this war of aggression – once admitted to exist at all – has repeatedly been construed as bilateral, as a civil war or an ethnic conflict, to the accompaniment of much international head scratching about why people cannot seem to get along and a lot of pious clucking about the human rights violations of "all sides" as if they were comparable. This three-pronged maneuver is familiar to those who work with the issue of rape: blame women for getting ourselves raped by men we know, chastise us for not liking them very well afterward, and then criticize our lack of neutrality in not considering rapes of men to be a comparable emergency.

One result of this approach is that the rapes in this war are not grasped as either a strategy in genocide or a practice of misogyny, far less both at once. They are not understood as continuous both with this particular ethnic war of aggression and with the gendered war of aggression of everyday life. Genocide does not come from nowhere, nor does rape as a ready and convenient tool of it. Nor is a continuity an equation. These rapes are to everyday rape what the Holocaust was to everyday anti-Semitism. Without everyday anti-Semitism a Holocaust is impossible, but anyone who has lived through a pogrom knows the difference.

What is happening here is first a genocide, in which ethnicity is a tool for political hegemony: the war is an instrument of the genocide; the rapes are an instrument of the war. The Bosnian Serbs under the command of Radovan Karadzic do not control the state; their war is against the people and the democratically elected government of Bosnia-Herzegovina. If you control the state and want to commit genocide, as the Nazis did under the Third Reich, you do not need a war. You do it with the state mechanisms at hand. This is being done now, quietly, to Hungarians and Croatians in occupied eastern Croatia and in Vojvodina, formerly an autonomous region now annexed to Serbia. This is virtually invisible to the world.

Now consider the situation of the Albanians in Kosovo. They are surrounded; they are within a state. When Serbia moves on them militarily, going beyond the segregation and oppression they suffer now, it may not look like a war to anyone else. It will not cross international borders, the way much international law wants to see before it feels violated. But it will be another facet of the campaign to eliminate non-Serbs from areas targeted for "cleansing," a genocide.

To call such campaigns to exterminate non-Serbs "civil war" is like calling the Holocaust a civil war between German Aryans and German Jews. If and when the reality in Vojvodina comes out, or Albanians are "cleansed," perhaps that too will be packaged for Western consumption as ancient ethnic hatreds, a bog like Vietnam, or some other formulation to justify doing nothing about it.

In this genocide through war, mass rape is a tool, a tactic, a policy, a plan, a strategy, as well as a practice. Muslim and Croatian women and girls are raped, then often killed, by Serbian military men, regulars and irregulars in a variety of formations, in their homes, on hillsides, in camps – camps that used to be factories, schools, farms, mines, sports arenas, post offices, restaurants, hotels, or houses of prostitution. The camps can be outdoor enclosures of barbed wire or buildings where people are held, beaten, and killed and where women, and sometimes men, are raped. Sometimes the women are also raped after they are killed. Some of these camps are rape/death camps exclusively for women, organized like the brothels of what is called peacetime, sometimes in locations that were brothels before the war.

In the West, the sexual atrocities have been discussed largely as rape *or* as genocide, not as what they are, which is rape as genocide, rape directed toward women because they are Muslim or Croatian. It is as if people cannot think more than one thought at once. The mass rape is either part of a campaign by Serbia against non-Serbia, or an onslaught by combatants against civilians, or an attack by men against women, but never all at the same time. Or – this is the feminist version of the whitewash – these atrocities are presented as just another instance of aggression by all men against all women all the time. If this were the opening volley in a counteroffensive against rape as a war against all women, it would be one thing. But the way it works here is the opposite: to make sure that no one who cares about rape takes a side in *this* war against *these* particular rapes. It does not so much galvanize opposition to rape whenever and wherever it occurs, but rather obscures the fact that these rapes are being done by *some* men against *certain* women for specific reasons, here and now. The point seems to be to obscure, by any means available, exactly who is doing what to whom and why.

The result is that these rapes are grasped in either their ethnic or religious particularity, as attacks on a culture, meaning men, or in their sex specificity, meaning as attacks on women. But not as both at once. Attacks on women, it seems, cannot define attacks on a people. If they are gendered attacks, they are not ethnic; if they are ethnic attacks, they are not gendered. One cancels the other. But when rape is a genocidal act, as it is here, it is an act to destroy a people. What is done to women defines that destruction. Also, aren't women a people?

These rapes have also been widely treated as an inevitable by-product of armed conflict. Every time there is a war, there is rape. Of course rape does occur in all wars, both within and between all sides. As to rape on one's own side, aggression elsewhere is always sustained by corresponding levels of suppression and manipulation at home. Then, when the army comes back, it visits on the women at home the escalated level of assault the men were taught and practiced on women in the war zone. The United States knows this well from the war in Vietnam. Men's domestic violence against women of the same ethnicity escalated – including their skill at inflicting torture without leaving visible marks. But sexual aggression against Asian women through prostitution and pornography exploded in the United States: U.S. American men got a particular taste for violating them over there. This must be happening to Serbian women now.

Rape *is* a daily act by men against women; it is always an act of domination by men over women. But the role of these rapes in this genocidal war of aggression is a matter of fact, not of ideological spin. It means that Muslim and Croatian women are facing two layers of men on top of them rather than one, one layer engaged in exterminating the other, and two layers of justification – "just war" and "just life." Add the representation of this war as a civil war among equal aggressors, and these women are facing three times the usual number of reasons for the world to do nothing about it.

All the cover-ups ignore the fact that this is a genocide. The "civil war" cover-up obscures the role of Belgrade in invading first Croatia, then Bosnia-Herzegovina, and now in occupying parts of both. A civil war is not an invasion by another country. If this is a civil war, neither Croatia nor Bosnia-Herzegovina is a nation; but they are both recognized as such. In a civil war, aggression is mutual. This is not a reciprocal genocide. Muslims and Croatians are not advancing and retreating into and out of Serbia. They are not carrying out genocide against Serbs on their own territories. There are no concentration camps for Serbs in Sarajevo or Zagreb. The term "civil war" translates, in all languages, as "not my problem." In construing this situation as a civil war at bottom, the international community has defined it in terms of what it has been willing to do about it.

It is not that there are no elements of common culture here, at least as imposed through decades of Communist rule, meaning Serbian hegemony. It is not that there are no conflicts between or within sides, or shifting of sides in complex ways. It is not that the men on one side rape and the men on the other side do not. It is, rather, that none of these factors defines this emergency, none of them created it, none of them is driving it, and none of them explains it. Defining it in these terms is a smoke screen, a propaganda tool, whether sincere or cynical, behind which Serbia continues to expand its territory by exterminating people and raping women en masse.

The feminist version of the cover-up is particularly useful to the perpetrators because it seems to acknowledge the atrocities – which are hard to deny (although they do that too) – and appears to occupy the ground on which women have effectively aroused outrage against them. But its function is to exonerate the rapists and to deflect intervention. If all men do this all the time, especially in war, how can one pick a side in this one? And since all men do this all the time, war or no war, why do anything special about this now? This war becomes just a form of business as usual.[3] But genocide is not business as usual – not even for men.

This is often accompanied by a blanket critique of "nationalism," as if identification with the will to exterminate can be equated with identification with the will to survive extermination; as if an ethnic concept of nation (like the Serbian fascist one) is the same as a multiethnic concept of nation (like the Bosnian one); and as if those who are being killed because of the nation they belong to should find some loftier justification for staying alive than national survival.

Like all rape, genocidal rape is particular as well as part of the generic, and its particularity matters. This is ethnic rape as an official policy of war in a genocidal campaign for political control. That means not only a policy of the pleasure of male power unleashed, which happens all the time in so-called peace; not only a policy to defile, torture, humiliate, degrade, and demoralize the other side, which happens all the time in war; and not only a policy of men posturing to gain advantage and ground over other men. It is specifically rape under orders. This is not rape out of control. It is rape under control. It is also rape unto death, rape as massacre, rape to kill and to make the victims wish they were dead. It is rape as an instrument of forced exile, rape to make you leave your home and never want to go back. It is rape to be seen and heard and watched and told to others: rape as spectacle. It is rape to drive a wedge through a community, to shatter a society, to destroy a people. It is rape as genocide.

It is also rape made sexy for the perpetrators by the power of the rapist, which is absolute, to select the victims at will. They walk into rooms of captive women and point, "you, you, and you," and take you out. Many never return. It is rape made more arousing by the ethnic hostility against the designated "enemy," made to feel justified by the notion that it is "for Serbia," which they say as they thrust into the women and make them sing patriotic songs.[4] It is rape made to seem right by decades of lies about the supposed behavior of that enemy – years and years of propaganda campaigns, including in schools, full of historical lies and falsified data. In this effort, rapes and murders carried out by Serbs against non-Serbs are presented to the Serbian population on television as rapes and murders of Serbs by Muslims and Croats. The way in which pornography is believed in the men's bodies as well as in their minds gives this war propaganda a special potency.

This is also rape made especially exciting for the perpetrators by knowing that there are no limits on what they can do, by knowing that these women can and will be raped to death. Although the orders provide motivation enough, the rapes are made sexually enjoyable, irresistible even, by the fact that the women are about to be sacrificed, by the powerlessness of the women and children in the face of their imminent murder at the hands of their rapists. This is murder as the ultimate sexual act.

It will not help to say that this is violence, not sex, for the men involved. When the men are told to take the women away and not bring them back, first they rape them, then they kill them, and then sometimes rape them again and cut off their breasts and tear out their wombs. One woman was allowed to live only as long as she kept her Serbian captor hard all night orally, night after night after night, from midnight to 5:00 AM. What he got was sex for him. The aggression was the sex.

This is rape as torture as well as rape as extermination. In the camps, it is at once mass rape and serial rape in a way that is indistinguishable from prostitution. Prostitution is that part of everyday nonwar life that is closest to what we see done to women in this war. The daily life of prostituted women consists of serial rape, war or no war. The brothel-like arrangement of the rape/death camps parallels the brothels of so-called peacetime: captive women impounded to be passed from man to man in order to be raped.

This is also rape as a policy of ethnic uniformity and ethnic conquest, of annexation and expansion, of acquisition by one nation of other nations. It is rape because a Serb wants your apartment. Most distinctively, this is rape as ethnic expansion through forced reproduction. African American women were forcibly impregnated through rape under slavery. The Nazis required Eastern European women to get special permission for abortions if impregnated by German men. In genocide, it is more usual for the babies on the other side to be killed. Croatian and Muslim women are being raped, and then denied abortions, to help make a Serbian state by making Serbian babies.

If this were racial rape, as Americans are familiar with it, the children would be regarded as polluted, dirty, and contaminated, even as they are sometimes given comparative privileges based on "white" blood. But because this is ethnic rape, lacking racial markers, the children are regarded by the aggressors as somehow clean and purified, as "cleansed" ethnically. The babies made with Muslim and Croatian women are regarded as Serbian babies. The idea seems to be to create a fifth column within Muslim and Croatian society of children – all sons? – who will rise up and join their fathers. Much Serbian fascist ideology simply adopts and adapts Nazi views. This one is the ultimate achievement of the Nazi ideology that culture is genetic.

The spectacle of the United Nations troops violating those they are there to protect adds a touch of the perverse. My correspondent added that some UN troops are participating in raping Muslim and Croatian women taken from Serb-run rape/death camps. She reports that "the UN presence has apparently increased the trafficking in women and girls through the opening of brothels, brothel-massage parlors, peep shows, and the local production of pornographic films." There are also reports that a former UNPROFOR commander accepted offers from a Serbian commander to bring him Muslim girls for sexual use. All this is an example of the male bond across official lines. It pointedly poses a problem women have always had with male protection: Who is going to watch the men who are watching the men who are supposedly watching out for us? Each layer of male protection adds a layer to violence against women. Perhaps intervention by a force of armed women should be considered.

Now, the use of media technology is highly developed. Before, the Nazis took pictures of women in camps, forced women into brothels in camps, and took pictures of naked women running to their deaths. They also created events that did not happen through media manipulation. In this war the aggressors have at hand the new cheap, mobile, accessible, and self-contained moving-picture technology. The saturation of what was Yugoslavia with pornography upon the dissolution of communism – pornography that was largely controlled by Serbs, who had the power – has created a population of men prepared to experience sexual pleasure in torturing and killing women. It also paved the way for the use on television of footage of actual rapes, with the ethnicity of the victims and perpetrators switched, to inflame Serbs against Muslims and Croatians. In the conscious and open use of pornography, in making pornography of atrocities, in the sophisticated use of pornography as war propaganda, this is perhaps the first truly modern war.

Although these acts flagrantly violate provision after provision of international law, virtually nothing has been done about them for well over two years. Now the international machinery seems finally to be lumbering into action, even as more men, women, and children are being liquidated daily. To explain this slow response, it is important to consider that most human rights instruments empower states to act against states, not individuals or groups to act for themselves. This is particularly odd given that international human rights law recognizes only violations of human rights by state actors. In other words, only entities like those who do the harm are empowered to act to stop them. It would have seemed clear after 1945 that states often violate the rights of those who are not states and who have no state to act for them. The existing structure of international law was substantially created in response to this. Yet its architects could not bring themselves to empower individuals and groups to act against individuals, groups, or states when their human rights were violated.

This problem is particularly severe for women's human rights because women are typically raped not by governments but by what are called individual men. The government just does nothing about it. This may be tantamount to being raped by the state, but it is legally seen as "private," therefore as not a human rights violation. In an international world order in which only states can violate human rights, most rape is left out. The role of the state in permitting women to be raped with impunity can be exposed, but the structural problem in addressing it remains.

There is a convergence here between ways of thinking about women and ways of thinking about international law and politics. The more a conflict can be framed as within a state – as a civil war, as domestic, as private – the less effective the human rights model becomes. The closer a fight comes to home, the more "feminized" the victims become, no matter what their gender, and the less likely it is that international human rights will be found violated, no matter what was done.[5] Croatia and Bosnia-Herzegovina are being treated like women,[6] women gang-raped on a mass scale. This is not an analogy; far less is it a suggestion that this rape is wrong only because the women belong to a man's state. It identifies the treatment of a whole polity by the treatment of the women there.[7]

In the structure of international human rights, based as it is on the interest of states in their sovereignty as such, no state has an incentive to break rank by going after another state for how it treats women – thus setting a standard of human rights treatment for women that no state is prepared to meet within its own borders or is willing to be held to internationally. When men sit in rooms, being states, they are largely being men. They protect each other; they identify with each other; they try not to limit each other in ways they themselves do not want to be limited. In other words, they do not represent women. There is no state we can point to and say, "This state effectively guarantees women's human rights. There we are free and equal."

In this statist structure, each state's lack of protection of women's human rights is internationally protected, and that is called protecting state sovereignty. A similar structure of insulation between women and accountability for their violations exists domestically. Raped women are compelled to go to the state; men make the laws and decide if they will enforce them. When women are discriminated against, they have to go to a human rights commission and try to get it to move. This is called protecting the community. It is the same with international human rights, only more so: only the state can hurt you, but to redress it you have to get the state to act for you. In international law there are a few exceptions to this, but in the current emergency in Bosnia-Herzegovina and Croatia they are of no use. Each state finds its reasons to do nothing, which can be read as not wanting to set a higher standard of accountability for atrocities to women than those they are prepared to be held to themselves.

Formally, wartime is an exception to the part of this picture that exempts most rape, because atrocities by soldiers against civilians are always considered state acts. The trouble has been that men do in war what they do in peace, only more so; so when it comes to women, the complacency that surrounds peacetime extends to wartime, no matter what the law says. Every country in this world has a legal obligation to stop the Serbian aggressors from doing what they are doing, but until Bosnia-Herzegovina went to the International Court of Justice and sued Serbia for genocide, including rape, no one did a thing.[8] In so doing, Bosnia-Herzegovina is standing up for women in a way that no state ever has. The survivors I work with also filed our own civil suit in New York against Karadžić for an injunction against genocide, rape, torture, forced pregnancy, forced prostitution, and other sex and ethnic discrimination that violates women's international human rights.[9]

A war crimes tribunal to enforce accountability for mass genocidal rape is being prepared by the United Nations. There are precedents in the Tokyo trials after World War II for command responsibility for mass rape. Beyond precedent, the voices of the victims have been heard in the structuring of the new tribunal. To my knowledge, no one asked Jewish survivors how the trials at Nuremberg should be conducted, nor do I think the women raped in Nanking were asked what they needed in order to be able to testify about their rapes. The issue of accountability to victims has been raised here formally for the first time: How can we create a war crimes tribunal that is accessible to victims of mass sexual atrocity? What will make it possible for victims of genocidal rape to speak about their violations?

The genocidal rapes of this war present the world with a historic opportunity: that this becomes the time and place, and these the women, when the world recognizes that violence against women violates human rights. That when a woman is raped, the humanity of a human being is recognized to be violated. When the world says never again – not in war, not in peace – and this time means it.

Author's Note: Earlier versions of this material were delivered at the United Nations World Conference on Human Rights, Vienna, on June 17, 1993, and at the Zagreb University Law School, Zagreb, on June 25, 1993. The intellectual and research collaboration of Natalie Nenadic and Asja Armanda, all the women of Kareta Feminist Group, and the survivors made this work possible.

Notes

1. Natalie Nenadic, letter to author, October 1992, from Zagreb, Croatia.

2. Citations are provided in Theodore Meron, "Rape as a Crime under International Humanitarian Law," *American Journal of International Law* 87 (1993): 424–28.

3. Susan Brownmiller, in "Making Female Bodies the Battlefield" (this volume), provides one illustration.

4. All the specific examples from this war are taken directly from my work with survivors. Supporting information is contained in Roy Gutman, *Witness to Genocide* (New York, 1993) and sources referenced in my "Crimes of War, Crimes of Peace," in *Of Human Rights,* ed. S. Shute and J. Gardner (New York, 1993).

5. This insight was first expressed to me by Asja Armanda of Kareta Feminist Group.

6. For an analysis that "in 1991/1992, Croatia is a woman," see Katja Gattin for Kareta, "Where have all the feminists gone?" (unpublished paper, January 20, 1992, Zagreb).

7. His Excellency Muhamed Sacirbey, ambassador and permanent representative of Bosnia and Herzegovina to the United Nations, brilliantly argued before the Security Council on August 30, 1993, that "Bosnia and Herzegovina is being

gang-raped" by being forced into submission by violence and aggression, including rape, deprived of the means of self-defense, and then being treated as if it were seduction, through forcing the victim to embrace the consequences and denying legal relief.

8. Order of Provisional Measures, *Application of the Convention on the Prevention and Punishment of the Crime of Genocide (Bosnia and Herzegovina v. Yugoslavia [Serbia and Montenegro])*, no.93/9 International Court of Justice (April 8, 1993).

9. *K. v. Karadzic*, Civ. No. 93–CN–1163 (S.D.N.Y. 1993).

Surfacing Gender: Reconceptualizing Crimes against Women in Time of War

Rhonda Copelon

Introduction

Historically, the rape of women in war has drawn occasional and short-lived international attention. Most of the time rape has been invisible, or comes to light as part of the competing diplomacies of war, illustrating the viciousness of the conqueror or the innocence of the conquered. When war is done, it is comfortably cabined as a mere inevitable "by-product of war," a matter of indiscipline, of soldiers revved up by war, needy, and briefly "out of control."

Military histories rarely refer to rape, and military tribunals rarely either charge or sanction it. This is true even where rape and forced prostitution are mass or systematic, as with the rape of women in both theaters of the Second World War;[1] it is even true where the open, mass, and systematic rape has been thought to shock the conscience of the world, such as in the "rape of Nanking"[2] or the rape of an estimated 200,000 Bengali women during the war of independence from Pakistan.[3] Though discussed in the judgment of the International Military Tribunal in Tokyo, rape was not separately charged against the Japanese commander as a crime. In Bangladesh, amnesty was quietly traded for independence.

The question today is whether the terrible rape of women in the war in the former Yugoslavia will likewise disappear into history or at best will survive as an exceptional case. The apparent uniqueness of the rape of women in Bosnia-Herzegovina, directed overwhelmingly against Bosnian-Muslim women, is a product of the invisibility of the rape of women through history as well as in the present. Geopolitical factors – that this is occurring in Europe, is perpetrated by white men against white, albeit largely Muslim women, and contains the seeds of a new world war – cannot be ignored in explaining the visibility of these rapes. By contrast, the rape of 50 percent of the women of the indigenous Yuracruz people in Ecuador by mercenaries of an agribusiness company seeking to "cleanse" the land is invisible, just as the routine rape of women in the the civil wars in Peru, Liberia, and Burma, for example, has gone largely unreported.[4]

Moreover, just as historically the condemnation of rape in war has rarely been about the abuse of women as a crime of gender, so the mass rape in Bosnia has captured world attention and remains there largely because of its association with "ethnic cleansing," or genocide. In one week, a midday women's talk show opened with the script, "In Bosnia, they are raping the enemy's women . . . ," and a leading Croatian-American scholar blithely distinguished "genocidal" rape from "normal" rape. Our ad hoc Women's Coalition against Crimes against Women in the Former Yugoslavia spoke of rape as a weapon of war whether used to dilute ethnic identity, destabilize the civilian population, or reward soldiers. But the public was nodding: Yes, when rape is a vehicle of genocide.

The elision of genocide and rape in the focus on "genocidal rape" as a means of emphasizing the heinousness of the rape of Muslim women in Bosnia is thus dangerous. Rape and genocide are separate atrocities. Genocide – the effort to destroy a people based on its identity as a people – evokes the deepest horror and warrants the severest condemnation. Rape is sexualized violence that seeks to humiliate, terrorize, and destroy a woman based on her identity as a woman. Both are based on total contempt for and dehumanization of the victim, and both give rise to unspeakable brutalities. Their intersection in the Serbian and, to a lesser extent, the Croatian aggressions in Bosnia defines an ineffable living hell for women. From the standpoint of these women, they are inseparable.

But to emphasize as unparalleled the horror of genocidal rape is factually dubious and risks rendering rape invisible once again. Even in war, rape is not fully recognized as an atrocity. When the ethnic war ceases or is forced back into the bottle, will the crimes against women, the voices of women, and their struggles to survive be vindicated? Or will condemnation be limited to this seemingly exceptional case? Will the women who are brutally raped for domination, terror, booty, or revenge – in Bosnia and elsewhere – be heard?

Whether the rape, forced prostitution, and forced impregnation of women will be effectively prosecuted before the recently created UN ad hoc International Tribunal,[5] whether the survivors will obtain redress, or whether impunity will again be the agreed-upon or de facto cost of "peace" is up for grabs. The pressure of survivors and their advocates, together with the global women's human rights movement, will make the difference. The situation presents a historic opportunity as well as an imperative to insist on justice for the women of Bosnia as well as to press for a feminist reconceptualization of the role and legal understanding of rape in war.

To do this, we must surface gender in the midst of genocide at the same time as we avoid dualistic thinking. We must critically examine the claim that rape as a tool of "ethnic cleansing" is unique, worse than or not comparable to other forms of rape in war or in peace, at the same time as we recognize that rape together with genocide inflicts multiple, intersectional harms.[6] This combination of the particular and the general is critical if the horrors experienced by women in Bosnia are to be appreciated and if that experience is to have meaning for women brutalized in lesser-known theaters of war or in the byways of daily life.

This chapter examines the evolving legal status of rape in war with attention to both the particular and the general as well as to the tension between them. The opening section focuses on the two central questions of conceptualization. The first is whether these gender crimes are fully recognized as war crimes under the Geneva Conventions, the cornerstone of what is called "humanitarian" law — that is, the prohibitions that have made war itself permissible. The second is whether international law does or should distinguish between "genocidal rape" and mass rape for other purposes. In this regard it examines the limitations and the potential in the concept of "crimes against humanity" as well as the relation between gender and nationality/ethnicity in the crimes committed against women in Bosnia. The second section looks at the viability of the ad hoc International Tribunal as well as the gender issues presented.

Reconceptualizing Rape, Forced Prostitution, and Forced Pregnancy in War

IS RAPE A WAR CRIME?

Although news of the mass rapes of women in Bosnia had an electrifying effect and became a significant factor in the demand for the creation of an international war crimes tribunal, the leading question for a time was whether rape and other forms of sexual abuse are "war crimes" within the meaning of the Geneva Conventions and the internationally agreed-upon norms that bind all nations whether or not they have signed the Conventions. The answer is not unequivocal.

The question is not whether rape is technically a crime or prohibited in war. Rape has long been viewed as a criminal offense under national and international rules of war.[7] The 1949 Geneva Conventions as well as the 1977 Protocols regarding the protection of civilians in war explicitly prohibit rape, enforced prostitution, and any form of indecent assault and call for special protection of women, including separate quarters with supervision and searches by women only.[8] Yet it is significant that where rape and other forms of sexual assault are explicitly mentioned, they are categorized as an outrage upon personal dignity, or crimes against honor.[9] Crimes of violence, including murder, mutilation, cruel treatment, and torture, are treated separately.

The concept of rape as a crime against dignity and honor as opposed to a crime of violence is a core problem. Formal sanctions against rape range from minimal to extreme. Where rape has been treated as a grave crime, it is because it violates the honor of the man and his exclusive right to sexual possession of his woman as property. Thus, in the United States the death penalty against rape was prevalent in southern states as a result of a combination of racism and sexism.[10] Similarly, the media often refer to the mass rape in Bosnia as the rape of "the enemy's women" – the enemy in this formulation being the male combatant and the seemingly all-male nation, religious, or ethnic group.

Under the Geneva Conventions, the concept of honor is somewhat more enlightened: rape is a crime against the honor and dignity of women.[11] But this too is problematic. Where rape is treated as a crime against honor, the honor of women is called into question and virginity or chastity is often a precondition.[12] Honor implies the loss of station or respect; it reinforces the social view, internalized by women, that the raped woman is dishonorable. And while the concept of dignity potentially embraces more profound concerns, standing alone it obfuscates the fact that rape is fundamentally violence against women – violence against a woman's body, autonomy, integrity, selfhood, security, and self-esteem as well as her standing in the community. This failure to recognize rape as violence is critical to the traditionally lesser or ambiguous status of rape in humanitarian law.

The issue then is not whether rape is a war crime, but whether it is a crime of the gravest dimension. Under the Geneva Conventions, the term is "grave breach." The significance of a war crime's being a "grave breach" is threefold. On the level of discourse it calls attention to the egregiousness of the assault. On the practical level, it is not necessary that rape be mass or systematic: one act of rape is punishable. Finally, only crimes that are grave breaches give rise to universal jurisdiction under the Geneva Conventions. Universal jurisdiction means that every nation has an obligation to bring the perpetrators to justice through investigating, arresting, and prosecuting offenders in its own courts or extraditing them to more appropriate forums. The existence of universal jurisdiction also provides a legal rationale for trying such crimes before an international tribunal and for the obligation of states to cooperate. If rape were not a "grave breach" of the Geneva Conventions, some international jurists would argue that it can be redressed only by the state to which the wrongdoer belonged or in which the wrong occurred, and not by an International Tribunal.[13]

The relevant portions of the Geneva Conventions do not specifically mention rape in the list of crimes considered "grave breaches." Included are "willful killing, torture, or inhumane treatment" and "willfully causing great suffering or serious injury to body or health."[14] Clearly these categories are broad and generic enough to encompass rape and sexual abuse.[15] But in addition to qualifying as "willfully causing great suffering or serious injury to body or health" or as "inhumane treatment," it is important that rape be recognized as a form of torture.

When the Geneva Conventions were drafted, the view that torture was a method of extracting information was dominant. Today, however, this distinction has been largely abandoned, although it endures in popular thinking. The historian Edward Peters writes: "It is not primarily the victim's information, but the victim, that torture needs to win – or reduce to powerlessness."[16] Recent treaties define torture as the willful infliction of severe physical or mental pain or suffering not only to elicit information, but also to punish, intimidate, or discriminate, to obliterate the victim's personality or diminish her personal capacities.[17] Thus torture is now commensurate with willfully causing great suffering or injury. Moreover, it is not simply or necessarily the infliction of terrible physical pain; it is also the use of pain, sensory deprivation, isolation, and humiliation as a pathway to the mind. Indeed, in the contemporary understanding of torture, degradation is both vehicle and goal.[18]

Although largely ignored until recently by human rights advocates, the testimonies and studies of women tortured by dictatorial regimes and military occupations make it clear that rape is one of the most common, terrible, and effective forms of torture used against women.[19] Rape attacks the integrity of the woman as a person as well as her identity as a woman. It renders her, in the words of Lepa Mladjenovic, a psychotherapist and Serbian feminist antiwar activist, "homeless in her own body."[20] It strikes at a woman's power; it seeks to degrade and destroy her; its goal is domination and dehumanization.

Likewise, the testimonies in this book of raped women, whether they were attacked once or forced into prostitution, make it clear that rape is both a profound physical attack and a particularly egregious form of psychological torture. They document the intersection of contempt for and conquest of women based on their sex as well as on their national, religious, or cultural identity. They demonstrate the significance of the threat, fear, or reality of pregnancy as well as of the fact that in Bosnia the rapists are in many cases former colleagues, neighbors, or even friends.

Indeed, torturers know well the power of the intimate in the process of breaking down their victim.[21] Because rape is a transposition of the intimate into violence, rape by acquaintances, by those one has trusted, is particularly world shattering and thus a particularly effective tool of ethnic cleansing. It is no wonder that local Bosnian Serbs are being incited and, in some cases, recruited to rape. Their stories in this collection, notwithstanding their self-justificatory quality, reflect the common methods of training torturers – exposure to and engagement in increasingly unthinkable violence and humiliation.[22]

Despite the fact that rape in Bosnia has drawn substantial international condemnation, the United Nations' position on the status of rape as a grave breach of humanitarian law is not clear. The UN Human Rights Commission condemned "the abhorrent practice of rape and abuse of women and children in the former Yugoslavia which, *in the circumstances,* constitutes a war crime" and urged all nations to "exert every effort to bring to justice . . . all those individuals directly or indirectly involved."[23] While this implies that rape is a "grave breach," the limitation to the particular "circumstances" could be read as a limitation to the context of ethnic cleansing. The Declaration of the 1993 World Conference of Human Rights in Vienna, though strongly worded, is limited to "systematic" rape and abuse.[24]

Most significantly, the Report subsequently adopted by the Security Council that constitutes the statute establishing the jursisdiction of the International Tribunal largely tracks the Geneva Conventions' definition of grave breach and does not explicitly list rape as a grave breach or describe it as implicit in the recognized categories.[25] But if, as a consequence of women's pressure, it is prosecuted as such and the various bodies of the UN begin to refer to rape as a grave breach, then this practice will effectively amend or expand the meaning of grave breach in the Conventions and Protocols. This emphasizes the importance, from a practical as well as a moral perspective, of insisting that all rape be subject to punishment, not only mass or genocidal rape. It should be noted that under the Geneva Conventions, responsibility is imputed to commanders where they knew, or should have known, of the likelihood of rape and failed to take all measures within their power to prevent or suppress it.[26]

It is also important to point out the importance of the Vienna Declaration's explicit inclusion of forced pregnancy in its condemnation of the mass atrocities in the former Yugoslavia. This is clearly a product of the intensive women's mobilization that preceded the World Conference. As the testimonies in this book indicate, forced pregnancy must be seen as a separate offense: the expressed intention to make women pregnant is an additional form of psychological torture; the goal of impregnation leads to imprisoning women and raping them until they are pregnant; the fact of pregnancy, whether aborted or not, continues the initial torture in a most intimate and invasive form; and bearing the child of rape, whether placed for adoption or not, has a potentially lifelong impact on the woman and her place in the community.[27]

GENOCIDAL RAPE VERSUS "NORMAL" RAPE:
WHEN IS MASS RAPE A CRIME AGAINST HUMANITY?

"Crimes against humanity" were first formally recognized in the Charter and Judgment of the Nuremberg Tribunal; they do not depend on adherence to a treaty, and they too give rise to universal jurisdiction. Since crimes against humanity can be committed in any war, it is irrelevant whether the war in the former Yugoslavia is international or internal.

Rape has been separately listed, and forced prostitution acknowledged, as a "crime against humanity" in the Report establishing the statute of the International Tribunal.[28] This is not without precedent. After the Second World War, Local Council Law No. 10, which provided the foundation for the trials of lesser Nazis by the Allied forces, also listed rape as a crime against humanity, although no one was prosecuted.[29] Nonetheless, the Security Council's reaffirmation that rape is a "crime against humanity," and therefore among the most egregious breaches of civilization, is profoundly important. But the meaning of this designation and its import for other contexts in which women are subjected to mass rape apart from ethnic cleansing are not clear. The danger, as always, is that extreme examples produce narrow principles.

The commentary on this aspect of the jurisdiction of the current Tribunal signals this danger. It explains crimes against humanity as "inhumane acts of a very serious nature, such as willful killing, *torture or rape, committed as part of a* widespread *or* systematic attack against any civilian population on national, political, ethnic, racial, or religious grounds."[30] Several aspects of this definition deserve comment.

First, on the positive side, the statute correctly encompasses violations that are widespread but not necessarily systematic. The law wisely does not require massive numbers but specifies patterns of abuse. Particularly with rape, numbers are unprovable: a small percentage of women will ultimately come forward, and the significance of rape threatens to become drowned in statistical claims. Moreover, the statute does not require that rape be ordered or centrally organized. Commanders can be held responsible where widespread violence is known and tolerated.[31] In Bosnia, rape is clearly a conscious tool of war and ethnic cleansing. It is politically and ethically important for the Tribunal to investigate and prove the chain of command, but it is likewise important that leaders can be held legally responsible without proof that rape was systematic or committed under orders.

Second, the commentary on the statute does rank rape with torture, at least where it is widespread or systematic. But it undercuts this by appearing to conflate what were originally understood as two separate and independent criteria of crimes against humanity: gross acts of violence *and* persecution-based offenses. Under the original concept, rape should qualify as a gross act of violence and accordingly, if widespread or systematic, would independently qualify as a crime against humanity. By merging the criterion of gross violence with persecution-based offenses, the commentary could limit prosecution to rape that is undertaken as a method of persecution on the specified grounds. Since the statute of the Tribunal lists rape and persecution separately, it is not clear, until put in practice, whether the broader understanding will prevail.

The narrow view is quite prevalent, however. The international and popular condemnation of the rapes in Bosnia tends to be either explicitly or implicitly based on the fact that rape is being used as a tactic of ethnic cleansing. Genocidal rape is widely seen not as a modality of rape but as unique. The distinction commonly drawn between genocidal rape and "normal" rape in war or in peace is proffered not as a typology, but rather as a hierarchy. But to exaggerate the distinctiveness of genocidal rape obscures the atrocity of common rape.

Genocidal rape often involves gang rapes, is outrageously brutal, and is done in public or in front of children or partners. It involves imprisoning women in rape "camps" or raping them repetitively. These are also characteristics of the most common rape in war – rape for booty or to boost the morale of soldiers; and they are common characteristics of the use of rape as a form of torture and terror by dictatorial regimes.[32]

The notion that genocidal rape is uniquely a weapon of war is also problematic. The rape of women is a weapon of war where it is used to spread political terror, as in the civil war in Peru. It is a weapon of war where, as in Bosnia and elsewhere, it is used against women to destabilize the society and force families to flee, because in time of war women are the mainstay of the civilian population, even more than in peacetime.[33]

The rape of women, where permitted or systematized as "booty" of war, is likewise an engine of war: it maintains the morale of soldiers, feeds their hatred and sense of superiority, and keeps them fighting. The Japanese military industrialized the sexual slavery of women in the Second World War: 200,000 to 400,000 mostly Korean, but also Philippine, Chinese, and Dutch women from Indonesia were deceived or disappeared into "comfort stations," raped repeatedly and moved from battlefield to battlefield to motivate as well as reward the Japanese soldiers. Genocide was not a goal, but it is believed that 70 to 90 percent of these women died in captivity, and among the known survivors, none were subsequently able to bear children.[34] For similar reasons, the United States military in Vietnam raped Vietnamese women and established brothels, relying on dire economic necessity rather than kidnapping to fill them.[35] Indeed, the foregoing testimonies of the Bosnian Serbian rapists reveal an admixture of all these goals.

At the same time, genocidal or ethnic cleansing rape, as practiced in Bosnia, does have some aspects that are particularly tailored to its goals of driving women from their homes or destroying their possibility of reproducing within and "for" their community. As the preceding testimonies suggest, that women are raped by men familiar to them exacerbates their trauma and the impulse to flee the community because trust and safety are no longer possible. This is particular to the Bosnian situation, where war and propaganda have made enemies out of neighbors.

The second and more generally distinctive feature of genocidal rape is the focus on women as reproductive vessels. The explicit and common threat to make Muslim women bear "Serbian babies" (as if the child were the product of sperm only) justifies repetitive rape and aggravates her terror and potential unacceptability to her community. Bengali women were raped to lighten their race and produce a class of outcaste mothers and children. Enslaved African women in the southern United States were raped as property to produce babies bartered, sold, and used as property.[36] While intentional impregnation is properly treated as a separate offense, it should also be noted that pregnancy is a common consequence of rape. In situations where women are raped repeatedly, most fertile women will become pregnant at some point. When the United States navy took over Saipan, for example, one observer reports that virtually all the women, who had been enslaved as comfort women for the Japanese army, were pregnant.[37]

These distinctive characteristics do not place genocidal rape in a class by itself; nor do they reflect the full range of atrocities, losses, and suffering that the combination of rape and ethnic cleansing inflicts. The women victims and survivors in Bosnia are being subjected to crimes against humanity based on ethnicity and religion, and based on gender. It is critical to recognize both and to acknowledge that the intersection of ethnic and gender violence has its own particular characteristics.

This brings me to the third concern: the complete failure of the United Nations and the international community in general to recognize that persecution based on gender must be recognized as its own category of crimes against humanity. The crystallization of the concept of crimes against humanity in the wake of the Holocaust has meant that "it" is popularly associated with religious and ethnic genocide. But the concept is a broader one, and the categories of persecution are explicitly open ended, capable of expanding to embrace new understandings of persecution.

With respect to women, the need is to acknowledge that gender has historically not been viewed as a relevant category of victimization. The frequency of mass rape and the absence of sanction are sufficient evidence. In the Holocaust, the gender persecutions – the rape and forced prostitution of women as well as the extermination of gay people – were obscured.[38] The absence of gender as a basis for persecution is not peculiar to the concept of crimes against humanity. A parallel problem exists in the international standards for political asylum, which require a well-founded fear of persecution, but do not explicitly recognize gender as a source of persecution.[39] The expansion of the concept of crimes against humanity to include gender is thus part of the broader movement to end the historical invisibility of gender violence as a humanitarian and human rights violation.

Moreover, the particular goals and defining aspects of genocidal rape do not detract from, but rather elucidate the nature of rape as a crime of gender as well as ethnicity. Women are targets not simply because they "belong to" the enemy, but precisely because they keep the civilian population functioning and are essential to its continuity. They are targets because they too *are* the enemy; because of their power as well as vulnerability as women, including their sexual and reproductive power. They are targets because of *hatred* of their power as women; because of endemic objectification of women; because rape embodies male domination and female subordination.

The crime of forced impregnation – central as it is to genocidal rape – also elucidates the gender component. Since under patriarchy women are viewed as little more than vessels for childbearing, involuntary pregnancy is commonly viewed as natural – divinely ordained perhaps – or simply an unquestioned fact of life. As a result, the risk of pregnancy in all rape is treated not as an offense, but as a sequela. Forced pregnancy has drawn condemnation only when it reflects an intent to harm the victimized race. In Bosnia, the taunt that Muslim women will bear Serbian babies is not simply an ethnic harm, particularly in light of the prevalence of ethnically mixed families. When examined through a feminist lens, forced pregnancy appears as an assault on the reproductive self-determination of women; it expresses the desire to mark the rape and rapist upon the woman's body and upon the woman's life.

Finally, that the rape of women is also designed to humiliate the men or destroy "the enemy" itself reflects the fundamental objectification of women. Women are the target of abuse at the same time as their subjectivity is completely denied. The persistent failure to acknowledge the gender dimension of rape and sexual persecution is thus a most effective means of perpetuating it.

In sum, the international attention focused on Bosnia challenges the world to squarely recognize sexual violence against women in war as torture. Moreover, it is not enough for rape to be viewed as a crime against humanity when it is the vehicle of some other form of persecution; it must also be recognized as a crime against humanity because it is invariably a persecution based on gender. This is essential if the women of Bosnia are to be understood as full subjects as well as objects in this terrible victimization and if the international attention focused on Bosnia is to have meaning for women subjected to rape in other parts of the world.

Seeking Gender Justice

The history of atrocities and oppression and of festering hatreds among the peoples of the former Yugoslavia underscores the necessity of the demand, articulated by feminist critics of the war, for "justice, not revenge."[40] It is troubling as well as significant that the United Nations has taken steps to establish an International Tribunal to try the perpetrators of war crimes and crimes against humanity in the former Yugoslavia. On the negative side, the choice of an ad hoc Tribunal rather than a permanent international criminal court reveals the shallowness of the international commitment to justice and opens the process to excessive politicization. At the same time, the creation of this Tribunal lessens the possibility that legal amnesty will be the price of peace. But it is no guarantee against de facto impunity; nor does it guarantee that the suffering of the women will be vindicated. This section outlines some of the problems with the Tribunal as it is at present envisaged and suggests some alternative routes, in response to Helke Sander's final ruminations in her letter to Lysistrata.

THE INTERNATIONAL TRIBUNAL

The potential efficacy of the new International Tribunal is riddled with doubt. Unless there is a radical change in the military context, this

Tribunal, unlike those at Nuremberg and Tokyo, will not sit in judgment of conquered aggressors, but will be called upon primarily to judge the victors – the Bosnian Serbs and the Serbian leaders. Since the Tribunal cannot compel the presence of the indicted criminals, it must count on their being arrested if they move beyond their own countries or those that protect them. Thus the rejection of the option of trials in absentia is likely to reduce the Tribunal to publishing detailed, formal indictments – an international wanted list – as a historical record and a constraint on the movement of the accused.

Beyond its formal powers, the United Nations has utterly failed to provide the Tribunal with the resources necessary to do the extensive and careful fact finding required. The UN Commission of Experts that laid the foundation for the Tribunal operated on a shoestring at a time when the survivors of atrocities were most accessible. To prosecute the leaders, the issues of command responsibility and Serbian complicity require investigation, and yet the UN relies on the investigations of a grossly underfinanced Special Rapporteur and independent human rights missions. Moreover, the Tribunal, modeled after Nuremberg, is likely to consider only thirty cases. There is no mechanism for trying the thousands of direct perpetrators and low-level commanders. The UN seems to have forgotten that most of the Nazis were tried under the Local Council Law, which established the lesser war crimes tribunals. Moreover, the statute creating the Tribunal makes no provision for compensation or rehabilitation of the survivors.

Beyond these general defects are the gender defects. In addition to the ambiguous status of gender crimes in the statute that defines the substantive power of the Tribunal, there are substantial process concerns as well. Will women come forward? And how will they be treated when they do? It is a given that women are terrified and, at best, reluctant to come forward to charge rape. Admitting rape in a sexist society is a public dishonoring and has consequences for the ability to continue or build relationships with one's community and with male partners. Most women are silent about it.[41] To charge rape is to risk retaliation and death, a risk heightened by war and by knowing and being known to the rapist. To charge rape usually is to risk being raped again – figuratively, at least – by the law enforcers. The callous, humiliating, and debilitating treatment of women refugees by some members of the press and some human rights missions in this war only confirms the expectation of abuse by official investigatory bodies.

The designers of the Tribunal have done nothing to mitigate these fears. Ensuring sensitive and empowering gender justice ought to have been a central concern in the creation of the Tribunal.[42] This would include, at a minimum, gender sensitivity training of all personnel as well as the establishment of a special sex crimes unit staffed primarily by women experienced in eliciting evidence in an empowering as opposed to a traumatizing way. In respect to indictments and trials, survivors should not be publicly identified without their consent; certain proceedings should be held in camera with safeguards to prevent abuse; victims should be able to testify without face-to-face confrontation with the perpetrators while preserving the accused's rights through video and one-way observation; rules of evidence should forbid reference to a woman's prior sexual conduct, restrict the consent defense, and control cross-examination to prevent abuse as well as distortion; expert testimony on trauma should be permitted but not required; and victims should be entitled to the assistance of their own counsel and counselors. But these concerns have been effectively ignored. The statute creating the Tribunal recognizes the need to protect victims and witnesses from retaliation and to design rules of procedure and evidence that take into account the protection of victims in cases of rape and sexual assault. But beyond calling for protection of the victims' identity, the statute leaves to the Tribunal the responsibility to develop the rules.

As part of a broader demand for participation at all diplomatic and international levels, and in light of the particular salience of gender to the Tribunal process, women have also called for gender parity in staffing the Tribunal at every level. It is likely, however, that women's participation will be token.[43] This alone attests to the lack of concern for encouraging the participation of women survivors. Moreover, that it will devolve upon the Tribunal to design the rules under which rape and sexual abuse will be prosecuted highlights the disregard of this effort for the rights of women. Without continuing pressure, it is likely that the integrity of this Tribunal as well as its receptivity to women will be sacrificed.

ALTERNATIVE ROUTES

At the same time, it is essential that women create their own strategies for vindication and redress. Women have, of course, the possibility of establishing independent tribunals to symbolically try the perpetrators in

Bosnia and other contexts. Beyond that, international law provides some other tools.

The concept of universal jurisdiction, which applies to grave breaches, torture, genocide, and crimes against humanity, confers upon the separate nations both the power and obligation to try violators when they enter their territory. The nations of the world, and particularly of Europe, where the perpetrators are most likely to travel, might have a significant effect if they simply announced that they would vigorously search out, investigate, arrest, and prosecute or extradite those who crossed their borders. The Tribunal cannot function without this, and given its meager resources, national courts are an essential alternative. The absence of such declarations to date underscores the questions raised about the political will to try the offenders.

There is also the possibility of a more women-controlled legal remedy – the filing of private civil lawsuits for compensatory and punitive damages against the perpetrators when they enter their countries. In the United States a line of cases, instigated largely by victims of torture by military or dictatorial governments, has established the right of aliens to sue for human rights violations occurring anywhere in the world so long as the alleged perpetrator can be physically sued in the United States. The possibility of such suits in other countries that either follow the principles of Anglo-American jurisprudence or incorporate international law in their domestic law is being explored.[44]

Two such lawsuits have been filed against the Bosnian-Serbian leader Radovan Karadzic on behalf of Bosnian Muslim and Croatian women, women's organizations, and unnamed victims of atrocities committed under his command.[45] Karadzic was sued during successive stays in New York City in connection with UN-sponsored peace negotiations. If the court rejects his initial contention that he is entitled to immunity from suit because he was here on UN business, the case is likely to reach the issue of his responsibility for gross violations of human rights and humanitarian law. At this stage it is common for human rights violators to refuse to appear before the court, which then results, after a factual hearing, in a judgment for the plaintiffs by default.

These lawsuits cannot stop ongoing atrocities or guarantee concrete relief, but they have a profound symbolic value. They provide an official forum for examining atrocities and the responsibility of individuals for them, and they usually result in a judgment of wrongdoing and an award of substantial money damages, usually millions of dollars. Only in rare cases where the wrongdoer has substantial assets that can be discovered will the survivors actually recover the money. But these cases are not brought primarily for money. They are pursued as a wedge against impunity and an opportunity for survivors to tell the story and obtain vindication. They also make the perpetrators a little less secure: they cannot travel without risking the revelation of their crimes and the compromise of their political standing, personal reputations, families, property, or wealth.

Such lawsuits require international coordination, for which the growth of the global women's movement provides the foundation. Yes, Lysistrata, the leaders responsible should be arrested, not feted, in the countries to which they travel, and the actual rapists should not enjoy vacations or carry out international business without sanction. The cost of their atrocities, if it is not prison, should at the least be confinement to their own countries. Women can build the capacity to do this. We can publicize the violators' identities, track their peregrinations, and mobilize the legal and political resources to pressure countries to arrest and prosecute them and find lawyers to bring private suits. We can do it for the raped women in the former Yugoslavia, and we can do it wherever women's human rights are violated.

Conclusion

Given the formidable pressure being brought to bear by women survivors and the women's movement globally, it may well be that some few men will be indicted and even tried before the International Tribunal or national courts, at least if impunity is not again the price of peace. This would be precedent setting in international law and offer symbolic vindication to the untold numbers of women this war has rendered homeless in so many senses. Unless the gender dimension of rape in war is recognized, however, it will mean little for women where rape is not also a tool of genocide.

Emphasis on the gender dimension of rape in war is critical not only to surfacing women as full subjects of sexual violence in war, but also to recognizing the atrocity of rape in the time called peace. When women charge rape in war they are more likely to be believed, because their status as enemy, or at least "the enemy's" is recognized and because rape in war is seen as a product of exceptional circumstances. When women charge rape in everyday life, however, they are disbelieved largely because the ubiquitous war against women is denied.

From a feminist human rights perspective, gender violence has escaped sanction because it has not been viewed as violence and because the public/private dichotomy has shielded such violence in its most common and private forms.[46] The recognition of rape as a war crime is thus a critical step toward understanding rape as violence. The next is to recognize that rape that acquires the imprimatur of the state is not necessarily more brutal, relentless, or dehumanizing than the private rapes of everyday life.

This is not to say that rape is identical in the two contexts. There are differences here, just as there are differences between rape for the purpose of genocide and rape for the purpose of booty. War tends to intensify the brutality, repetitiveness, public spectacle, and likelihood of rape. War diminishes sensitivity to human suffering and intensifies men's sense of entitlement, superiority, avidity, and social license to rape. But the line is not so sharp. Gang rape in civilian life shares the repetitive, gleeful, and public character of rape in war. Marital rape, the most private of all, shares some of the particular characteristics of genocidal rape in Bosnia: it is repetitive, brutal, and exacerbated by betrayal; it assaults a woman's reproductive autonomy, may force her to flee her home and community, and is widely treated as legitimate in law and custom. Violation by a state official or enemy soldier is not necessarily more devastating than violation by an intimate.[47]

Every rape is a grave violation of physical and mental integrity. Every rape has the potential to profoundly debilitate, to render the woman homeless in her own body and destroy her sense of security in the world. Every rape is an expression of male domination and misogyny, a vehicle of terrorizing and subordinating women. Like torture, rape takes many forms, occurs in many contexts, and has different repercussions for different victims. Every rape is multidimensional, but not incomparable.

The rape of women in the former Yugoslavia challenges the world to refuse impunity to atrocity as well as to resist the powerful forces that would make the mass rape of Muslim women in Bosnia exceptional and thereby restrict its meaning for women raped in different contexts. It thus demands recognition of situational differences without losing sight of the commonalities. To fail to make distinctions flattens reality; and to rank the egregious demeans it.[48]

Notes

1. See, e.g., Susan Brownmiller, *Against Our Will: Men, Women, and Rape* (New York, 1975), pp.31–113.

2. The "rape of Nanking" refers to the brutal taking of Nanking by Japanese soldiers, which involved mass and open killing, looting, and rape that went on for several months. It is estimated that twenty thousand women were raped in the first month. See Friedman, *The Law of War: A Commentary/History,* vol. 2 (New York, 1972), p.46.

3. Brownmiller, *Against Our Will,* pp.78–86. Among the motives for these rapes was a genocidal one – to destroy the racial distinctiveness of the Bengali people.

4. Presentation of Guadelupe Leon, Panel on Military Violence and Sexual Slavery, 1993 UN Conference on Human Rights, NGO Parallel Activities, June 1993; Americas Watch and Women's Rights Project, *Untold Terror: Violence against Women in Peru's Armed Conflict* (New York, 1992); Asia Watch and Women's Rights Project, *Burma: Rape, Forced Labor, and Religious Persecution in Northern Arakan* (Washington, D.C., 1992); Shana Swiss, *Liberia: Women and Children Gravely Mistreated* (Boston, 1991). For other examples, see Shana Swiss and Joan E. Giller, "Rape as a Crime of War," *JAMA* 270 (August 4, 1993): 612.

5. The full title is International Tribunal for the Prosecution of Persons Responsible for Serious Violations of International Humanitarian Law Committed in the Territory of the Former Yugoslavia since 1991. See *Report of the Secretary-General Pursuant to Paragraph 2 of the Security Council Resolution 808 (1993),* S/25704 (May 3, 1993), para. 25, p.8.

6. On the concept of the significance of the intersection of categories of oppression, see Kimberle Crenshaw, "Demarginalizing the Intersection of Race and Sex: A Black Feminist Critique of Anti-Discrimination Doctrine, Feminist Theory, and Antiracist Politics," *University of Chicago Legal Forum,* 1989, pp.139–67.

7. See, e.g., Yougindra Khusalani, *Dignity and Honour of Women as Basic and Fundamental Human Rights* (Boston, 1982).

8. *Geneva Conventions relative to the Protection of Civilian Persons in Time of*

War, common art. 3, 1(a) and (c); arts. 27 and 76, 97 (hereafter, *Geneva Convention IV*); *Protocol Additional to the Geneva Conventions of 12 August 1949, and relating to the Protection of Victims of International Armed Conflicts (Protocol I)*, art. 76, and *Protocol Additional to the Geneva Conventions of 12 August 1949, and relating to the Protection of Victims of Non-International Armed Conflicts (Protocol II)*, art. 4, reprinted in Center for Human Rights, *Human Rights: A Compilation of International Instruments*, vol. 1 (second part) (New York, 1993), pp.799–939.

9. See, e.g., Ibid., *Geneva Convention IV*, art. 27, para. 2; *Protocol II*, art. 4.

10. This was recognized by the U.S. Supreme Court in striking the death penalty in *Coker v. Georgia*, 433 U.S. 584 (1977).

11. Khusalini, *Dignity and Honour*, pp.39–76.

12. See, e.g., Americas Watch and Women's Rights Project, *Untold Terror*.

13. It should be noted here that the concept of "grave breach" applies only to international conflict and not to civil war. Although there is debate about whether the conflict in the territory of the former Yugoslavia is international or internal, the UN has taken the position that the warring parties have agreed to abide by the rules governing international conflicts. *Report of the Secretary-General*, para. 25, p.8.

14. *Geneva Convention IV*, art. 147; *Protocol I*, arts. 11 and 85(3).

15. Khusalani, *Dignity and Honour*, pp.39–76.

16. Edward Peters, *Torture* (New York, 1985), p.164.

17. *UN Convention against Torture*, art. 1; *Inter-American Convention against Torture*, art. 2, reprinted in J. Herman Burgers and Hans Danelius, *The United Nations Convention against Torture – A Handbook on the Convention against Torture and Other Cruel, Inhuman and Degrading Treatment or Punishment* (Boston, 1988), appendix.

18. Amnesty International, *Report on Torture* (New York, 1974).

19. See, e.g., Ximena Bunster-Burotto, "Surviving beyond Fear: Women and Torture in Latin America," in *Women and Change in Latin America,* ed. June Nash and Helen Safa (Boston, 1986), pp.297–325; F. Allodi and S. Stiasny, "Women as Torture Victims," *Canadian Journal of Psychiatry* 35 (March 1990): 144–48; Inge Lunde and Jorge Ortmann, "Prevalence and Sequelae of Sexual Torture," *Lancet* 336 (August 1990): 289–91. While not the subject here, the rape of men is also a devastating crime of gender, designed as it is to humiliate through feminization.

20. Testimony before the Global Tribunal on Violations of Women's Human Rights, part of the NGO. Parallel Activities, 1993 World Conference on Human Rights, Vienna, June 15, 1993.

21. See Amnesty International, *Report on Torture;* Elaine Scarry, *The Body in Pain: The Making and Unmaking of the World* (New York, 1985), p.41; Judith Lewis Herman, *Trauma and Recovery* (New York, 1992).

22. See, e.g., Stanley Milgram, "Some Conditions of Obedience and Disobedience to Authority," *Human Relations* 18 (1965): 57–74. On the training of torturers, see Amnesty International, *Torture in Greece: The First Torturers' Trial, 1975* (New York, 1977); Mika Haritos-Fatouros, "The Official Torturer: A Learning Model for Obedience to the Authority of Violence," *Journal of Applied Social Psychology* 18 (1988): 1107–20.

23. UN Commission on Human Rights, *Rape and Abuse of Women in the Territory of the Former Yugoslavia,* report on the 49th sess., February 1–March 12, 1993, Economic and Social Council suppl. no.3, E/CN4/1993/122 (emphasis supplied).

24. The Conference agreed: "Violations of the human rights of women in situations of armed conflict are violations of the fundamental principles of international human rights and humanitarian law. All violations of this kind, including in particular murder, systematic rape, sexual slavery, and forced pregnancy, require a particularly effective response." *Report of the Drafting Committee, Addendum, Final Outcome of the World Conference on Human Rights,* A/conf.157/PC/add. 1 (June 24, 1993) (hereafter "Vienna Declaration").

25. Article 2 identifies as grave breaches "(a) wilfull killing; (b) torture or inhuman treatment, including biological experiments; (c) wilfully causing great suffering or serious bodily injury to body or health." *Report of the Secretary-General,* art. 2, paras. 37–40, pp.10–11.

26. *Protocol I,* art. 86.

27. Anne Tierney Goldstein, *Recognizing Forced Impregnation as a War Crime under International Law* (New York: Center for Reproductive Law and Policy, 1993), examines forced impregnation under the Geneva Conventions and as a means of genocide and enslavement.

28. *Report of the Secretary-General,* art. 5, paras. 47–49, p.13.

29. Khusalani, *Dignity and Honour,* pp.13–38, esp. p.23.

30. *Report of the Secretary-General,* art. 5, para. 48, p.13.

31. Ibid., art. 7, *Draft Code of Offenses against Peace and Security of Mankind,* UN GAOR, 6th sess. (1951), suppl. 9, doc. A/1858, art. 2(11).

32. See, e.g., Brownmiller, *Against Our Will;* Bunster-Burrotto, "Surviving beyond Fear"; Amnesty International, *Women on the Frontline* (New York, 1991).

33. Americas Watch and Women's Rights Project, *Untold Terror;* Swiss and Giller, "Rape as a Crime of War."

34. Testimony of Bok Dong Kim before the Global Tribunal on Violations of Women's Human Rights, NGO Parallel Activities, 1993 World Conference on Human Rights, Vienna, June 15, 1993. See also *Hearings before the United Nations Secretary-General (February 25, 1993)* (testimony of Hyo-chai Lee, MA, Soon-Kum Park, and Chung-Ok Yum, MFA, Korean Council for the Women Drafted for Military Sexual Service in Japan); Lourdes Sajor, "Women in Armed Conflict Situations," MAV/1993/WP.1 (September 21, 1993), prepared for Expert Group Meeting on Measures to Eradicate Violence against Women, UN Division for the Advancement of Women.

35. Brownmiller, *Against Our Will*, pp.86–113.

36. Angela Y. Davis, *Women, Race and Class* (New York, 1983), p.172.

37. Conversation with D. B.

38. See Brownmiller, *Against Our Will*, pp.48–78, for the unrecognized sexual violence against women on the part of Allied as well as Axis forces. See also Erwin J. Haeberle, "Swastika, Pink Triangle, and Yellow Star: The Destruction of Sexology and the Persecution of Homosexuals in Nazi Germany," in *Hidden from History: Reclaiming the Gay and Lesbian Past,* ed. Martin Duberman, Martha Vicinus, and George Channcez Jr. (New York, 1990), pp.365–79 (noting the gender aspect of the Nazi attacks on homosexuals reflected in the use of the pink triangle and charges of emasculation).

39. The Convention relating to the Status of Refugees recognizes persecution based on race, religion, nationality, membership in a particular social group, or political opinion. The "social group" category is currently being expanded to encompass gender claims, but this is not enough. See Pamela Goldberg and Nancy Kelly, "International Human Rights and Violence against Women," *Harvard Human Rights Journal* 6 (spring 1993).

40. Testimony of Slavika Kusic, Center for Women War Victims in Zagreb, before the Global Tribunal (see note 20).

41. At the Global Tribunal in Vienna, Fadila Memisevic of the Center for the Registration of War Crimes and Genocide in Zenica spoke of a woman in the refugee camp who was hated by the other women because she spoke out about the practice of rape and therefore cast the stigma on her sisters, who did not want to talk about it. For a discussion of the tensions between human rights documentation and the needs of survivors, see Swiss and Giller, "Rape as a Crime of War."

42. See International Women's Human Rights Law Clinic, *Gender Justice and the Constitution of the War Crimes Tribunal Pursuant to Security Council Resolution 808,* photocopy, 1993, on file with author.

43. For example, a list of twenty-three names proposed to the General Assem-

bly for the eleven judgeships contained only two women. Both were elected, but not easily. None of the nominees for chief prosecutor were women, and expertise in the issue of violence against women was not a criterion of selection.

44. The original case, *Filartiga v. Pena-Irala,* 630 F. 2d 876 (second circuit, 1980), resulted in a $10.4 million award against a Paraguayan torturer who was sued by the affected family after he was arrested by the Immigration and Naturalization Service, as a result of pressure from the Paraguayan community, because he was discovered residing illegally in the United States. Information on subsequent cases and on bringing such cases is available from Beth Stevens, Michael Ratner, or Peter Weiss at the Center for Constitutional Rights, 666 Broadway, New York, N.Y. 10012; FAX (212) 614–6499.

45. *Jane Doe v. Radovan Karadzic,* Civil Action no.93 Civ. 0878 (PKL)(U.S. Southern District of New York, filed 1993); *S. Kadic v. Radovan Karadzic,* Civil Action no.93 Civ. 1163 (PKL)(U.S. Southern District of New York, filed 1993).

46. See, e.g., Charlotte Bunch, "Women's Rights as Human Rights: Toward a Revision of Human Rights," *Human Rights Quarterly* 12 (1990): 486; Rhonda Copelon, "Intimate Terror: Understanding Domestic Violence as Torture"; and Celina Romany, "State Responsibility Goes 'Private': A Feminist Critique of the Public/Private Distinction in International Human Rights Law," in *International Women's Human Rights,* ed. Rebecca Cook (Philadelphia, 1994).

47. Herman, *Trauma and Recovery.*

48. As the Tribunal proceeds, you can write to United Nations Secretary-General Boutros Boutros-Ghali, to your country's ambassador to the United Nations, and to the judges and chief prosecutor of the Tribunal, which will be situated in The Hague. The two women judges are Gabrielle Kirk-MacDonald (United States) and Elizabeth Odio-Benito (Costa Rica).

Afterword
Have the Bosnian Rapes Opened a
New Era of Feminist Consciousness?

Cynthia Enloe

t is always dangerous to imagine that one is on the brink of something new – especially if what is imagined as new is also imagined as
good. It dulls one's attentiveness to the persisting bad old ways. It
lures one into underestimating the stamina of past distortive habits.
Nonetheless, in the early 1990s one could be excused for feeling as though
we're standing on – perhaps just precariously perched on – the threshold
of a significant breakthrough in the international politics of violence
against women.

The very horror of the post–Cold War war in Bosnia has put rape on
the international agenda. This in itself is not what is new, not what signals a new era of political consciousness. Rape has been on the international agenda before. It is not new that stories of men's rapes of women in
wartime have been translated into media headlines. And it is not new that
stories of soldiers' sexual assaults on women have been invested with such
significance that they could be used to shape the current course and later
meaning of a political conflict. Stories of the rapes of Belgian women by
German soldiers in World War I and of rapes of Chinese women by Japanese soldiers and of German women by Russian soldiers in World War II
became so widely known as to affect the international politics of each of
these conflicts.[1] In scores of civil and interstate conflicts, from ancient
Greece through the period of white American westward expansion and
into the recent era of disputes over ideology and sovereignty in Bangladesh, Sri Lanka, Mozambique, and El Salvador, stories of rape have

been a staple of war reporting. "Murder, pillage, and rape" is a litany that has been repeated over and over by war reporters as if rape naturally accompanied pillaging. Moreover, in all these conflicts tales of rape have been instruments wielded overwhelmingly by men, especially by those men positioned to shape the larger political conflict. The rapes have been reported as violations of "our" women's honor, as threats to "our" manhood as fathers, husbands, and sons, challenges to "our" collective masculinized honor as an ethnic community, as a nation. Thus merely the news of rape is not sufficient to mark the present era as new. Indeed, stories of rape heretofore have been translated into the mortar that has kept the bricks of patriarchal international politics in place.

What may be new now is, first, that the rapes in Bosnia have been documented by women's organizations, organizations that are primarily concerned with the raped women's own welfare. Furthermore, these women's organizations have helped create an international political network of feminists who are using news of the Bosnian women's victimization not to institutionalize women as victims, not to incite men to more carnage, but to explain anew how war makers rely on peculiar ideas about masculinity. Finally, they are documenting these rapes so that internationally recognized human rights can be redefined in women's favor. And this time the feminist reporters are using news of wartime sexual assaults by male soldiers to rethink the very meanings of both sovereignty and national identity as each is protected – or challenged – by the workings of the international community. If they succeed in all these ambitious projects, and it is by no means clear that they will have the power required to succeed, the postwar lives of women in the states of the former Yugoslavia will be very different than they would be in a Balkan collection of sovereign patriarchal states. If they succeed, the construction of the entire international political arena will be significantly less vulnerable to patriarchy.

Women's organizations in El Salvador and Sri Lanka previously tried valiantly to get out the word about male combatants' sexual assaults on civilian women. They too had to struggle against a deadly combination of internal conflicts and external intrusions. But the women's groups in Croatia, Serbia, and Bosnia have been particularly successful in getting the news out through international channels in their own terms. There are several reasons for this. The war in the former Yugoslavia broke out after the United Nations Decade on Women, that is, after the burgeoning of international networks of women, providing these women with at least potentially, though far from automatically, available news pipelines that were only in their fledgling forms when earlier conflicts occurred. Also, this war occurred at a time when a significant number of women within Europe (especially feminist and peace activist women) had begun to use the emerging European Community structures to expand and refine their own ideas about "European" feminism, a politics that they hoped would be shaped far less by the still-potent loyalties, hatreds, and fears stoked by selective memories of World War II. Thus this book's origins in Germany four decades after the end of that war and three years after the fall of the Berlin Wall and two years after the signing of the Maastricht Treaty on European integration is not happenstance. German feminists in the early 1990s perhaps have a special stake in figuring out just what it means for German women and Bosnian women to share "Europeanness."

The politics of rape always occur in a historical context. The victims, the reporters, the readers – they, we, all exist in very particular historical settings that will determine whether we are assaulted and by whom, whether we ever hear about the assaults on others and from whom. And these same particular historical contexts we live in also will help determine whether, on the one hand, we take rape seriously, see it as a conscious attempt to control and humiliate women, or on the other hand, adopt the patriarchal convention of imagining men's rapes of women as merely a natural part of wartime's politically dulling litany of "murder-pillage-rape." Nor are the men who are raping women in Bosnia in the early 1990s outside time. Even the most misogynist forms of masculinity are historicized. Thus those Serbian militiamen who gave and followed orders to sexually assault women are men who have grown up under a particular kind of state system, a system supported by particular forms of party, army, and ideological structures. Not all of these militiamen have experienced those historically peculiar structures in identical ways. Borislav Herak, the textile factory worker turned militarized rapist, is not a Yugoslavian Everyman. Yet by listening to him carefully in this volume's amazing interview, we can begin to chart exactly what had to come together in 1992 to achieve this horrifying transformation. Thus, too, the women who have helped collect, distribute, and analyze the information about the rapes in Bosnia are historically rooted, at the very time they are attempting to redirect history by their actions.

By the early 1990s, many more women with a feminist consciousness were established as journalists in mainstream television and print media. Others were managing their own media, such as *Ms.* magazine, *Sojourner*, and *Off Our Backs* in the United States and *Everywoman* in Britain, deliberately choosing to use a feminist analysis to cover events.[2] These magazines, in addition, had become much more internationally minded by the early 1990s, thanks in large part to Third World feminists' 1980s critiques of European and North American feminists' parochialism. So it was not mere coincidence that Croatian feminist groups existed at the outbreak of the war and that they had personal contacts with the editors of *Ms.* that they could use to get out to Americans not only the news of the rapes in Bosnia, but a distinctly feminist interpretation of that news.

New as well is the thinking about all forms of violence against women, including rape. By the time Croatians, Serbs, and Bosnians were at war, there had been two decades of feminist work on rape, work in the form of gathering information and thinking about what it meant, and work in the form of counseling and supporting women who had suffered rape. On rape crisis lines, which emerged only in the 1970s, in courtrooms where feminist lawyers and legal activists began practicing in the late 1970s, in classrooms and academic journals, as well as on Take Back the Night Marches organized in North America and Europe in the early 1980s, serious analytical work was being done to make sense of rape from the vantage point of women who had been assaulted and women whose daily routines and personal identities were controlled in large measure by the fear of being raped.

As ideas, experiences, and strategies were shared and compared, startlingly fresh concepts were introduced. "Marital rape" no longer was deemed an oxymoron, nor was "date rape." Each was possible. Each could be documented – and challenged. Exploring date rape and marital rape, furthermore, could expose the underpinnings of entire state systems and social orders that perpetuated women's marginality.

Likewise, in the years preceding the war in Bosnia feminists became more confident that their long-standing hunches about warfare's reliance on particular ideas about femininity and masculinity, and on a patriarchal state's control of women, were valid. It was this empirically grounded confidence that spurred them to question the standard notion that rapes of women perpetrated by male soldiers in the midst of war were inconsequential, like discharged ammunition, or inevitable. In other words, while some feminists were showing that "marital rape" was not a contradiction in terms, other feminists were showing that "martial rape" was not natural. Both, feminists showed, were processes designed to sustain masculine privilege. Both, that is, were political.

Rapes in World War I Belgium or World War II China might have been publicized for the sake of mobilizing citizens to fight. But until such 1980s feminist challenges, wartime rapes that did not support the dominant party's own agenda were easy to dismiss or cover up. Anything that is considered "natural" can be written off as inconsequential, the very opposite of "news." Thus rape during the Vietnam War attracted virtually no public attention during either that war's French phase or its American phase.[3] But in 1982, seven years after the end of the Vietnam War, five hundred Australian women made history by defying authorities and inserting their own contingent into the usually celebratory and patriotic ANZAC Day memorial march. They insisted that rapes that took place during the Vietnam War (to which the Australian government contributed troops to assist its American ally) were not natural, that they were news, that exposing them and listening to the voices of the women on whom those rapes were perpetrated would reveal the politics of that war more accurately. The Australian women marchers therefore proclaimed that they were marching not to memorialize fallen Australian male soldiers, but rather "in memory of all women of all countries in all wars who were raped."[4]

As rape was assigned more importance by feminists trying to dismantle patriarchy's wall, they began to make connections outward in two directions. First, they began to wonder how rape as a form of masculinist domination supported other patriarchal mechanisms that might on the surface seem far removed from such overt violence: sexual harassment in the workplace, women's geographic confinement, commercialized notions about beauty and sexual desire, male privilege in legislatures and police departments, women's stifled literary voices. In this first process, rape became less exceptional; feminists insisted that rape be seen as a violent form of a much more pervasive – and much more subtle – mode of domination. Rape thereby gained even deeper political meaning. It is for this reason that the women who have suffered wartime rapes in Bosnia are being spoken about by feminists in many countries in ways unthought of only a generation ago: these women are not just rape victims; they are being portrayed by feminists as simultaneously women with particular sorts of positions within their evolving communities' political systems; they are women who have voices that are expected to be heard – or to be silenced; they are women with self-perceptions of their own bodies and sexuality shaped by cultural norms and commercial exchanges. If this feminist understanding is widely accepted, Bosnian women who have been raped will hereafter have to be treated – and listened to – not as conveniently one-dimensional cartoons but as actors in their own complexly gendered political communities.

At the same time, feminists starting with a determination to describe the full scope of wartime rape, to pursue its long-range repercussions and to excavate its causes, charted a second path of outward analysis. They wondered what taking rape seriously would reveal about large social structures, structures that most commentators seemed perfectly comfortable describing without ever mentioning rape. Feminists traced the connections between patterns of rape, on the one hand, and racial stratification in their own societies. They sought to expose how societal and international systems of racism need particular forms of sexualized violence in order to survive. Feminists also pursued the misogynist politics of rape straight through the entire judicial system. They showed that this social structure rests not just on ideas about law, but on beliefs about male rationality and male sexuality. Still other feminists used women's experiences of rape as a searchlight to reveal the inner workings of their country's military structure. Using rape as a starting point, these women discovered the military's heavy reliance not just on men as soldiers, but on misogynist forms of masculinist soldiering. As they learned more, feminists became ever more intellectually daring. They claimed that to make sense of the causes of wartime rape, they as feminists should be heard when they analyzed whole economies and the state. This usually required a physical risk taking to match their intellectual daring. When feminists ask new questions about who rapes women and for what reason and with whose condoning, they are likely to be harassed, imprisoned, driven underground or into exile, or assassinated. These are not merely discussions in an academic seminar. When these feminists came together to talk and strategize, women in Chile, the Philippines, Canada, India, Britain, the United States, and Germany found that taking rape seriously had compelled them to think about the links between beauty and the market economy, geographic mobility and masculinity, sexuality and soldiering. Feminists may have been caught off guard by the ferocity of the conflict in Bosnia, but they were prepared for it intellectually and politically. They attempted, not always successfully, to ensure that these wartime rape victims would not become mere propaganda fodder; nor would they let these rapes be swept under the patriarchal rug.

A third development had been occurring that had attracted less popular attention, but that has now reached the point where it has helped ensure that the women raped in Bosnia won't be forgotten or, alternatively, publicized merely for the sake of inciting men on all sides to fight even more fiercely. This is the feminist transformation of internationally recognized human rights.

Human rights is not a new idea. Eleanor Roosevelt, a self-conscious femininst, was among the leaders in entrenching human rights guarantees in the founding articles of the post–World War II United Nations. But it was only in the 1980s that human rights became the basis for widespread domestic political organizing in countries as diverse as Czechoslovakia, Argentina, South Korea, and Kenya. During that same decade, many peace activists in Europe and North America began building institutions designed to monitor human rights in those countries whose authoritiarian regimes their own governments were aiding in the name of Cold War rivalries. Genuine peace, these activists argued, would come only when the rights of free expression and due process of law were both supported by local authorities and rewarded by their powerful foreign allies. Still, these two developments by themselves did not ensure that rape would be taken seriously in the public arena or that women subjected to rape would have their voices heard in the circles where post–Cold War international alliances were being reforged.

In fact, much of human rights activism was dominated until the early 1990s by the legal profession, a profession, especially in its international enclaves, that was notably unwelcoming to women, feminist or nonfeminist. Moreover, the human rights treaties legitimated by United Nations recognition were the products of intergovernmental diplomatic negotiations. They were imbued with ideas articulated by men who imagined outside monitoring of relations between their own countries' women and men to be a violation of their "national sovereignty" and their "national identity." Free press and free elections might – just might – be liable to the international community's scrutiny, but violence against women? *That* was each nation's, each government's, own "family affair." In this post–World War II political conception of international human rights, the patriarchal family and the sovereign nation were glued tightly together.

But then, about 1980, something began to change. Women active in their own countries' antimilitarism movements began to question whether it was enough – analytically or strategically – to portray all citizens outside an oppressive regime's circle of co-optation as suffering identically. What would happen to one's understanding of a militaristic government's use of coercion against its citizens if one acknowledged that rape was being used systematically against its female prisoners?[5] Meanwhile, the women staff people and women volunteers who had become the backbone of human rights organizations such as Amnesty International, the Helsinki Citizens Assembly, and Human Rights Watch began to insist that their emerging feminist analyses of rape be applied to their human rights work.

In early 1992, Amnesty International's London headquarters published a slim but devastating report on "police rape." Another oxymoron was being turned on its head. Building on the pioneering work of Indian, Peruvian, and the Filipina feminists who had been monitoring their respective police forces' systematic sexual assaults on women during alleged security sweeps, Amnesty added its considerable international influence to the call for police rape to be considered as much a denial of human rights as election fraud.[6]

Women activists in other male-led human rights groups not only followed with more substantial reports, but began to demasculinize the formal structures of their organizations. Women inside the U.S.-based Human Rights Watch organized a new unit devoted to the violations of women's human rights. In 1992 they helped publish a report documenting both rebels' and government forces' sexual intimidation of women in Peru. The following year they published a similar report on male combatants' sexual assaults on women in the contested Indian state of Kashmir.[7]

At the same time, veteran feminist activists began to conceptualize their campaigns in terms of international human rights. For instance, Georgina Ashworth, of the London-based feminist institute Change, incorporated human rights analysis into her advocacy for gender fairness in development aid programs; American feminist Kathleen Barry, a leading campaigner for the abolition of the internationalized prostitution industry, began to reinterpret human rights law as a strategic part of that campaign; her compatriot Charlotte Bunch, director of a university center to train women for public leadership, made violence against women as a human rights issue central to that enterprise; and Peruvian feminist Roxanne Carrillo helped redirect the United Nations agency Development Fund for Women (UNIFEM) into a new realm of advocacy, human rights.[8]

While the war in Bosnia continues to destroy people's lives, the United Nations sponsored its first international conference on human rights in over a decade. The conferees converging on Vienna in June 1993 included not only mostly male delegations representing governments, but scores of nongovernment groups, a substantial proportion of which were feminist. And the dangerous work done by women in Bosnia, Croatia, and Serbia – women pulled daily in opposite directions by the different consequences of Western sanctions, by local male officials' policies, by their unequal access to local supporters – together with their allies in Germany, Britain, and the United States, had an impact. But it was not just the horrific stories coming out of Bosnia that produced this impact on a still state-dominated, still deeply masculinized and legalistic international conference. It was that those stories were being told with at least a large dose of feminist interpretation and that that interpretation had been made possible because women in Europe and North America had allowed themselves to be educated by Indian, Filipina, Salvadoran, Sri Lankan, and Peruvian feminists about militarized rape.

So despite evidence that many journalists and editors have adopted the well-worn strategy of exploiting news of rape to sell their product, there are also encouraging signs that rape will be taken seriously in its own right, that is, as a significant political phenomenon worthy of actions beyond mere propagandist exploitation.[9] But for Bosnian women, as well as women in other countries where male combatants have tried to make male sexual assualt on women an instrument of war, the proof of the feminist pudding will probably come in the postwar years. Most of the men who have raped women – or ordered that men under their command rape women – will survive this war. Many of them, according to recent reports, will have in their closets the video films made of their assaults.[10] Will they hide those films after the war? Will they watch them furtively or with male friends to remind themselves of what it felt like to be "real men"? to be "nationalists"? Will these men feel somehow less manly after the war ends?

It will be in the postwar years, when the horrible excitement of the war has subsided and the restless media and diplomatic corps have turned their attention elsewhere, that Croatian, Serbian, and Bosnian women and their foreign supporters will face a special challenge. The politics of rape do not cease when the guns grow cold. The politics of rape may look different, less visible, less outrageous, but they still continue to play themselves out. This is because the politics of rape do not end when the assault itself ends; they do not end when the woman, if she has survived, manages to reach a safe refuge. The politics of rape extend for as long as that woman sees herself in part as a rape survivor, as long as others – friends, brothers, mothers, police officials, social workers, nationalist politicians, lovers – see her through the lens of rape; they extend for as long as the power relations between this woman and others are in any way shaped by their respective ideas about men as rapists and women as potential and actual rape victims. In these tricky postwar months and years some of those women who have suffered at the hands of wartime rapists will be pressured to marry; others will be pressured to give up the idea of marrying. After the war the politics of rape likely will be played out in such a way that some women will be rewarded for staying silent; others, perhaps, will find themselves in postwar situations in which they will be rewarded for telling their stories – or for telling only sanitized versions of their full stories. Some women will experience postwar demands that they honor only certain of their wartime supporters – perhaps their own ethnic group's men but not "foreign" women. Some women will be expected to define themselves henceforth only in terms of their having been raped and thus to identify with one national community and despise another.

A postwar era in any country is a time when lessons – potentially deadly lessons – are crafted and distributed for instructing the next generation of women and men about what to fear, what to cherish, who to blame, and who to count on for protection. Human rights doctrines and policies, even those newly informed by feminist thinking, will not alone ensure that this postwar period is an empowering one for Bosnian women who have experienced rape. Beyond legal theory and international agencies, it will take women's ongoing local autonomous organizing to name and challenge all forms of rape. It will take a deeper analysis of men's anxieties about their manliness, anxieties that make so many of them open to misogyny and militarism. And if the postwar years as lived by Bosnian women are to be an empowering time, then those of us who today are so riveted by their experiences will have to develop much longer attention spans. For the actual politics of the rapes in Bosnia will extend far beyond the peace agreement between nationalist male elites, far beyond the demobilization of the militias. When Sarajevo once again has running water and enjoys quiet nights, the politics of the wartime rapes so graphically described in this volume will still be playing themselves out. Who will be attentive then?

Notes

1. Susan Brownmiller examines in detail how the rape stories coming out of Belgium and later out of China were used for propaganda purposes: see Susan Brownmiller, *Against Our Will* (New York, 1975), pp. 34–38, 54–62. Regarding the reports of the Soviet Red Army soldiers' rapes of German women in the final weeks of World War II and the impact these reports had on German women in Berlin, the freshest analysis is from Columbia University historian Atina Grossman in her paper "A Question of Silence: The Rape of German Women by Occupation Soldiers," presented at the Ninth Berkshire Conference on the History of Women, Vassar College, Poughkeepsie, New York, June 12, 1993.

2. See for instance, *Off Our Back*'s special supplement, "Serbia's War against Croatia," May 1993.

3. For the most detailed account of a rape of a Vietnamese woman by a group of American soldiers and its subsequent bureaucratic cover-up, see Daniel Lang, *Casualties of War* (New York, 1969).

4. "Australia: Women in Wars," *Spare Rib*, July 1982, p. 16.

5. The groundbreaking scholarly article providing both evidence and feminist analysis of Latin American military officials' deliberate use of rape as state torture is Ximena Bunster, "Surviving beyond Fear: Women and Torture in Latin America," in *Women and Change in Latin America*, ed. June Nash and Helen Safa (South Hadley, Mass., 1986), pp. 297–325.

6. Amnesty International, *Rape and Sexual Abuse: Torture and Ill Treatment of Women in Detention* (New York, 1992).

7. Americas Watch and the Women's Rights Project, *Untold Terror: Violence against Women in Peru's Armed Conflict* (New York, 1992). Asia Watch and Physicians for Human Rights, *Rape in Kashmir: A Crime of War* (New York, 1993). Two more recent reports detail the uses of rape in communal and ethnic conflicts: Joyoti Grech, "Resisting War Rape in Bangladesh," *Trouble and Strife* 26 (sum-

mer 1993): 17–21, and Svati Chakravarti Bhatkal, "Sisterhood and Strife," *Women's Review of Books* 10 (July 1993): 12–13. A detailed account by an Iraqi democratic critic of the Saddam Hussein regime's security agency's systematic use of rape against Iraqi women is contained in: Samir al-Khalil, *Republic of Fear* (New York, 1993).

8. See, for instance, Georgina Ashworth, *Of Violence and Violation: Women and Human Rights* (London, 1985); Kathleen Barry, *Prostitution of Sexuality,* forthcoming; Charlotte Bunch, "Women's Rights as Human Rights: Toward a Revision of Human Rights," *Human Rights Quarterly* 12 (1990): 486–98; Rebecca J. Cook, "Women's International Human Rights: A Bibliography," *New York University Journal of International Law and Politics,* forthcoming; Stanlie M. James, "Toward a Theoretical Articulation of Human Rights with Women's Rights," (1993), unpublished paper available from Professor James, Department of Afro-American Studies, University of Wisconsin, Madison. Additional information is available from the Coalition against Trafficking in Women, Calder Square, P.O. Box 10077, State College, Pa. 16805, and from Global Campaign for Women's Human Rights, Douglass College, Rutgers University, New Brunswick, N.J.

Because some of the most outspoken resistence to the universalizing of human rights standards has come from male government officials in Asia, it is especially helpful to look at Asian feminists' analysis of human rights: Asia Pacific Forum on Women, Law, and Development, *Women's Rights, Human Rights: Asia-Pacific Reflections* (Kuala Lumpur, 1992). See also Ramla Khalidi and Judith Tucker, *Women's Rights in the Arab World* (Washington, D.C., 1993); Joanna Kerr, ed., *Ours by Right: Women's Rights as Human Rights* (Highland, N.J., 1993); and Katarina Tomasevski, *Women and Human Rights* (Highland, N.J., 1993). I am indebted to Vasuki Nesiah, Sri Lankan feminist of Harvard Law School, for making me aware of much of the new work being done by feminists in the human rights arena.

9. For a feminist analysis of mainstream media's exploitation of the Bosnian rape stories, see "Abused and Misused: Women and Their Political Exploitation," *Connexions* 42 (1993): 12–14.

10. Catherine A. MacKinnon, "Turning Rape into Pornography: Postmodern Genocide," *Ms.* 4 (July–August 1993): 24–30 (reprinted in this book).

The Contributors

Susan Brownmiller is the author of the pivotal work *Against Our Will: Men, Women, and Rape*, as well as *Femininity* and a novel, *Waverly Place*. She is currently working on a book about rape and the Vietnam War.

Rhonda Copelon is a professor of law and the codirector of the International Women's Human Rights Law Clinic at the City University of New York School of Law. She is coauthor, with Babcock et al., of *Sex Discrimination and the Law*.

Cynthia H. Enloe is a professor of government at Clark University. Among her works are *Does Khaki Become You? The Militarization of Women's Lives; Bananas, Beaches, and Bases: Making Feminist Sense of International Politics;* and *The Morning After: Sexual Politics at the End of the Cold War*.

Marion Faber is a professor of comparative literature at Swarthmore College and the translator of Nietzsche's *Human, All Too Human* (Nebraska, 1984) and Sarah Kirsch's *Panther Woman* (Nebraska, 1989).

Vera Folnegovic-Smalc is chief physician at the Center for Clinical Psychiatry at the Vrapce Psychiatric Hospital in Zagreb. She is also a professor of psychiatry at the medical school of the University of Zagreb.

Roy Gutman is a foreign correspondent for *Newsday* and won the 1993 Pulitzer Prize for his reports from Bosnia, described in *A Witness to*

Genocide. He is also the author of *Banana Diplomacy: The Making of American Foreign Policy in Nicaragua 1981–1987.*

Catharine A. MacKinnon is a professor of law at the University of Michigan. She is the author of *Only Words, Toward a Feminist Theory of the State; Feminism Unmodified: Discourses on Life and Law;* and *Sexual Harassment of Working Women: A Case of Sex Discrimination.*

Paul Parin served as a physician with Tito's partisans during the liberation of Yugoslavia. He trained in neurology and psychoanalysis in Zurich and did ethnopsychiatric research in West Africa. He received the Erich Fried Prize in 1992.

Helke Sander is a film director and an author; she is also a professor at the Hochschule für bildende Künste in Hamburg and codirector of the Bremem Institute for Film and Television.

Ruth Seifert is an assistant professor at the German Federal Army's Institute for Social Science. She has taught military sociology, feminist theory, women's studies, and labor sociology.

Alexandra Stiglmayer has been a freelance correspondent in Bosnia-Herzegovina for German and American media since January 1992. Previously she worked with the WDR (West German Radio and Television) in Cologne.

Azra Zalihic-Kaurin was a student in legal studies at the University of Sarajevo. Having been a freelance journalist and reporter with various Sarajevo newspapers and Bosnian TV, she fled from Sarajevo in May 1992 and is now a reporter for the Croatian daily newspaper *Vecernji List.*